Tinnie Ellsworth

Our Society Cook Book

Embracing About 1200 Tried, Reliable and Economical Recipes

Tinnie Ellsworth

Our Society Cook Book
Embracing About 1200 Tried, Reliable and Economical Recipes

ISBN/EAN: 9783744786461

Printed in Europe, USA, Canada, Australia, Japan

Cover: Foto ©Andreas Hilbeck / pixelio.de

More available books at **www.hansebooks.com**

OUR SOCIETY

Cook ✳ Book,

EMBRACING

ABOUT 1200 TRIED, RELIABLE AND ECONOMICAL

RECIPES.

ESPECIALLY ADAPTED TO THE WANTS OF THOSE WHO DESIRE
HEALTHFUL COOKERY AND WHOSE OBJECT IS
THE ELEVATION OF THE ART.

———————

"When roasted crabs hiss in the bowl."

—*Love's Labour's Lost.*

———————

" Bid them cover the table, serve in the meat, and we will come to dinner "

—*Merchant of Venice.*

———————

HARRISBURG, PA.:

PENNSYLVANIA PUBLISHING CO.

1888.

———-) TO (———

Those Housewives

WHO DELIGHT

IN MAKING HOME A PLACE OF PEACE, COMFORT

AND ENJOYMENT,

THIS BOOK IS RESPECTFULLY DEDICATED.

PREFACE.

N the compilation of this work, we have striven to give the greatest amount of information possible, consistent with the plan adopted, and to so arrange it that any subject sought can be easily and quickly found; and, when found, that it shall contain just the information sought. The tendency of the age is toward the practical, and he who would gain the attention of the public must be concise and to the point.

Our aim is to assist in the management of the household, but especially would we enter our plea for improved cookery. Ill-cooked meals are a source of discomfort. Bad cooking is waste—waste of money and loss of comfort. Among the "common things" which educators should teach the rising generation, this should not be overlooked. It is the commonest and yet the most neglected of the branches of female education.

In this department we have endeavored to give only those recipes which have stood the test of actual use and received the endorsement of the best cooks and caterers of the day, and all of them can be depended upon as being just what they purport to be.

We have considered it unnecessary to add the names of the contributors, as most of them would be nearly or quite unknown to the reader, and, therefore, would carry no weight of authority with them, and would serve but to occupy space, which is better used for additional recipes.

ILLUSTRATIONS.

SOCIETY COOK BOOK.

CHAPTER I.

BREAD MAKING.

F it be true that bread is the staff of life, no one can be insensible to the statement which has been made by authors on the subject so many times of late, that we make a great mistake, from a dietetic point of view, in the kind of flour which we select for making bread. The most nutritious bread is not the whitest, but rather the reverse, since the branny portion of wheat, which is systematically rejected, contains very valuable substances and salts that, taken into the body, go to form bone, flesh, and nerve, as well as to assist in the digestion of starchy matters. The central portion of wheat, or that portion which forms the ordinary flour of commerce, consists solely of starch, which is not a flesh-forming substance, but a heat-giving principle of food. The bran contains phosphates, of which bones and nerves are so largely made up; gluten, or flesh-forming substance; and cerealine, a peculiar body which has the character of a ferment, changing starchy matter in such a way as to be more readily absorbed and utilized by the system in the act of digestion.

It stands to reason, therefore, that flour made from the entire wheat contains the very substances which are needed to make it nutritious, and that the removal of the bran in the making of flour,

OUR

SOCIETY COOK BOOK.

CHAPTER I.

BREAD MAKING.

F it be true that bread is the staff of life, no one can be insensible to the statement which has been made by authors on the subject so many times of late, that we make a great mistake, from a dietetic point of view, in the kind of flour which we select for making bread. The most nutritious bread is not the whitest, but rather the reverse, since the branny portion of wheat, which is systematically rejected, contains very valuable substances and salts that, taken into the body, go to form bone, flesh, and nerve, as well as to assist in the digestion of starchy matters. The central portion of wheat, or that portion which forms the ordinary flour of commerce, consists solely of starch, which is not a flesh-forming substance, but a heat-giving principle of food. The bran contains phosphates, of which bones and nerves are so largely made up; gluten, or flesh-forming substance; and cerealine, a peculiar body which has the character of a ferment, changing starchy matter in such a way as to be more readily absorbed and utilized by the system in the act of digestion.

It stands to reason, therefore, that flour made from the entire wheat contains the very substances which are needed to make it nutritious, and that the removal of the bran in the making of flour, as ordinarily practiced, entails the loss of very important items of diet. Further, it is clear that the physiologist is right in recommending the use of whole grain flour, provided that there is no special drawback on account of its physical character. But this is just what has been the case hitherto. When the bran is mixed with the ordinary flour and taken, it is found to be difficult of digestion, and, in some cases, to irritate; the latter result being due to the mechanical action of the bran scales upon the intestines, and hence there has been a real difficulty in extending the consumption of brown bread. But recent improvements in milling machinery have to a great extent overcome these difficulties, and as a consequence, the consumption of wheat in its many and various preparations is correspondingly increased.

For good bread three things are essential — good flour, good yeast, and great care.

Yeast that will not Sour.

Good bread cannot be made from poor yeast, and here is a recipe that will not sour: One bowl of flour, one bowl of sugar, one cup of salt, one tablespoonful ginger. Take a double handful of hops and pour over them five quarts of water, boil an hour, and have as much water on at the last, and pour scalding hot through a strainer on to the other ingredients, stirring briskly; when cold add a cup of good yeast and let rise thirty-six hours, pour into a perfectly sweet jug, and keep in a cool place. A cupful of this added to a quart of lukewarm water, with flour enough to make a stiff batter, will make two loaves of bread. Set this at night and knead in more flour the next morning, keep in a place where it will be of even temperature, raising it as fast as possible; when raised again, knead a good deal, using but little flour, and put into bread pans; when well raised bake slowly three-fourths of an hour. Part of this taken out and raised once or twice, with sufficient butter or lard, and the white of an egg added, makes excellent rolls for tea.

A Good Reliable Yeast.

Steep slowly, in a porcelain or bright tin kettle, one large handful of hops, tied in a cloth, boil six large potatoes, sliced thin, in two quarts of water; when done very soft, mash till smooth and creamy. Have ready one pint of flour, wet and rubbed to a smooth paste; pour into this the potato water, boiling hot, stirring smoothly; let it boil a few minutes, stirring all the time; add the hop water and potatoes, two tablespoonfuls of salt, and one cup of white sugar; stir thoroughly, and set away to cool. When milk warm, stir in one cup of yeast; let it rise in a warm place twelve hours; put it into an air-tight vessel, previously well scalded, and set in the cellar. This will keep from four to six weeks. Always make new yeast before the old is gone, in order to have some to start with. Be very particular with every new batch of yeast, to have the vessel in which it is kept well cleaned, and scalded with hot saleratus water. Much depends upon keeping this sweet and clean.

Another Good Yeast.

Boil two potatoes with a good handful of hops, tied in a bag; mash the potatoes when done, in the yeast dish, and add two teacupfuls of flour, and scald with the potato water; when cool, add a yeast cake soaked in warm water. Dry hop yeast can always be found at grocery stores.

Good Home-made Bread.

The superiority of good home-made bread has long been acknowledged, yet how few know how to make a really good article of bread, therefore so many housekeepers depend on the baker, which is at least very expensive, to say nothing of the injury the constant use of baker's bread causes to the health of delicate persons and children, as all baker's bread contains alum, which causes the loaves to increase in weight, as it makes the flour absorb more water. Therefore a pound loaf of baker's bread will contain less nourishment than a loaf of home-made bread of equal weight. Economy.

therefore, should make every housekeeper her own bread maker, as baker's bread dries and becomes stale much quicker than home-made.

To make first-rate bread, the sponge should be set over night in a warm place and raised and kneaded three times; the first time from fifteen to twenty minutes—the more the better. If this rule is followed the bread will present an even surface when sliced off, and not the loose, crumbly appearance which is so often seen in bread.

Take three quarts of good flour, sift and warm; make a cavity in the center, add a large teaspoonful of salt; take one pint of new milk, or water boiling hot, pour into this and stir quickly; cool off with one quart of cold milk or water; add one cup of yeast; mix well together; then cover well and set in a moderately warm place (if in cold weather); this will be ready to knead up before break-fast, if set over night. Slashing the dough with a sharp knife adds to its lightness and texture. When well kneaded the first time cover tightly, watch closely, and as soon as light knead as before, but be very careful not to work in much flour; only keep enough on the board to prevent sticking, as all the flour that is added after the first kneading only makes the bread hard and dry. As soon as it is light the second time divide into loaves and reserve a portion for biscuit so that the bread will not be cut till cold. Mold smoothly, put into tins, let rise fifteen or twenty minutes in a warm place; bake half an hour in moderately hot oven. When done, set on hearth, cover with double thick cloth five minutes, turn out on same cloth; let stand until cool; put in stone jar and keep covered. Always keep a cloth folded in the bottom of the jar to take up the dampness which naturally collects.

YEAST BREAD.

To three quarts water add one teacupful of yeast, stir into enough sifted flour to make a stiff batter; do this in the evening and set in a warm place. In the morning mix stiff; it will soon rise, then mold out into the tins. No certain time can be given for the time of rising, as that depends on the temperature.

POTATO BREAD.

Pare and boil six good-sized potatoes, drain off the water, mash fine and pour over them about three pints of cold water and run through a colander; add flour until this is a thin batter, then put in a coffee cup of yeast from the jug; let stand until it rises, then stir into it flour as much as you can with a spoon and let it rise again; work in enough more flour to make stiff enough for bread, and then let rise the third time; when light this time, work into loaves and let rise. All the flour must be sifted.

ANOTHER.

Boil four potatoes to the loaf; mash when done and add two tea-cupfuls of flour and scald with the potato water; when cool add the yeast and let stand till bed time, then sponge and knead in the morning; make quite stiff and knead fifteen or twenty minutes; let rise again and mold into loaves.

MILK SPONGE BREAD.

Put a pint of boiling water into a pitcher with a teaspoonful of sugar, one-fourth teaspoonful of salt, and the same of soda; let it stand till you can bear your finger in it, then add flour to make a thick batter; beat it hard for two minutes. Now place the pitcher in a kettle of hot water—not hot enough to scald the mixture; keep the water at the same temperature till the emptyings are light. If set early in the morning and carefully watched they will be ready by eleven o'clock to make a sponge the same as for other bread, with a quart of very warm milk. Let this sponge get very light, then make into loaves and set to rise again, taking care that they do not get too light this time before putting into the oven, or the bread will be dry and tasteless. The emptyings pitcher and bread pan or tray must be perfectly clean and sweet. Scald them out with saleratus or lime water.

SALT RISING BREAD.

In the evening scald two tablespoonfuls of corn meal, a pinch of salt and one of sugar, with sweet milk, and set in a warm place till morning; then scald a teaspoonful of sugar, one of salt, half as much soda, with a pint of boiling water, add cold water till luke-warm, then put in the mush made the night before, and thicken to a batter with flour; put in a close vessel in a kettle of warm water (not too hot); when light, mix stiff, adding a little shortening; mold into loaves. It will soon rise, and will not take as long to bake as yeast bread.

SALT RISING BREAD, No. 2.

In the morning take a quart dish and scald it out, then put in a pint of warm water; put in a teaspoonful of salt and a little pinch of soda, two or three tablespoonfuls of corn meal, and flour enough to make a thick batter. Stir well, and set the dish in a kettle of warm water, and keep at the same temperature (just so you can bear your hand in it). If water rises on the top, stir in briskly one or two tablespoonfuls of flour, and put back into the kettle. If the flour is good the emptyings will be light within three or four hours; then take flour enough in a bread pan to make three or four loaves of bread, make a hole in the center, put in the emptyings, and fill the same dish with warm water; add a little salt, stir it in with a spoon, mix a thick sponge and cover it with some of the flour, and set in a warm place to rise. When light, mold it into loaves and set to rise again (it does not require as much kneading as yeast bread). Bake from a half to three-fourths of an hour. Railroad emptyings are made in the same way, of middlings instead of flour.

CORN BREAD.

One pint sweet milk, one pint sour milk, one pint flour, two pints meal, one teaspoonful syrup, one teaspoonful salt, one teaspoonful soda. Steam three hours.

CORN BREAD, No. 2.

Two eggs well beaten, one cup sugar, half cup butter, one cup sweet milk, half cup sour milk, half cup wheat flour, one and a half cups corn meal, two teaspoonfuls of any good baking powder.

CORN BREAD, No. 3.

One pint buttermilk, two eggs, one pint corn meal, two table-spoonfuls melted butter, a little salt, and one teaspoonful soda.

CORN BREAD, No. 4.

One pint corn meal, one pint flour, one pint buttermilk, one tea-cupful molasses, one teaspoonful soda, one teaspoonful salt. Bake just two hours.

GRANDMOTHER'S INDIAN BREAD.

Three cups sweet milk, three cups corn meal, one cup wheat flour, one half cup molasses, one teaspoonful of soda, one teaspoonful salt. Put into a buttered bake-dish, and set in a steamer and steam three hours.

QUICK GRAHAM BREAD.

One and a half pints sour milk, two-thirds cup cooking molasses, a half teaspoonful salt, two even teaspoonfuls of saleratus dissolved in a little hot water, and as much Graham flour as can be stirred in evenly with a spoon. Put into a well-greased pan, and bake immediately. It will require from an hour and a half to two hours to bake.

BAKING POWDER GRAHAM BREAD.

One and one-half pints Graham flour, one-half pint flour, one tablespoonful of sugar, one teaspoonful of salt, two teaspoonfuls baking powder; mix with a pint and a half of milk, or equal parts of milk and water. Sift together Graham, flour, sugar, salt, and baking powder; add the milk, or milk and water, mix rapidly into a soft dough, put into a greased tin, bake in rather hot oven for forty minutes. Protect the loaf with paper the first fifteen minutes.

Brown Bread of Graham Flour.

Take one cup of milk; add hot water to warm; thicken with sifted flour, sufficient to make a sponge; stand over night in a warm place; in the morning add half a cup of milk, with a cup of hot water, one cup molasses, one cup butter, one teaspoonful salt; mix in Graham flour till thick, and smooth with a spoon; pour into bread pans half full; let stand in a warm place until the pans are nearly full; bake an hour in a moderately hot oven. Keep a steady fire.

Graham Bread.

To a scant quart of warm water add a heaping teaspoonful of salt, a good half cup of brown sugar; stir in a pint of the sponge made of flour for potato bread; add as much Graham flour as can be stirred in; put into baking pans and let rise until light; bake in a moderate oven, and when done wrap in a damp towel until cool.

Graham Bread, No. 2.

Take one and two-thirds cups of water or milk and a small piece of butter or lard; mix quite thick with Graham flour or Arlington wheat meal, which is better; add half a cup of good yeast and set to rise over night. In the morning dissolve one-half teaspoonful soda in a little water and add one-half cup of molasses; stir this into the bread, mix quite soft and put in baking tin to rise. Bake thoroughly. A nice rye and wheat loaf may be made in the same way, using one and one-half cups sifted rye and the rest wheat flour. If you wish a light colored loaf use only one cup of rye and sweeten with sugar.

Brown Bread.

Take two quarts of corn meal; scald with one quart of boiling milk or water; when cool add one quart of Graham flour, one large spoonful salt, one cup brown sugar or best molasses, one cup home-made yeast, one cup flour. Mix with warm water as stiff as can easily be stirred; put in deep basins; steam two hours and bake one. Before baking baste with a few spoonfuls of sweet cream or milk; this makes a soft, tender crust.

Biscuit is made from the same dough as the bread, rolled out and spread with a small quantity of lard, which must be very fresh and sweet. Double the dough together, roll and spread again three times; then cut in small biscuits; place on buttered tins; let stand half an hour; bake fifteen minutes until a very light brown. Cover with cloth a few minutes and slip off on the same until ready for use. All bread, biscuit, loaf cake or doughnuts made from yeast should rise after being mixed before being baked; if put into the oven or fried directly they are never light, as the dough has no chance to recover its elasticity.

Brown Bread, No. 2.

One pint of rye meal sifted, one pound of coarse yellow Indian meal sifted, one quart of sour milk, salt, half cup of molasses or less, one heaping teaspoonful of saleratus dissolved in a little hot water. Steam three hours and-a-half in a tin pail set in a kettle of boiling water.

Boston Brown Bread.

Flour one-half pint, one pint corn meal, one-half pint rye flour, one teaspoonful salt, one tablespoonful brown sugar, two teaspoonfuls baking powder, one-half pint water; sift flour, corn meal, rye flour, sugar, salt and baking powder together thoroughly; peel, wash, and well boil two mealy potatoes, rub them through the sieve, diluting with water. When this is quite cold use it to mix the flour, etc., into a batter like cake; pour it into a well-greased mold, having a cover (a tin pail will do), place it in a kettle or sauce pan half full of boiling water, when the loaf may steam or simmer one hour; then take off the cover and bake in the oven a half hour.

Rye Bread.

Make a sponge as for wheat bread, and let it rise over night; then add two-thirds cup molasses, one teaspoonful salt, one quart milk and water—equal parts—and mix with rye flour, not as stiff as wheat bread, and bake.

RYE AND INDIAN BREAD.

Scald two quarts Indian meal by pouring over it just boiling water enough to wet it, one quart rye meal or flour, one-half tea-cupful molasses, two teaspoonfuls salt, one of soda, one cup of yeast; make as thick as can be stirred with a spoon, mixing with warm water, and let rise over night; put in a bake tin, let stand a half hour, and bake from four to six hours.

RYE BREAD WITH BAKING POWDER.

One pint rye flour, one-half pint corn meal, one-half pint flour, one teaspoonful sugar, one teaspoonful salt, two teaspoonfuls baking powder, one tablespoonful lard, nearly one pint milk. Sift together rye flour, corn meal, flour, sugar, salt and powder, rub in the lard cold, add the milk and mix into a smooth batter, as for cake; pour into a well greased tin, and bake in a moderate oven three-quarters of an hour; protect with a paper the first quarter.

HOYLETON BREAD.

Five cups Indian meal, seven cups wheat flour, two cups rye meal, four cups buttermilk, two cups sweet milk, one-half cup molasses, two teaspoonfuls salt, two teaspoonfuls soda. Put it in a three quart pail that has a cover; let it stand near the fire thirty minutes with the cover off, to rise, then put on cover, and bake or steam four hours.

NORWEGIAN BREAD, FOR DYSPEPTICS.

One pint barley meal, one-half pint Graham, one-half pint flour, one teaspoonful salt, two teaspoonfuls baking powder, one pint milk. Sift together barley meal, Graham, flour, salt and powder. Mix into a firm batter with the milk, pour into a greased tin, and bake in a moderate oven forty minutes; cover with a greased paper the first twenty minutes.

OAT MEAL BREAD.

One-half pint oat meal, one and-a-half pints flour, half teaspoonful salt, three teaspoonfuls baking powder, three-fourths pint milk; boil the oat meal in one and-a-half pints salted water for one hour. Then dilute it with the milk. Set aside to get perfectly cold. Sift together flour, salt, powder, and when the oat meal preparation is cold place it in a bread bowl; add to it the flour, etc.; mix smoothly together, pour from the bowl into the greased tin, and bake in a moderate oven three-fourths of an hour; protect the loaf with paper the first twenty minutes.

RICE BREAD.

Boil one cupful of rice in a pint of water; when tender, add one-half pint milk; when cold, add one and-a-half pints flour sifted, with a teaspoonful sugar, half teaspoonful salt, two teaspoonfuls baking powder; mix together smoothly, pour into greased tin, and bake forty minutes.

2

CHAPTER II.

BREAKFAST AND TEA CAKES.

LIGHT BISCUIT.

IN kneading bread, set aside a small loaf for biscuits. Into this work a heaping tablespoonful of lard and butter mixed, and a teaspoonful of sugar. The more it is worked, the whiter it will be. As it rises, mold it down twice before making into biscuit. Roll out and cut with a biscuit cutter. The dough should be quite soft.

BUTTER BISCUIT.

Sift one quart of flour into a pan, and make a hollow in the center large enough to admit a pint of milk and a coffee-cup of yeast; mix into a sponge, set it to rise; in the morning add one pound of melted butter, and knead as much flour as will, with another pint of warm milk or water, make a soft dough; make out the biscuit in pans to rise; when sufficiently light, bake in a well-heated oven.

SODA BISCUIT.

One quart of sifted flour, an even teaspoonful of soda dissolved in a pint of buttermilk, or sour milk, heaping tablespoonful of lard, a pinch of salt. Bake in an oven—not too hot—after raising fifteen or twenty minutes. If sour cream is to be had, use it instead of milk, leaving out the shortening.

DIXIE BISCUIT.

Three pints of flour, two eggs, two tablespoonfuls of lard, one small cup of yeast, one cup of milk; mix at 11 o'clock, roll out at 4 o'clock, and cut with two sizes of cutters, putting the smaller one on top; let rise until supper. Bake twenty minutes.

18

BAKING POWDER BISCUIT.

To begin with, have a hot oven; have the flour sifted, and roll dough as soft as it can be handled. Then more baking powder is needed than is usually given. For each teacupful of flour use a teaspoonful of powder; butter the size of a hen's egg is sufficient for a quart of flour; after rubbing powder and butter into the flour, mix soft with cold water or milk, stirring with a spoon; roll lightly and bake at once.

CREAM OF TARTAR BISCUIT.

One quart flour, a tablespoonful of butter, and a tablespoonful of lard, a half teaspoonful of salt, one teaspoonful of soda, two teaspoonfuls of cream of tartar. Sift the flour and cream of tartar together, rub the butter and lard very thoroughly through it; dissolve the soda in a pint of milk or water (if water, use more shortening); mix all together. Roll out, adding as little flour as possible; cut with a biscuit cutter, and bake immediately in a quick oven.

ENGLISH BISCUIT.

One and a-half pints of flour, one coffee-cup full corn starch, three tablespoonfuls sugar, a large pinch of salt, two large teaspoonfuls baking powder, three tablespoonfuls lard, one egg, one-half pint milk, one-half cup currants, one tablespoonful coriander seed (if desired). Sift together flour, corn starch, sugar, salt, and baking powder; rub in the lard cold; add the eggs beaten, milk, currants well cleaned; mix into a smooth dough soft enough to handle, flour the board, turn out the dough, roll it out to half an inch thickness, cut out with a round cutter, lay them on a greased baking tin, and bake in a rather hot oven twenty minutes; rub over with a little butter on a clean piece of linen when taken from the oven.

GRAHAM BISCUITS.

Take one quart water or milk, butter the size of an egg, three tablespoonfuls sugar, half cup yeast, and a little salt; take enough white flour to mix a batter with the water; add the other ingredients, and as much Graham flour as can be stirred in with a spoon; set it away until morning; then grease a pan, flour hands, take a lump of dough the size of a hen's egg, roll lightly between the palms; let them rise twenty minutes, and bake in a rather hot oven.

COLD BISCUITS.

Three pints flour, two tablespoonfuls sugar, one teaspoonful salt, two heaping teaspoonfuls baking powder, four tablespoonfuls lard, two tablespoonfuls caraway seeds, two eggs, one pint milk. Sift together flour, sugar, salt and powder, rub in lard cold, add the seeds, beaten eggs, and milk; mix into a smooth, firm dough, flour the board, turn out the dough, give it a few quick kneadings, and roll out to the thickness of a quarter of an inch, cut into large biscuits, prick with a fork, lay on a greased tin. Bake in hot oven fifteen minutes; when cold, store for use.

BUNNS.

Break an egg into a cup, and fill the cup up with sweet milk; mix with it a half cup yeast, half cup butter, one cup sugar, enough flour to make a soft dough; flavor with nutmeg; let rise till very light, then mold into biscuits with a few currants; let rise the second time and bake, and when nearly done glaze with a little molasses and milk.

BUNNS.

One cup butter, one cup sugar, half cup yeast, half pint milk, make stiff with flour, and mold into biscuits; when light, bake.

BUNNS.

One cup yeast, one egg, one tablespoonful molasses, flour to make a batter; let it rise, then add one pint milk, one pint sugar dissolved in the milk, half pint butter, two eggs; stir in flour stiff enough to make the buns, and let them rise in the pans before baking.

CINNAMON CAKE.

Take yeast bread dough when light, knead and roll out three-fourths of an inch thick; put thin slices of butter on the top, sprinkle with sugar, and then with cinnamon; let rise, and bake.

Graham Cakes.

To one quart Graham flour add one teaspoonful of salt, five tablespoonfuls molasses, three tablespoonfuls yeast, or a yeast cake dissolved in warm water. Stir as thick as pound cake; let stand over night; when ready to bake, add a well beaten egg, a tablespoonful lard and a teaspoonful of soda. Bake in cups half an hour.

Rye Drop Cakes.

One egg, two cups rye flour, two cups flour, half a cup sugar, a teaspoonful salt, two teaspoonfuls cream of tartar, one teaspoonful soda—or three teaspoonfuls baking powder,—a tablespoonful melted butter, and one of lard, one and a half cups milk; drop from a spoon and bake half an hour.

Corn Cakes.

One pint sour milk, two cups Indian meal, one cup flour, one egg, two tablespoonfuls molasses, one teaspoonful salt, one teaspoonful soda; mix thoroughly and bake twenty-five minutes in shallow pans.

Johnny Cake.

One quart corn meal, one quart milk, two eggs, two tablespoonfuls shortening, half cup sugar, teaspoonful salt, three teaspoonfuls baking powder—or substitute one quart sour milk and a large teaspoonful soda.

Newport Breakfast Cakes.

Three eggs, three spoonfuls sugar, one and-a-half pints milk, half cup butter, three teaspoonfuls baking powder. Stir stiff with flour and bake in loaves, like cakes.

Potato Cakes.

Peal enough good sized potatoes for a meal for the family, grate on a coarse grater, and stir in from three to five eggs, salt and mix stiff enough to mold into cakes, and fry in hot lard or drippings.

GRIDDLE CAKES.

STALE BREAD GRIDDLE CAKES.

Soak one pint bread crumbs in warm water, when soft drain off the water and add one pint sour milk with a teaspoonful soda stirred in, half teaspoonful salt, a beaten egg, and thicken with flour to make a batter.

CORN MEAL GRIDDLE CAKES.

One pint corn meal, one of sour milk or buttermilk, one egg, one teaspoonful soda, one of salt. Bake on a griddle.

RICE GRIDDLE CAKES.

One and one-half pints boiled rice, the same of flour, one-half teacupful sour milk, one teacupful sweet milk, one teaspoonful soda, salt, three eggs, and butter the size of a walnut.

FLOUR GRIDDLE CAKES.

Make a thick batter with one quart of sour milk and flour. Let it stand over night and in the morning add two well-beaten eggs, salt, and a teaspoonful of soda dissolved in a tablespoonful warm water. Bake immediately.

GREEN CORN GRIDDLE CAKES.

Six ears grated corn, two eggs, one pint milk, one pint flour, one tablespoonful butter, a little salt. Bake on a griddle.

HOMINY GRIDDLE CAKES.

To one pint warm boiled hominy add a pint of milk, or milk and water, and flour enough to make a thin batter; beat up two or three eggs and stir them into the batter with a little salt. Fry as other griddle cakes.

CRUMB CORN CAKES.

Soak a quart of bread crumbs in a quart of sour milk over night; in the morning rub through a colander and add four well-beaten eggs, a heaping teaspoonful soda dissolved in a little warm water,.

one tablespoonful shortening, and corn meal to mix into a nice batter. It is better to beat yolks and whites of eggs separately, stirring the whites in lightly just before baking.

FLANNEL CAKES.

Three eggs, one quart sweet milk, one quart sifted flour, with three teaspoonfuls baking powder, a small spoonful salt; beat the yolks and half of the milk, salt and flour together, then the remainder of the milk, and last, the whites of the eggs, well beaten; a teacup of boiled rice improves them.

BUCKWHEAT CAKES.

Take, of equal parts of buttermilk and water, one quart, half cup yeast, a little salt; stir into a batter with buckwheat flour, let rise over night; in the morning add half teaspoonful soda dissolved in a little water. Bake on a hot griddle.

GRAHAM GRIDDLE CAKES.

One pint Graham flour, half pint corn meal, half pint flour, one heaping teaspoonful sugar, half teaspoonful salt, one egg, one pint buttermilk, one teaspoonful soda.

SQUASH, PUMPKIN AND APPLE GRIDDLE CAKES.

Cold stewed squash, pumpkin or apple, rubbed through a colander, half pint; mix with two well-beaten eggs and half pint milk. Sift together half pint Graham flour, half pint corn meal, half teaspoonful salt, heaping teaspoonful baking powder. Mix smooth and thoroughly into a batter and bake on a hot griddle.

BERRY GRIDDLE CAKES.

Take of huckleberries, blackberries, or raspberries a half pint, one and one-half pints flour, one teaspoonful salt, one tablespoonful brown sugar, two teaspoonfuls baking powder, two eggs, and one pint milk. Sift together flour, sugar, salt and powder; add beaten eggs, milk and berries; mix into a batter; have the griddle hot enough to form a crust as soon as the batter touches it. In order to confine the juice of the berries turn quickly in order to form a crust on the other side; turn once more on each side to complete the baking.

Egg Cracknels.

One quart flour, one-half teaspoonful salt, five tablespoonfuls sugar, one teaspoonful baking powder, four tablespoonfuls butter, and five eggs. Sift together flour, sugar, salt and powder; rub in the butter cold; add the eggs beaten, and mix into a firm, smooth dough. Flour the board, turn out the dough, and give it a few minutes' rapid kneading; cover with a damp towel fifteen minutes; then roll it out to the thickness of one-eighth of an inch. Cut out with biscuit cutter. When all are cut out, have a large pot of boiling, and a large tin pan of cold water. Drop them a few at a time into the boiling water. When they appear at the surface and curl at the edges, take them up with a skimmer, and drop them in the cold water. When all are thus served, lay them on greased baking tins and bake in a fairly hot oven fifteen minutes.

Oatmeal Crackers.

One pint very fine oatmeal, one-half pint Graham flour, one-half teaspoonful salt, one-half teaspoonful sugar, one-half teaspoonful baking powder, one-half pint cream. Sift together the oatmeal, Graham, salt, sugar and powder; add the cream and mix into a dough, rather too soft to handle. Let it stand half an hour, by which time it will have absorbed the extra moisture, and handling it will be easy. Flour the board with Graham, roll out to the thickness of one-third inch, prick with a fork, lay on greased baking tin, and bake in a moderate oven ten minutes. They must be watched during baking, as they burn quickly, and when baked handled with care; they break easily.

Graham Crackers.

Sift together one quart Graham flour, one tablespoonful sugar, half teaspoonful salt, half teaspoonful baking powder; mix with two tablespoonfuls butter and a good half pint milk, into a smooth dough, and knead well for five minutes; roll it to the thickness of one-quarter inch, cut into crackers round or square. Bake in rather hot oven ten minutes; when cold store for use.

CRUMPETS.

Mix together thoroughly while dry one quart sifted flour, two heaping teaspoonfuls baking powder, a little salt, then add two tablespoonfuls melted butter and sweet milk enough to make a thin dough. Bake quickly in muffin rings or patty pans.

LONDON CRUMPETS.

Sift together one and one-half pints flour, one-half teaspoonful salt, one teaspoonful sugar, and two teaspoonfuls baking powder; add one beaten egg, a scant pint of milk and cream in equal parts, a little ground cinnamon or a teaspoonful extract of cinnamon; half fill greased muffin rings, place on a hot, well-greased griddle. Bake on one side only. Serve hot with cottage cheese.

KENTUCKY CORN DODGERS.

Place your griddle where it will heat, for this is much better than a bread pan, there being less danger of scorching at the bottom. Take an even pint of sifted meal, a heaping tablespoonful of lard, a pinch of salt, and a scant half pint of cold water; mix well and let it stand while you grease your griddle and sprinkle some meal over it. Make the dough into rolls the size and shape of goose eggs, and drop them on the griddle, taking care to flatten as little as possible, for the less bottom crust the better. Place in the oven and bake until brown on the bottom. Then change to the grate, and brown on top, taking from twenty to thirty minutes for the whole process. Eaten while hot with plenty of good butter, they are better than any other bread.

The same amount of meal, lard and salt mixed with boiling water, till of the consistency of thick batter, will give you delightful hot cakes, to be cooked like any other batter bread.

FRITTERS.

GREEN CORN FRITTERS.

Grate green corn from the cob, and allow an egg and a half for every cupful, with a tablespoonful of milk or cream; beat the eggs well; add the corn by degrees, beating very hard; salt to taste. Put a tablespoonful of melted butter to every pint of corn; stir in the milk, and thicken with just enough flour to hold them together —say a tablespoonful for every two eggs. You may fry in hot lard, as you would fritters, or cook upon a griddle like batter cakes. Eaten at dinner or breakfast, these always find a cordial welcome.

GREEN CORN FRITTERS, No. 2.

Two cups of grated corn, two eggs, one cup of milk, flour for thin batter, a pinch of soda, salt, one tablespoonful melted butter. Mix and fry as you would griddle cakes.

APPLE FRITTERS.

Beat three eggs very lightly, then stir in one teaspoonful of salt, one-half cup of sugar, one pint of milk, two cups of chopped apple and two cups of flour. Flavor with nutmeg. Stir all well together and fry in lard as pancakes. Sift sugar over them and send to the table.

CELERY FRITTERS.

Boil some thick but tender stalks of celery in salted water; when done dry them on a cloth, cut them in equal lengths about one and a-half inches; fry them in batter to a golden color, sprinkling fine salt well over, and serve.

OYSTER FRITTERS.

Drain them thoroughly, chop fine, season with pepper and salt. Make a batter of eggs, milk and flour; stir the chopped oysters in this and fry in hot butter; or fry them whole, enveloped in batter, one in each fritter. In this case the batter should be thicker than if they were chopped.

CLAM FRITTERS.

Twelve clams, minced fine; one pint milk; three eggs. Add the liquor from the clams to the milk; beat up the eggs and put to this, with salt and pepper, and flour enough for thin batter; lastly, the chopped clams. Fry in hot lard, trying a little first to see if the fat and batter are right. A tablespoonful will make a fritter of moderate size. Or you can dip the whole clams in batter and cook in like manner. Fry quickly, or they are apt to be too greasy.

LOBSTER FRITTERS.

Put one lobster in two quarts boiling water with half a cup salt; boil twenty-five minutes; when cold remove the meat and fat, cut into small slices; put one tablespoonful butter, one tablespoonful flour, one cup cream, a little celery, salt, thyme, white pepper, and a salt-spoon of parsley, into a stew-pan; let boil two minutes; add yolks of four eggs, and the lobster; mix and set it back to simmer five minutes; pour it out on a well-greased dish and set it away to get firm by cooling; cut into slices, dip into common batter and fry to a light brown in hot lard. Serve on the fritters a few sprigs of parsley, quite dry, fried in the lard fifteen seconds.

RICE FRITTERS.

Boil one cup of rice in one pint of milk until soft; add the yolks of three eggs, one tablespoonful sugar, two tablespoonfuls butter, two tablespoonfuls flour; when cold add the whites of the eggs whipped to a stiff froth; drop in spoonfuls in plenty of hot lard and fry to a light brown color. Serve with cream, wine or lemon sauce.

BLACKBERRY FRITTERS.

Mix one cup blackberries with one and a-half cups common batter and drop by tablespoonfuls into hot lard.

All berry fritters can be made as directed for the above and served with spiced sauce made as follows: Set on the fire three-fourths pint of water, one cup sugar; boil twenty minutes, remove from the fire and add one teaspoonful each of extract cloves, mace, and ginger.

GEMS.

GRAHAM GEMS.

One pint milk, one pint Graham flour, salt-spoonful salt; beat well; heat the gem pan hot, butter it and drop the dough into the sockets with a spoon, filling each one-half full.

GRAHAM GEMS, No. 2.

One pint buttermilk, one teaspoonful soda, a little salt, one egg, one-half cup sugar, tablespoonful lard; thicken with Graham flour, and bake in gem tins.

GRAHAM GEMS, No. 3.

One pint milk, one cup flour, one cup Graham flour, one egg, a little salt. Have the irons hot before using.

COLD WATER GEMS.

Take cold water, Graham flour, and a little salt, make rather a stiff batter; heat and grease the irons, or tins, and bake twenty minutes.

MIXED GEMS.

One-half pint Graham, half pint corn meal, half pint rye flour, half pint buckwheat flour, one teaspoonful salt, two heaping teaspoonfuls baking powder, one pint rich milk; mix into a thin batter, then half fill well-greased gem pans. Bake in hot oven fifteen minutes.

CORN GEMS.

One pint corn meal, one pint flour, one teaspoonful salt, two large teaspoonfuls baking powder, one pint milk; mix into a firm batter, two-thirds fill well-greased gem pans and bake in a hot oven fifteen minutes.

OATMEAL GEMS.

Soak one cup oatmeal over night in one cup water; in the morning add one cup sour milk, one teaspoonful soda, one cup of flour, a little salt, bake in gem irons. If on trial they are a little moist or sticky, add a little more flour.

MUFFINS.

To one quart of milk add two well-beaten eggs, a lump of butter half the size of an egg, a little salt, and flour enough to make a stiff batter; stir in half a pint of yeast. Let them stand until they are perfectly light and then bake on a griddle in rings made for the purpose. These are merely strips of tin three-fourths of an inch wide, made into rings two and a half or three inches in diameter, and without bottoms, the ring being simply placed on the griddle and the batter being poured in to fill it.

MUFFINS, No. 2.

One pint flour, one cup milk, two eggs, two teaspoonfuls baking powder, butter the size of an egg; beat the yolks of the eggs with the butter, then add the whites well beaten. Sift baking powder with the flour, and mix all together into a batter. Bake in muffin rings.

MUFFINS, No. 3.

One pint new milk, one egg, one tablespoonful sugar, one table-spoonful butter, half teaspoonful salt, one cake yeast (or better, half cup home-made yeast); mix with flour until a very stiff batter is formed; leave in a warm place over night and bake in the morning in rings.

RICE FLOUR MUFFINS.

One and one-half cups rice flour, two cups wheat flour, one pint milk, one egg, three teaspoonfuls baking powder, a little salt, a small piece of butter. Bake as usual.

RICE MUFFINS.

One pint sifted flour, two heaping teaspoonfuls baking powder and a little salt. Thoroughly mix together; then add one cup cold boiled rice, two eggs, one tablespoonful butter, and enough sweet milk to make a thick batter. Bake immediately.

GRAHAM MUFFINS.

Two cups sour milk, one teaspoonful saleratus, two eggs, a little salt, butter half the size of an egg, three cups Graham flour. Bake in rings.

GRAHAM MUFFINS, No. 2.

Two cups Graham flour, one cup sweet milk, one-third cup sugar, one egg, butter the size of an egg, two teaspoonfuls baking powder. Bake in rings twenty or thirty minutes in hot oven.

CORN MEAL MUFFINS.

One and one-half cups of corn meal, the same of flour, two heaping teaspoonfuls baking powder, one-half cup sugar, one-half teaspoonful salt, one tablespoonful butter, two eggs, and milk enough to make a stiff batter.

MUSH.

CORN MUSH.

Take boiling water (soft water is preferable), salt to the taste, add meal very slowly so as to prevent any lumps being formed; cook thoroughly.

OATMEAL MUSH.

Put four tablespoonfuls oatmeal into one quart cold water; add one teaspoonful salt, let it cook slowly for from one to two hours, adding hot water when needed; just before serving stir in one teaspoonful butter, or soak the meal over night and add boiling water and cook in the morning.

CRACKED WHEAT MUSH.

To one quart salted water add three-fourths cup cracked or rolled wheat, and boil two hours; or it may be soaked over night and boil one hour.

Cracked Wheat Mush, No. 2.

Moisten one and one-half cups cracked wheat with cold water, add one-half teaspoonful salt, place in a muslin bag, leaving half the space for the wheat to swell; put into a small colander and place in a kettle of water and keep boiling from three to four hours. Serve with syrup and butter or cream and sugar. It is nice sliced and fried when cold.

Fried Mush for Breakfast.

Night before, stir into two quarts of boiling water a little salt and one pound of farina, boil for ten minutes, and pour it into a shallow dish to cool; next morning cut it into slices, and fry in lard light brown. This is far superior to corn meal mush.

Hominy.

Take one cup hominy to one quart salted water and soak over night and boil three-fourths of an hour. Serve with milk and sugar. Slice and fry when cold.

PUFFS.

Puffs.

Two eggs, two cups of milk, two cups of flour, and a little salt. Pour into hot roll pans and bake in a quick oven. Fill the pans about half full.

German Puffs.

Two cups of sweet milk, two cups of flour, three eggs, and a little salt.

Graham Puffs.

One egg, one pint sweet milk, one pint Graham flour, and a pinch of salt; beat the eggs thoroughly; add the milk, then the flour gradually; beat the whole mixture briskly with an egg-beater; pour into cast-iron gem pans, well-greased, and hot; bake in very hot oven; this mixture is just sufficient for twelve gems.

OATMEAL PUFFS.

Sift together one-half pint oatmeal, one-half pint Graham, one-half pint flour, one teaspoonful sugar, one-half teaspoonful salt, and two teaspoonfuls baking powder; add three beaten eggs and one pint milk; mix into a thin batter; half fill well-greased gem pans and bake in hot oven ten or fifteen minutes.

POTATO PUFFS.

To each two cupfuls of mashed potatoes take one tablespoonful of melted butter and beat to a cream; put with this two eggs whipped light, and a cupful of milk, salting to taste; beat all well; pour into greased baking dish and bake quickly to a light brown. Serve in the dish in which it is cooked.

CREAM PUFFS.

One-half pint boiling water, one cup of butter, two cups of flour. Let the water and butter boil, then stir in the flour; let it cool; add five eggs well beaten; beat all well; drop in muffin rings; bake thirty minutes. Boil one pint of milk; beat together one cup of flour, one cup of sugar, and two eggs; add this to the boiling milk and boil three minutes; cut a hole in the top of each cake and fill with cream, putting the piece of crust back.

PUFFETS.

One quart flour, one pint milk, two eggs beaten light, butter size of an egg, three tablespoonfuls sugar, three teaspoonfuls baking powder; bake quickly.

PROVERBS.

One cup rich milk, one egg, two cups flour, one teaspoonful baking powder, a little salt; beat together thoroughly, fill buttered cups half full and bake in a hot oven.

POCKET BOOKS.

One quart warm water or milk, two eggs, three teaspoonfuls sugar, one cup yeast, four tablespoonfuls melted butter, add flour to make a sponge, and set to rise; when it is risen work it over and set to rise again; when light put in a piece of soda the size of a bean; roll out, spread the surface with butter, cut in squares and double over to form a pocket book shape; put in a pan and let stand till light, then bake.

ROLLS.

How to make Rolls.

When mashing potatoes for dinner, put a tablespoonful of it into one pint of the water they were boiled in, and set aside till bedtime; then strain it through a colander, add one pint of milk, one large spoonful nice lard, one large spoonful white sugar, one teaspoonful salt, one penny-worth of yeast, and flour to make a stiff batter. Leave it in a moderately warm place. In the morning add flour enough to make a soft dough, working it well. Let it rise again, roll out half an inch thick, cut into round cakes, fold together, drawing a buttered knife through as you fold them. Let them rise again for half an hour, or until light; bake in a quick oven for fifteen or twenty minutes. In cold weather the milk should be luke-warm; in hot weather the milk should be scalded and cooled. The potatoes must be pared before boiling, and the kettle in which they are boiled must be perfectly clean.

Rolls No. 2.

Take a piece of bread dough when molded; roll out half an inch thick; spread with butter, and sprinkle with sugar; roll up and cut off the size you want; let rise and bake.

Parker House Rolls.

Two quarts flour, one cup yeast, one pint milk, boiled, then cooled to milk-warm, one tablespoonful of shortening, one of sugar; lay a sponge, leaving out enough flour to mix in when rolling out; if for tea, mix in the morning; bake as soon as ready.

Cinnamon Rolls.

Take light dough, as for bread; mix in shortening, an egg, and a

little sugar; roll out to about one-quarter inch in thickness; spread with butter, then sprinkle with sugar and cinnamon; roll up and cut as you would a jelly cake; put in pans like biscuit; set to rise. When light, put a little lump of butter, and sugar and cinnamon on each one, and bake.

White Mountain Rolls.

Sixteen cups of flour, half cup of sugar, cup of butter, cup of yeast, the whites of four eggs beaten to a stiff froth, and four cups of boiling milk; melt the butter and sugar in the milk, have the milk blood warm and mix the bread, adding the whites of eggs after mixing in part of the flour; knead stiff and let rise in a warm place over night. In the morning knead into rolls and let rise till light; rub the beaten white of an egg over the tops of rolls, and bake thirty minutes.

Vienna Twist Rolls.

Break pieces off dough (as prepared for common rolls) the size of an egg, and divide each piece into two unequal pieces, the largest piece form with the hands into a plain roll tapering at each end; lay them, thus formed, on a greased baking tin so as not to touch each other; flatten each a little and wash over with milk; divide the remaining pieces each into three, roll the pieces out under the hands into strips a little longer than the roll already made, and braid them; then lay each braid, as soon as formed, on top of the plain roll; when all are made, wash over with milk. Bake in a hot oven twenty minutes—a very handsome roll for a dinner party.

Oatmeal Rolls.

Sift together one-half pint oatmeal, one-half pint Graham, one pint flour, one teaspoonful salt, two teaspoonfuls baking powder, and mix with three-fourths pint milk into a smooth dough; turn out and give one or two quick kneadings to complete its quality; roll out to the thickness of half an inch, cut out with large round cutter, fold through the centre laying one half over on the other, lay them on a greased baking tin so they do not touch, wash over with milk and bake in a good hot oven fifteen minutes.

ITALIAN ROLLS.

Take a piece of bread dough and one-fourth the amount of butter, work the butter thoroughly into the dough and roll out to about one-half an inch in thickness; cut into strips about six inches long; sift over them fine corn meal, place them, separated, on a buttered baking tin, and when light bake in a quick oven.

GRAHAM BREAKFAST ROLLS.

Take six potatoes, boiled and pressed through a colander, one pint warm water, one-half cup sugar, one-half teaspoonful salt, one-half cup yeast; mix into a stiff dough with Graham flour, and let rise over night; in the morning mold into rolls and bake when light.

FRENCH ROLLS.

Into one pound of flour rub two ounces of butter and the whites of three eggs well-beaten; add a tablespoonful of good yeast, a little salt, and milk enough to make a stiff dough; cover and set in a warm place till light; cut into rolls, dip the edges into melted butter to keep them from sticking together, and bake' in a quick oven.

TREMONT HOUSE ROLLS.

Take two quarts of flour, add one teaspoonful salt; make a hole in the middle and put into it one tablespoonful of sugar, butter about the size of an egg, one pint of boiled milk, and one teacupful of yeast. Do not stir, but put them together at night, and set in a cool place until morning. Then mix all together and knead fifteen minutes. Set in a cool place again for six hours, and roll out about one-half an inch thick and cut with a biscuit cutter; moisten one edge with butter, and fold together like rolls; lay in the pan so that they will not touch, set for half an hour in a warm place to rise, and bake in a quick oven.

Rosettes.

To three eggs, the yolks beaten very light, add one quart of milk, a piece of butter the size of an egg cut in little pieces into the milk and eggs, three coffee cups of flour, a little salt, three teaspoonfuls of baking powder, and lastly the whites of the eggs beaten very light and stirred quickly into the mixture. Bake in a quick oven.

RUSKS.

Sweet Rusks.

In one large coffee cup of warm milk dissolve one cake of compressed yeast; then add three eggs and one cup of sugar, and beat all together; use only flour enough to roll out, to which add two ounces of butter; let it rise. When very light, knead, mold into shape, and set in a warm place. When light, bake in a hot oven; when done, cover the top with sugar dissolved in milk.

Sweet Rusks, No. 2.

One pint of warm milk—new is best—one-half cup of butter, one cup of sugar, two eggs, one teaspoonful of salt, two tablespoonfuls of yeast; make a sponge with the milk, yeast, and enough flour to make a thin batter, and let rise over night. In the morning add the sugar, butter, eggs, and salt, well-beaten together, with enough flour to make a soft dough. Let it rise again, then make into round balls, and rise a third time. Bake in a moderate oven.

Rusks.

Half pint of sweet milk, one teacup of yeast, two eggs; mix with sufficient flour for a stiff batter and raise; then add one cup of butter, half cup of sugar, one teaspoonful of soda, and a little nutmeg; let rise, and knead out into biscuits; let rise and bake. Just before taking out of the oven beat up the white of an egg and rub over the top, then sprinkle with sugar; put into the oven again for a moment, and serve hot.

Baking Powder Rusks.

Thoroughly mix with one quart sifted flour, two heaping tea-spoonfuls baking powder, and one teaspoonful salt; then mix the beaten yolks of three eggs with a half cup butter and one cup sugar; now stir up the flour prepared as above with water, making a dough of the proper consistency for bread; then add the eggs, butter and sugar, and mix all well together. Form into little cakes and rub the tops with sugar and water, and then sprinkle dry sugar over them and bake immediately.

Scones.

Thoroughly mix one quart sifted flour, two heaping teaspoonfuls baking powder; then rub into one-fourth pound butter and enough sweet milk to make a smooth paste; roll out the paste to one-fourth of an inch in thickness and cut it into triangular pieces, each side of which is about four inches long; put them into a greased tin and bake immediately in a very hot oven; when half done, brush them over with sweet milk.

Scotch Scones.

Sift together one quart flour, one teaspoonful sugar, one-half teaspoonful salt, two heaping teaspoonfuls baking powder; rub in a large tablespoonful lard cold; add two beaten eggs and nearly one-half pint milk; mix into a smooth dough, knead up quickly and roll out to one-third of an inch in thickness, cut out with a knife into squares larger than soda crackers, fold each in half to form three-cornered pieces, bake on a hot griddle eight or ten minutes; brown on each side.

Sally Lunn.

One quart of flour, a piece of butter the size of an egg, three tablespoonfuls of sugar, two eggs, two teacups of milk, two tea-spoonfuls of cream of tartar, one of soda, and a little salt. Scatter the cream of tartar, the sugar and the salt into the flour; add the eggs, the butter melted and one cup of milk; dissolve the soda in the remaining cup, and stir all together steadily a few moments. Bake in two round pans.

SALLY LUNN, No. 2.

Sift together one quart flour, one teaspoonful salt, two teaspoonfuls baking powder; rub in two-thirds cup butter cold; add four beaten eggs, one-half pint milk; mix into a firm batter like cup cake, pour into two round cake tins, and bake twenty-five minutes in a pretty hot oven.

PLAIN SHORT CAKE.

One quart flour, one saltspoonful salt, two heaping teaspoonfuls baking powder; mix thoroughly; then add one-quarter pound butter, and one-eighth pound lard, and enough cold water to make a thick paste. Roll out about a quarter of an inch thick, and cut into squares; prick with a fork and bake immediately.

SCOTCH SHORT CAKE.

Sift together one and a half pints flour, four tablespoonfuls sugar, one-half teaspoonful salt, a heaping teaspoonful baking powder; rub in four tablespoonfuls butter cold, add three beaten eggs, nearly one cupful milk, a teaspoonful extract of orange, or lemon; mix into a smooth dough without much handling, and roll out to the thickness of a quarter inch, and cut into shape of small envelopes; wash over with milk, and lay on each three thin slices of citron, and a few caraway seeds. Bake in a moderate oven twenty minutes.

SANDWICHES.

HAM SANDWICHES.

Take well-boiled ham, one-third fat and two-thirds lean, chop it until it is as fine as paste, then stir in the yolk of an egg. To one teaspoonful mustard, mix one tablespoonful Worcestershire sauce. Use this or more in such proportions as you may require.

EGG SANDWICHES.

Take slices of buttered bread and grate hard-boiled eggs on each slice with a coarse grater, sprinkle with pepper and salt; then lay two slices together.

This sandwich may be varied by grating a layer of cold smoked tongue or ham over the egg on one slice and not on the other. These require a light and dexterous hand to keep the egg from being crushed.

SARDINE SANDWICHES.

Open a can of sardines, remove the skin and bones, lay bits of the fish on well-spread bread and butter; squeeze lemon over it; lay a slice of buttered bread on top.

SCHOOL LUNCH SANDWICHES.

Beat three eggs, three tablespoonfuls of milk, saltspoonful of salt, and a dash of pepper; fry it as you would a griddle cake, and lay between buttered bread or biscuit, or slice hard-boiled eggs or nice stewed codfish left cold, and lay between slices of bread and butter.

OYSTER SANDWICHES.

Chop one quart raw oysters very fine, season with pepper, salt, a little nutmeg; mix with one-half cupful melted butter, the same of rich cream, whites of three eggs beaten, and eight powdered crackers. Heat them over steam in an oatmeal boiler or over the fire until a smooth paste; set away until very cold; then cut and lay between buttered slices of bread.

TONGUE OR HAM SANDWICHES.

Chop fine the lean of cold boiled tongue or ham, season with prepared mustard and black pepper; add melted butter and sweet cream until smooth like a paste, then spread between buttered slices of bread.

TOAST.

CREAM TOAST.

Take slices of stale bread, one quart of milk, three tablespoonfuls butter, whites of three eggs beaten stiff, salt, and three tablespoonfuls flour. Toast the bread to a golden brown, have a dish half full of boiling water in which a tablespoonful of butter has been melted; as each slice is toasted dip it in this for a second and lay in the deep heated dish in which it is to be served. Have ready, by the time the bread is all toasted, the milk scalding hot, but not boiling; thicken this with the flour; let simmer until cooked; put in the remaining butter, and when this is melted the beaten whites of the eggs; boil up once and pour over the toast, lifting the slices that the cream may run between; cover closely; set in the oven a few moments before sending to the table.

BREAKFAST TOAST.

Mix two tablespoonfuls of sugar, a little salt, and a well-beaten egg, in one-half pint of milk. In this mixture dip slices of bread and fry them on a buttered griddle until they are light brown on each side.

CHEESE AND EGG TOAST.

Put a cupful of cheese crumbs into half a pint of rich milk; boil until it melts. Have two eggs well beaten. Season the milk with salt, pepper and butter to taste; turn in the eggs; stir rapidly for a few minutes; remove from the fire and spread it over some hot slices of toasted bread. Cut them in halves and quarters and serve on a hot platter.

HAM TOAST.

Melt in a stew pan a small piece of butter till it is browned a little; put in as much finely-minced ham as will cover a round of buttered toast, and add gravy enough to make moist. When quite hot stir in quickly with a fork one egg. Place the mixture over the toast, which cut into pieces of any shape you may fancy.

Spanish Toast.

Beat three eggs to a foam; toast a few slices of bakers' bread; dip them in the egg, and fry them to a light brown.

Fried Bread.

Take dry bread, dip it in hot water quickly, and lay on a hot pancake griddle, which has some lard or butter melted, salt; when nicely browned on one side, turn on the other and brown; add more butter when needed. Some prefer the bread dipped in egg first.

WAFFLES.

One quart of sweet milk, warm, four eggs, a piece of butter the size of an egg, one teaspoonful of salt, teacup of yeast, flour enough to make a stiff batter; let it rise three hours. Bake in waffle-irons.

Waffles, No. 2.

Four eggs, whites beaten separately; two tablespoonfuls short-ening, one quart milk, one teaspoonful soda, salt; add the whites last; add two teaspoonfuls cream of tartar to flour enough to make thin batter.

Waffles, No. 3.

One pint sour cream (or part milk), two eggs, one spoonful soda, half spoonful salt; then make same as above.

Waffles, No. 4.

One pint of buttermilk, flour enough to make a thin batter, one tablespoonful of salt, one teaspoonful of soda; mix your milk, flour and salt, then sift the soda over the batter; break the white of one egg in a plate and put the yolk in the batter; beat in well; now whip the white of the egg to a stiff froth and stir in thoroughly—do not beat it in. Have the waffle-iron smoking hot and grease with lard or other grease, which should be free from either water or salt, as both make the waffles stick. If the milk be very sour, use more soda to sweeten it. Sour batter will stick to the irons, too.

BREAD WAFFLES.

Crusts and pieces can be put in a pitcher and milk poured over them; when needed, add more milk, and a little flour, to make the right consistency; enough soda to make sweet, salt, and make waffles, or pancakes.

RICE WAFFLES.

One and one-half cups of boiled rice, the same of flour, one cup sour milk, a scant teaspoonful soda, a little salt, three eggs, and butter the size of a walnut.

GRAHAM WAFERS.

Put a pinch of salt into one-half pound of Graham flour; wet it with one-half pint of sweet cream; mix quickly and thoroughly; roll out as thin as possible; cut in strips, prick, and bake in a quick oven.

SWEET WAFERS.

One pint flour, one cup sugar, three eggs, one tablespoonful butter; flavor with lemon; mix into a batter with a little milk to the consistency of sponge cake, and bake in wafer-irons.

CHAPTER III.

CAKE.

ALMOND CAKE.

FOUR cups sifted flour, three teaspoonfuls baking powder, two cups powdered sugar, one cup butter, ten eggs (the yolks and whites whipped separately, the yolks strained), one-half pound sweet almonds blanched and pounded, one tablespoonful orange-flower water, nutmeg. Beat butter and sugar until they are like whipped cream, add the strained yolks, rub the baking powder into the flour and add alternately with the whites, then the almond paste in which the nutmeg and orange-flower water have been mixed; beat well and bake as "snowballs" in small, round, rather deep pans, with straight sides; when done cover with almond frosting. Very rich.

ALMOND CAKE, No. 2.

One and one-half cups sugar, half cup butter, four eggs, half cup milk, two cups of flour, two teaspoonfuls baking powder; bake in sheets. Icing—whites of three eggs beaten stiff, three tablespoonfuls white sugar, one cup chopped nut meats; flavor to taste and put these between and on top of layers.

ADELAIDE CAKE.

One cup butter, one and one-half cups sugar, four eggs, one pint flour, two teaspoonfuls of baking powder, one cup dried stoned cherries, one-half cup milk, one teaspoonful vanilla; mix smoothly into a firm batter by beating the sugar, butter and eggs together, and adding the flour with the baking powder and the other ingredients. Bake about forty minutes.

Apple Cake.

Two eggs, whites and yolks beaten separately, one and one-half cups sugar, scant three-fourths cup butter, half cup sweet milk, three cups flour, one teaspoonful cream of tartar sifted in the flour, one-half teaspoonful soda in the milk. Bake in jelly tins or cut for dressing.

Dressing for Same.

Three good sized sour apples grated, the juice and grated rind of one lemon, one egg beaten, one cup sugar. Cook all together three minutes and spread between the layers.

Angels' Food.

Take the whites of eleven eggs, one and one-half tumblerfuls of granulated sugar, one tumblerful of flour, one teaspoonful of vanilla, and one teaspoonful of cream of tartar; sift the flour four times, then add the cream of tartar, and sift again; but have the right measure before putting in the cream of tartar. Sift the sugar and measure. Beat the eggs to a stiff froth on a large platter; on the same platter add the sugar lightly, then the flour very gently, then the vanilla; do not stop beating until you put it in the pan to bake; bake forty minutes in a very moderate oven, try with a straw, and if too soft, let it remain a few minutes longer. Turn the pan upside down to cool, and when cold, take out by loosening around the sides with a knife. Use a pan that has never been greased, and there must be on the edge three projections of tin an inch or two deep, so that there will be a space between the pan and the table when it is turned upside down. The tumbler for measuring must hold two and one-quarter gills.

Andalusia Sponge Cake.

Three eggs, well beaten, one cup white sugar, one cup flour, and one teaspoonful baking powder; flavor to suit the taste. Beat quickly and bake at once.

Black Fruit Cake.

Two pounds raisins, one pound currants, one-half pound citron.

four cups sugar, two cups butter, one cup molasses, eight eggs, two teaspoonfuls soda, one wine glass brandy, five cups flour, spice to taste. Half of this receipt makes two small loaves.

BRIDE CAKE.

The whites of sixteen eggs beaten to a stiff froth, one pound of sugar, one pound of flour, one-half pound of butter. Flavor with almond. Mix the butter and sugar to a cream, then add the eggs, then the flour.

BRIDE CAKE, No. 2.

One and one-half pounds butter, one and three-fourths pounds sugar (half New Orleans sugar), two pounds eggs well-beaten, four pounds raisins seeded and chopped, English currants, thoroughly cleaned, five pounds, citron shaved fine two pounds, sifted flour two pounds, two nutmegs, and an equal quantity of mace, one gill of alcohol, in which are put fifteen drops of oil of lemon. Cut the butter in pieces and put it where it will soften; stir it to a cream, then add the sugar and work till white; next beat the yolks of the eggs, and add them to the sugar and butter; have the whites beaten to a stiff froth and add them to the mixture, then the spices and flour, and last of all the fruit except the citron, which is to be put in in about three layers, one an inch from the bottom, one an inch from the top, and one between; smooth the top of the cake by putting on a spoonful of water. Bake three or four hours.

BREAD CAKE.

Four cups light dough, two cups sugar, one cup butter, three eggs, one cup raisins, a little nutmeg, one-half teaspoonful cloves, the same of cinnamon, one-half teaspoonful soda, dissolved in hot water. Let it rise a short time before baking, then put in the raisins and bake in a very slow oven.

BLACK CAKE.

Two cups brown sugar, one cup butter, one cup molasses, one cup sour milk, in which dissolve one teaspoonful soda, the yolks of eight eggs, four cups of browned flour, and spice to your taste.

BRIDGEPORT CAKE.

One cup butter, two cups brown sugar, one cup sour milk, three and one-half cups flour, four eggs, one teaspoonful saleratus, one cup raisins, spice and one glass brandy.

BUTTERNUT CAKE.

One and one-half cups sugar, one-half cup butter, two cups flour, three-fourths cup sweet milk, one cup meats of nuts, whites of four eggs, and two teaspoonfuls baking powder.

BOSTON CREAM CAKE.

One-half pint water, one-fourth pound butter, six ounces flour, five eggs. Boil the butter and water together, adding the flour while they are boiling; when thoroughly stirred take it from the fire; when it is cold add the eggs, one at a time, beating the mixture until it is entirely free from lumps. Wet the baking pan with a little soda water, drop the mixture onto the pan by spoon fuls. Bake twenty minutes in a hot oven; avoid opening the oven door while baking. When the cakes are cool, open them on one side and fill with the following mixture: One cup sugar, one-half cup flour, two eggs, and one pint milk. Beat the eggs, sugar, and flour together, and stir them into the milk while it is boiling, stir ring constantly until it thickens; when cold, flavor to suit the taste

COCOANUT CAKE.

Two beaten eggs, one cup sugar, rolled fine, one-third cup butter, one-half cup milk, two cups flour, sifted with two teaspoonfuls baking powder. Bake in layers and put together with frosting and a layer of desiccated cocoanut which has been previously soaked in milk; frost the top of the cake and sprinkle thickly with the cocoanut.

COCOANUT CAKE, No. 2.

One cup butter, three cups sugar, whites of six eggs, four and one-half cups sifted flour, two and one-half teaspoonfuls baking powder, one grated cocoanut, and one cup milk. Rub the butter and sugar to a cream, add the whites of the eggs, then the milk; mix the baking powder with the flour by sifting. After all are mixed together put in the cocoanut, mixing thoroughly, and bake immediately. This cake will keep for some time, retaining its freshness.

CHOCOLATE CAKE.

One-half cup butter, two cups sugar, four eggs, one cup sweet milk, two teaspoonfuls cream of tartar, one teaspoonful soda, one teaspoonful vanilla. Bake in layers.

Paste for Same.—One-half cake chocolate warmed in the oven ten minutes, one heaping teaspoonful white sugar, one teaspoonful cinnamon, one-half teaspoonful ground cloves, a pinch of ginger, and two teaspoonfuls vanilla. Pour a little water on the sugar, put it on the chocolate, heat on the stove and put in the spice when boiled.

CORN STARCH CAKE.

Take whites of three eggs, one cup white sugar, one-third cup butter, one-half cup milk, one cup flour, one cup corn starch, one teaspoonful soda and two of cream of tartar; flavor with lemon or vanilla.

CORN STARCH CAKE, No. 2.

Whites of six eggs, beaten to a stiff froth, one cup butter, two cups sugar, one cup sweet milk, one cup corn starch, two cups flour, two teaspoonfuls cream of tartar, one teaspoonful soda; flavor to suit the taste.

COFFEE CAKE.

Take two eggs, well beaten, one-half cup butter, one-half cup sugar, one cup molasses, one cup strong cold coffee, one teaspoonful cinnamon, one teaspoonful cloves, one teaspoonful allspice, one teaspoonful soda stirred into the molasses, one cup of raisins, flour to make of the consistency of pound cake.

CHOCOLATE ECLAIRS.

Make a batter as for "Boston Cream Cake," form it with a spoon on the baking pan into long narrow cakes, leaving a space between; when baked and cold make an opening in the side and put in the cream, which must also be cold. Make the cream as follows: Break, dissolve, and mix smoothly one ounce of chocolate with three tablespoonfuls warm water in a bowl; set over a boiling tea-kettle, add gradually a cup of milk and leave it to scald; beat one egg and add to it one-half cup of sugar, and two tablespoonfuls corn starch; mix well and stir into the scalded milk, then put the whole into the bowl over the boiling water, and stir till it is much thicker than boiled custard; add a very little salt and half a teaspoonful of vanilla; after filling the cakes with the custard, frost with hot icing with two ounces of chocolate dissolved in it. Frost the top only.

CHARLOTTE CACHEE.

One thick loaf of sponge or plain cup cake, two kinds of fruit-jelly, tart and sweet, whites of five eggs, one heaping cup of powdered sugar, juice of one lemon. Cut the cake into horizontal slices of uniform width; spread each with jelly—first the tart, then the sweet—and fit into their former places; ice thickly with a frosting made of the whites, sugar, and lemon-juice; set in a sunny window or slow oven, to harden. The former is the better plan.

CIDER CAKE.

One cup of sugar, half cup of butter, one egg, well-beaten, one large cup of cider, one teaspoonful of soda, flour sufficient to make it as thick as pound cake. One cup of raisins can be added if desired.

CAKE WITHOUT EGGS.

One cup butter, three cups sugar, one pint sour milk or cream, three cups flour, one pound raisins, one teaspoonful saleratus; spice to taste.

CREAM PUFFS.

Melt one-half cup of butter in a cup of hot water, and while boiling beat in one cup of flour. Take it from the fire and when cool stir in three eggs, one at a time, without beating them. Drop the mixture on tins in small spoonfuls and bake in a moderate oven.

Custard for the Filling.—One and one-half cups of milk, two eggs, four tablespoonfuls of flour, sugar to the taste, and flavor with vanilla. Beat up the eggs and sugar and stir in the milk with the flavoring, and when it comes to a boil stir in the flour, previously mixed smooth in a little milk. Cool and fill the puffs by opening them a very little.

CITRON CAKE.

One cup of butter, two of sugar, three of flour, four eggs, one cup of milk, one teaspoonful of soda, two of cream of tartar, and a pinch of salt Make the cake as above, put in the pan, cut the citron thin and put in the cake endways; push down until the batter covers the citron, and this will prevent the citron from falling to the bottom of the pan.

CREAM CAKE.

Three eggs, one cup of sugar, one cup of flour, one teaspoonful of baking powder, one-half cup of sweet cream. Bake like jelly cake. Put one cup of pulverized white sugar into one-half cup of very thick sweet cream, and spread between the cakes; flavor both the cake and cream to suit taste. This is delicious.

CHOCOLATE CAKE, No. 2.

One cup white sugar, one-half cup sweet milk, one-half cup melted butter, whites of four eggs beaten stiff, one and one-half

4

cups flour, with three teaspoonfuls of baking powder sifted in. Bake on three tins. Take whites of two eggs and make a frosting as for any other cake; add one teaspoonful vanilla and two-thirds cake of German sweet chocolate grated. Spread between layers but not on the top one. Take white of one egg to ice the top and sides. Do not frost the cake until cool. The same cake recipe may be used for cocoanut.

CHRISTMAS CAKE.

Take five pounds of flour, mix with it a dessert-spoonful of salt, rub in three-quarters of a pound of butter and one pound of lard.

CHRISTMAS CAKE.

Put in half a pint of good fresh brewers' yeast, and knead as for common bread. If there is any difficulty about the yeast, baking powder may be used, allowing a heaped teaspoonful of ordinary baking powder for every pound of material. If yeast is used, let the dough rise before adding the other ingredients. Mix in three pounds of currants, one and one-half pounds of moist sugar, a whole nutmeg, a quarter of a pound of candied lemon peel finely minced, a tablespoonful of brandy, and four eggs, well-beaten. Butter the mold and bake in a moderate oven for about two hours.

CINNAMON CAKE.

Three-fourths of a cup of butter, a cup of white sugar, one and one-half cups flour, four eggs (yolks and whites beaten separately), a tablespoonful of sweet milk, one and one-half teaspoonfuls baking powder, lemon, and a little salt. Rub the baking powder into the flour.

CINNAMON CAKE.

One cup sour cream, one cup sugar, one-half cup melted butter, one egg, one-half teaspoonful soda. Mix as for cookies, roll out, and spread ground cinnamon over the top; then roll up as a roll jelly cake and slice off with a sharp knife and bake. Any good cookie recipe will do.

CUP CAKE.

Rub to a cream one cup of butter and two cups of sugar, add four beaten eggs, and three cups of flour, into which one and one-half teaspoonfuls of baking powder have been sifted, season with extract of almonds; mix into a smooth batter and bake in well-greased cups or muffin pans.

COCOANUT POUND CAKE.

Beat half a pound of butter to a cream; add gradually one pound of powdered sugar, four well-beaten eggs, one pound of flour sifted with two tablespoonfuls baking powder, a pinch of salt, a teaspoonful of grated lemon peel, one-fourth pound of prepared cocoanut, and a cup of milk; mix thoroughly, butter the tins, and line them with buttered paper; pour the mixture in to the depth of one and one-half inches, and bake in a good oven; when baked spread icing over them. Return the cake to the oven a moment to dry the icing.

CLOVE CAKE.

One pound of brown sugar, one pound of flour, one pound of raisins, one-half pound of butter, one cup of milk, two large teaspoonfuls of baking powder stirred well into the flour, one tablespoonful of cloves, one tablespoonful cinnamon, one tablespoonful of nutmeg, four eggs; chop the raisins. For less quantity divide proportionately.

DELICATE CAKE.

One and one-half cups of granulated sugar, one cup of butter, two-thirds cup of milk, whites of six eggs beaten to a stiff froth, three even cups of flour, three teaspoonfuls of baking powder pu* in the flour and mixed; stir butter and sugar well together, to them add the milk, then put in the flour, and last add the beaten eggs; flavor with lemon. Stir the whole mixture well.

DELICIOUS CAKE.

Two cups of white sugar, one cup of butter, one cup milk, three eggs, one teaspoonful soda, two teaspoonfuls cream of tartar, three cups of sifted flour. Stir butter and sugar together, then add the beaten yolks of the eggs, then the beaten whites; dissolve the soda in the milk, rub the cream of tartar into the flour and add; flavor with extract of bitter almond.

DROP CAKE.

One pound of sugar, three-fourths of a pound of butter, one and one-fourth pounds flour, five eggs. To be dropped by the table-spoonful on buttered pans and baked.

DOUGH CAKE.

Two cups light dough, two cups sugar, one cup butter, half cup milk, two eggs, one and a half cups flour, one teaspoonful soda, one cup raisins; flavor with nutmeg and cinnamon.

DOVER CAKE.

Rub to a cream one cup of butter and two cups of sugar, add six eggs, two at a time, beating five minutes between each addition, one cup of milk, one and one-half pints of flour, sifted with two teaspoonfuls baking powder; season with one teaspoonful each of extract of cinnamon and orange; bake in rather hot oven forty minutes.

DUNDEE CAKE.

Whip to a cream one and one-half cups of butter and the same amount of sugar; add eight eggs, two at a time, beating five minutes between each addition, one-half cup of cream or milk, one and one-half pints of flour, sifted with two teaspoonfuls baking powder, one-half of a lemon peel cut in thin slices, one cup of washed, picked, and dried currants, one and one-half cups sultana raisins, one teaspoonful each of extract nutmeg, cloves, and vanilla; mix into a firm batter, pour into a shallow, square cake pan; chop one cup of almonds coarsely and sprinkle over the top; then bake one hour in a moderate oven.

DRIED APPLE CAKE.

Two cups of dried apples, chopped fine and soaked in water over night, then cook in one cup of molasses until soft; add one cup each of butter, sugar, and sour milk, two teaspoonfuls of soda, one teaspoonful each of cinnamon, cloves and lemon extract, one nutmeg. A cup of raisins may be added. Bake in a greased cake dish in a moderate oven. Flour for stiff batter.

ELECTION CAKE.

Beat one and one-half cups of butter and two cups of sugar to a white, light cream; add three eggs, beating a little longer, one and one-half pints of flour sifted with two teaspoonfuls baking powder, two cups of raisins, stoned, one cup of currants well cleaned, one-half cup chopped citron, one-half of a lemon peel, chopped, one-half cup of almonds, blanched and cut into shreds, one teaspoonful each of extract of vanilla and of bitter almonds, one cup of milk; mix into a consistent batter, put into a paper-lined tin and bake in a moderate, steady oven one and one-half hours.

EVERYDAY FRUIT CAKE.

One cup of butter, two cups of sugar, two cups of sour milk, two cups of raisins, five cups of flour, one teaspoonful saleratus, salt, cinnamon, cloves, citron and wine to suit the taste.

EGGLESS CAKE.

One and one-half cups of sugar, one cup of sour milk, three level cups of flour, one-half cup of butter, one teaspoonful of soda, one-half teaspoonful of cinnamon, one-half teaspoonful of grated nutmeg, and one cup of chopped raisins.

ENGLISH CHRISTMAS CAKE.

Sift five pounds of flour; mix with it one tablespoonful of salt, one and one-half pounds of butter and half a pint of fresh brewer's yeast, or five teaspoonfuls of baking powder; if yeast is used, allow dough to rise before adding other ingredients; mix in three pounds of washed currants, one and one-half pounds of "A" sugar, one nutmeg grated, one-fourth pound of chopped candied lemon peel, one wine glass of brandy, and four well-beaten eggs; butter the tins and line them with buttered paper; bake in a moderate oven for two hours. The quantity of brandy recommended will serve to keep these cakes fresh for an indefinite time.

FRUIT CAKE FROM DOUGH.

Two cups of sugar, one cup of butter, one pint of dough, two eggs, one teaspoonful of soda, as much fruit as you wish, spices to suit the taste; use flour enough to make as stiff as common fruit cake; set in a warm place to raise. When light bake in a moderate oven.

FRUIT CAKE.

One pound of sugar, one pound of butter, one pound of flour, eight eggs, two pounds of raisins, one pound of currants, one-fourth pound of citron, one tablespoonful of molasses, one cup of sour milk, one teaspoonful of soda, and spices of all kinds. Bake two hours in a moderate oven.

FRUIT CAKE, No. 2.

One cup of butter, two cups of sugar, three and a half cups of flour, one cup of molasses, one cup of cream, four eggs, one pound of raisins, citrons and currants according to taste, one teaspoonful of saleratus, spice to taste. Warranted to keep a year.

FRUIT JELLY CAKE.

Two cups of sugar, two-thirds cup of butter, same of sweet milk, four eggs, three cups of flour, three teaspoonfuls of baking powder; stir together, then divide into three equal parts. Into one part stir one tablespoonful of molasses, one cup of chopped raisins, one teaspoonful each of cloves, cinnamon and nutmeg. Bake, and put together with jelly or frosting.

Favorite Lemon Jelly Cake.

Take two cups of sugar, one-half cup of butter, one cup of milk, three eggs, two teaspoonfuls of cream of tartar, one teaspoonful of soda, three cups of flour; mix and bake in fine, thin layers. For the jelly grate the rind of three small or two large lemons and add the juice of the same with one cup of sugar, one egg, one cup of water, one teaspoonful of butter, one tablespoonful of flour; mix with a little water and boil till it thickens, then place between the layers of the cake. Make before needed for use.

Fig Cake.

Three cups of sugar, one cup each of butter and sweet milk, four cups of flour, two teaspoonfuls of baking powder, twelve beaten eggs; bake in layers. Take one pound of figs, boil till smooth and put between each layer with or without frosting. Frost the top.

Fig Cake, No. 2.

A large cup of butter, two and one-half cups of sugar, one cup of sweet milk, three pints of sifted flour, with three teaspoonfuls of baking powder, the whites of sixteen eggs, one and one-fourth pounds of figs cut into strips like citron and well floured.

French Loaf Cake.

Two cups of sugar, half cup of butter, one-half cup of sweet milk, teaspoonful of soda, two of cream of tartar, three eggs, three cups of flour; flavor with lemon.

Feather Cake.

Beat to a cream one-half cup of butter, add to it two cups of sugar and beat well together; one cup of milk with one teaspoonful of soda dissolved in it; beat well together; then add one cup of sifted flour with two teaspoonfuls of cream of tartar previously rubbed into it; add next the well-beaten yolk of three eggs, beat the whites separately until stiff, add them and then two more cups of flour;

beat well between each successive addition; butter two middle-sized
tins, put in the cake and bake for twenty minutes or half an hour
in a moderate oven.

FEATHER CAKE, No. 2.

One cup of white sugar, one teaspoonful of melted butter, one
egg, two-thirds cup of milk, two even cups of sifted flour, two even
teaspoonfuls of cream of tartar, one of soda; flavor with lemon; sift
cream of tartar and soda into the flour. You will be surprised when
you come to make this cake, it is so delicious.

GOLD CAKE.

The yolks of eight eggs, two cups of sugar, one cup of butter,
one-half cup of sweet milk, three cups of flour, two teaspoonfuls of
baking powder; flavor with orange extract.

GENTLEMAN'S FAVORITE.

Seven eggs, whites and yolks beaten separately, two cups of
sugar and one-half cup of butter worked to a cream, one tablespoonful of water, two teaspoons, level full, of baking powder, two
cups of flour, one-half teaspoonful of salt; bake in jelly-cake tins.

Jelly for Same.—One egg, one cup of sugar, three grated apples
without the peelings, one lemon; stir till it thickens. Cool before
using.

GINGER DROP CAKE.

Two cups of sugar, one cup of New Orleans molasses, one cup of
butter, six cups of flour, one cup of hot water, two teaspoonfuls of
soda, one teaspoonful of ginger, and one of cinnamon. Drop in
hot tins and bake in a hot oven.

GINGERBREAD LOAF.

One cup of butter, one of molasses, one of sugar, half of cold
water, one tablespoonful of ginger, one tablespoonful of cinnamon,
one of soda dissolved in boiling water; melt the butter, slightly
warm the molasses, spice and sugar, and heat together ten minutes;
then put in the water, soda and flour; stir very hard and bake in
three loaves. Brush them over with syrup while hot, and eat fresh.

GINGER-BREAD.

One pint of molasses, one glass of sour milk or cream, one table-spoonful of soda, one-half pint of melted lard; put the soda into the milk and molasses and beat to a foam. Make the dough very soft.

SOFT GINGER-BREAD.

One cup of sugar, one cup of butter, one cup of sour cream, one cup of New Orleans molasses, four cups of sifted flour, one table-spoonful of ginger, one teaspoonful of soda, the grated rind of one lemon, three eggs, well beaten; stir the butter and sugar together, then add eggs, milk and flour.

SOFT GINGER-BREAD, No. 2.

One coffeecup each of sugar, molasses, and butter, four cups of flour, one cup of sour milk, two large teaspoonfuls of ginger, two teaspoonfuls of cinnamon, one-half teaspoonful of cloves, one tea-spoonful of saleratus dissolved in the sour milk; stoned raisins may be added. Bake in sponge-cake tins.

GINGER CUP CAKE.

Mix two cups of powdered sugar with two cups of warmed butter; add three well-beaten eggs, a cup of molasses, four heaping cups of flour, a tablespoonful of fresh-ground ginger, one teaspoon-ful of dissolved saleratus; mix thoroughly and pour into buttered molds or patty pans; bake in a moderate oven.

GROOM'S CAKE.

Ten eggs beaten separately, one pound each of butter, white sugar, and flour, two pounds of almonds blanched and chopped fine, one pound of seeded raisins, one-half pound of citron shaved fine; beat the butter to a cream, add the sugar gradually, then the well-beaten yolks; stir all till very light, then add the chopped almonds; beat the whites stiff and add gently with the flour; take a little more flour and sprinkle over the raisins and citron, then put in the cake pan, first a layer of cake batter, then a layer of raisins and

citron, then cake, and so on until all is used, finishing off with a
layer of cake. Bake in moderate oven two hours.

GRAHAM CUP CAKE.

Rub to a light cream two-thirds cup of butter and one cup of
sugar; add two beaten eggs, one-half cup of cream, two cups of
Graham flour, one heaping teaspoonful of baking powder, one teaspoonful of extract of lemon; mix into a moderately thin batter;
bake in well-greased cups, or muffin pans, in a moderate oven.

HICKORY-NUT CAKE.

Two cups of white sugar, one-half cup of butter, three cups of
flour, three-fourths cup of sweet milk, one-half teaspoonful of soda
dissolved in the milk, one teaspoonful of cream of tartar put into
the flour, the whites of eight eggs. Just before baking add two
cups of hickory-nut meats.

HICKORY-NUT DROP CAKE.

Whites of six eggs beaten to a stiff froth; add one pound of
rolled sugar, one cup of hickory-nut meats, one teaspoonful of
baking powder, with flour to stiffen so as to drop. Drop by spoonfuls on a buttered tin and bake in a quick oven.

HUCKLEBERRY CAKE.

Rub together one cup of butter and two cups of sugar; add four
beaten eggs, one and one-half pints of flour sifted with two teaspoonfuls baking powder, one cup of milk, two cups of huckleberries, one teaspoonful each of extract of cinnamon, cloves and
allspice; put in a paper-lined bake tin and bake in a quick oven
fifty minutes.

HONEY CAKE.

Mix together one cup of honey and one cup of sugar; add one-
half cup of melted butter, two beaten eggs, one pint flour sifted
with two teaspoonfuls of baking powder, one teaspoonful of caraway seeds. Mix into a smooth batter and bake in a hot oven
thirty minutes.

Imperial Cake.

One pound each of sugar and flour, three-fourths pound of butter, one pound of almonds blanched and cut fine, one-half pound of citron, one-half pound of raisins, the rind and juice of one lemon, one nutmeg and ten eggs.

Ice-Cream Cake.

To the whites of five eggs, lightly beaten, add two cups of sugar, one cup of butter, one cup of milk, three cups of flour, and three teaspoonfuls of baking powder; bake in thin layers and use as a cream, to spread between, two and a half cups of sugar and one-half cup of water boiled together; beat the whites of three eggs to a stiff froth, and when the syrup will hair, pour it into the whites and stir as fast as possible; flavor with lemon or vanilla and spread between the layers and over the top.

Jelly Cake.

Beat to a cream three-fourths cup of butter and two cups of sugar; add five eggs, two at a time, beating five minutes between each addition, one and one-fourth pints of flour sifted with one and one-half teaspoonfuls of baking powder, one cup of milk; mix to a smooth batter and bake in jelly-cake tins; spread with currant or other fruit jelly.

Jelly Rolls.

One cup of sugar, one cup of flour, three eggs, one teaspoonful baking powder. Stir well and spread thin on a long baking tin or dripping pan. Bake quickly, turn out on a cloth, spread with jelly and roll up.

Kaffee Kuchen.

One pound light raised dough, one ounce of sugar and three of butter, one egg; cream the butter and beat well with the sugar and the egg; add the dough and mix thoroughly with the hand; put it in a warm place to rise; when light, pour it in a small dripping pan (when baked it should not be more than two-thirds of an inch thick) and let it stand ten or fifteen minutes; put in the oven and while baking prepare this icing:

Blanch two almonds and shred them; add to the beaten whites of two eggs one cup of sugar; stir in the almonds, and when the cake is baked cover it with the icing and dry in the oven. The almonds may be browned a little if liked.

KNICKERBOCKER CAKE.

Beat one-half pound of fresh butter to a cream; add one-half pound of powdered sugar, three-fourths pound of sifted flour, a tablespoonful of orange-flour water, and one of brandy, and four ounces of washed currants; add five well-beaten eggs, and beat the mixture until very light. Line some shallow cake tins with buttered paper, pour in the mixture until they are one-half full, and bake in a quick oven.

LEMON CAKE.

Five eggs beaten with three cups of sugar and one of butter, one cup of milk, five cups of sifted flour, one lemon rind grated, half a teaspoonful soda dissolved well in the milk, and one teaspoonful of cream of tartar in the flour; after all is well beaten, add the juice of the lemon and bake immediately.

LEMON CAKE, No. 2.

To four well-beaten eggs, add two cups sugar, two tablespoonfuls butter, one-half cup of milk, two cups of flour sifted with two teaspoonfuls of baking powder; bake in jelly tins and put together with a frosting made of the white of one egg, the juice and grated rind of one lemon, and sugar enough to stiffen.

LEMON JELLY CAKE.

Beat together two eggs, one cup of sugar, one-third cup of butter, one-half cup milk, two cups flour sifted, with a heaping teaspoonful baking powder; bake in jelly-cake tins.

Jelly for Same.—Two-thirds cup of water, one cup sugar, the juice and grated rind of one lemon; mix together and let boil; then stir in two well-beaten eggs. When cold, spread between the layers of cake; also upon the top, or the top may be frosted.

LADY CAKE.

Rub to a cream two-thirds cup of butter and three cups of sugar; add one cup of milk, one pint flour, one-half teaspoonful of baking powder, one teaspoonful extract of bitter almond; then add the whites of eight eggs whipped to a froth; when thoroughly mixed, put into a paper-lined tin and bake in a steady oven forty minutes, When cool, ice the bottom and sides with white icing.

LUNCH CAKE.

Beat thoroughly two cups of butter and two cups of sugar; add two cups of egg well beaten, one and one-half pints of flour sifted with a heaping teaspoonful baking powder, one gill of wine, one teaspoonful each of extract of rose, cinnamon and nutmeg; mix into a smooth batter and bake in a moderate oven one hour; when cold, ice with white icing.

LIGHT CAKE.

Beat six eggs, yolks and whites separately; beat with the yolks one pound white sugar, and three-fourths pound of butter; add one pound of flour sifted with a teaspoonful of cream of tartar, and one cup sweet milk with one-half teaspoonful of soda, one pound raisins, a little citron, and lemon peel, then the whites of the eggs beaten to a froth. Bake in a paper-lined cake tin one hour in a moderate oven.

LOAF CAKE.

Six cups of bread dough, five eggs, three cups of sugar, one cup of butter, two teaspoonfuls of ground cloves and cinnamon mixed, and half of a nutmeg, one and one-half pounds of raisins. Bake in a moderate oven.

MARBLED CAKE.

Light part: One and one-half cups of white sugar, one-half cup of butter, one-half cup of sweet milk, one half teaspoonful of soda, one teaspoonful **cream of** tartar sifted with two and one-half cups flour, whites of four eggs; beat and mix thoroughly.

Dark part: One cup of brown sugar, one-half cup of butter, one-half cup of sour milk, one-half teaspoonful of soda, two and one-half cups of flour, yolks of four eggs, one-half teaspoonful each of cloves, allspice, cinnamon, and nutmeg.

With a spoon drop the two batters alternately into a papered cake-tin.

MOUNTAIN CAKE.

One cup of sugar, one-half cup of butter, one-half cup of sweet milk, one-half cup of corn starch, one cup of flour, whites of six eggs, a little vanilla, two teaspoonfuls baking powder. Bake in layers.

Frosting for Above.—Whites of five eggs, twenty tablespoonfuls sifted sugar, beaten very light, and a little vanilla. Spread between layers and on the outside of the cake.

MADEIRA CAKE.

Beat together two and one-half cups of butter and two cups of sugar; add seven well-beaten eggs, one and one-half pints flour sifted with one heaping teaspoonful baking powder; mix with one gill of Madeira wine into a smooth batter and bake in a paper-lined cake-tin in a steady oven about one hour, and ice with transparent icing.

MOLASSES CAKE.

Beat together one cup of butter and one cup of brown sugar; add one-half cup of molasses, one cup of milk, one egg, one and one-half pints of flour sifted with one and one-half teaspoonfuls of baking powder; mix into a consistent batter and bake about forty minutes.

MOLASSES CAKE.

Beat together one-half cup of sugar, a piece of butter the size of an egg, and one egg; add one-half cup of molasses, one-half cup of sour milk, one-half teaspoonful of soda, two cups of flour, sifted, spices to suit the taste, and a cup of chopped raisins. Bake in a moderate oven.

Marbled Chocolate Cake.

One cup of butter, two cups of sugar, three cups of flour, four well-beaten eggs, one cup of milk, two teaspoonfuls of baking powder; take out one cup of this batter and mix with four table-spoonfuls of chocolate dissolved with a little cream; cover the bottom of the pan with the white batter and drop upon it in places a spoonful of the chocolate, forming rings, then another layer of the batter, and so on until all is used. Bake in a moderate oven.

Moreton Farm Cake.

Two pounds of butter, softened throughout, but not melted; add two pounds of nice, white, soft sugar, and mix together until creamed; take out one-half and reserve it in a separate bowl until wanted. To the rest add one quart of pretty warm, sweet milk; stir in gradually four pounds of 'flour, then mix in very thoroughly a teacupful of lively, home-made yeast. Let it stand in a warm place until very light, which will take about four hours; then add the remainder of the butter and sugar, and a little more flour if needed; add two pounds of raisins nicely stoned, a little pulverized mace, and, if at hand, some candied lemon peel; let it rise again, and when well raised mix it well, using the hands, and proportion it off into well-buttered pans; let them stand in a moderately warm place until beginning to rise; put them into a steady oven and bake them fully an hour, or longer if only one or two pans are used. There are no eggs used in this cake—none are needed. It is an excellent cake for economical housekeepers to make in winter, when eggs are scarce and high-priced. If the top and sides are frosted it will keep moist for a long time. Brown paper is nice to wrap cake in before putting it into the cake box.

Nut Cake.

One cup of butter, two cups of white sugar, four cups of flour, one cup of sweet milk, the whites of eight eggs, three teaspoonfuls of baking powder, and two cups of chopped nut meats.

Nut Cake, No. 2.

Two eggs, one cup of sugar, one-half cup of butter; beat together and add one-half cup of sweet milk, one and one-half cups of sifted flour, two teaspoonfuls baking powder, one large cup of chopped walnuts; frost when baked; mark in squares and put half a nut meat on each square.

White Nut Cake.

Whites of twelve eggs beaten to a froth, one cup of butter, two cups of sugar, three and one-half cups of flour, teaspoonful of yeast powder. After the butter is well mixed add one large cocoanut, grated; one large tumblerful of the kernels of pecans, and one tumblerful of blanched almonds, the almonds to be slightly mashed in a mortar.

Neapolitan Cake.

Black: Take one cup of butter, two cups of brown sugar, one cup of molasses, one cup of strong coffee, four and a half cups of sifted flour, four eggs, two teaspoonfuls of soda, two of cinnamon, two of cloves, one of mace, one pound of raisins, one of currants, and a quarter of a pound of citron.

White: One cup of butter, four cups of white sugar, two cups of sweet milk, two cups corn-starch mixed with four and-a-half cups of sifted flour, whites of eight eggs, two tablespoonfuls of baking powder, one-half teaspoonful of extract of bitter almonds.

Bake the cakes in round jelly pans with straight edges; the loaves should be one and a-half inches thick after baking. When the cake is cold, each black loaf should be spread with a thick coating of lemon and sugar, made as follows: The white of one egg thoroughly beaten, the grated rind of two and the juice of three lemons; powdered sugar enough to make a thick frosting; lay a white loaf on each black one and frost as you would any other cake.

Lady Fingers.

Rub half a pound of butter into a pound of flour; add half a pound of sugar; grate in the rind of two lemons, and squeeze in the juice of one; then add three eggs; make into a roll the size of the middle finger; it will spread in the oven to the size of a thin cake; dip in chocolate icing.

ORANGE CAKE.

Two cups of sugar, one cup of butter, one cup of sweet milk, three cups of flour, yolks of two eggs and whites of five, three tea-spoonfuls baking powder, grated peel and juice of one orange. Bake in four layers.

Filling.—Whites of three eggs, juice of one orange, fifteen table-spoonfuls of sugar. Beat together, spread between the layers and on the outside of cake. Pare and divide in small sections two oranges and put on top of cake.

ORANGE CAKE, No. 2.

Three eggs, one tablespoonful of butter, one and a-half cups of sugar, two cups of flour, with two teaspoonfuls of baking powder sifted with the flour, one-half cup of rich milk, a very little salt, orange juice, or some extract of lemon. Bake on jelly-cake tins.

Jelly for Orange Cake.—Take two good oranges, grate a part of the rind of one, then peel them and grate them all; remove the seeds and add one cup of sugar, two tablespoonfuls of water, and scald in a tin pail set in a kettle of hot water. Take one table-spoonful of corn starch, mix smooth with a few spoonfuls of cold water and stir into the orange and cook just enough to cook the corn starch; when nearly or quite cold, beat the whites of two eggs and add powdered sugar for frosting; leave out a little of this for the top of the cake if you like, and stir the rest into the orange, and you will have a jelly that will not run off or soak into the cake.

PERFECTION CAKE.

Three cups of sugar, three cups of flour, one cup of butter, one cup of milk, one cup of corn starch, the whites of twelve eggs beaten to a stiff froth. Before sifting the flour put in three tea-spoonfuls of baking powder; sift all together. Dissolve the corn starch in the milk and add it to the butter and sugar well beaten together; then add the flour and whites of the eggs. Never beat in a tin dish.

PORK CAKE.

Take one pound fat salt pork free from lean or rind, chop as fine as to be almost like lard, pour upon it one-half pint of boiling water; add two cups of sugar, one cup of molasses, one teaspoonful of soda stirred into the molasses, one pound of raisins, one-fourth pound of citron shaved fine; stir in sifted flour enough to make of the consistency of common cake batter; season with one spoonful each of nutmeg and cloves and two teaspoonfuls cinnamon. Bake in a moderate oven.

PORTUGUESE CAKE.

Beat together one and one-half cups of butter and four cups of sugar, add eight eggs, two at a time, beating five minutes between each addition, one pint flour sifted with a heaping teaspoonful of baking powder, three cups of almonds blanched and pounded to a paste with a little water, one cup of seedless raisins, one cup of currants; season with nutmeg; mix into a batter and bake in a well-papered tin in a steady oven for one and one-half hours.

PUFF CAKE.

Two cups of sugar, three eggs, one cup of butter, one cup of sweet milk, two teaspoonfuls cream of tartar, one teaspoonful of soda, and three cups of flour. Bake in a quick oven.

PINE-APPLE CAKE.

One cup of butter, two cups of sugar, one cup of milk, three cups of flour, whites of six eggs and yolks of four, three teaspoonfuls of baking powder well mixed through flour; bake in jelly-cake pans; grate a pine-apple; sprinkle with sugar, spread between the layers; pine-apple jam may be substituted; frost the outside; beat two tablespoonfuls of the pine-apple into the frosting.

Pound Cake without Soda.

One pound of powdered sugar, one-half pound of butter, eight eggs, whites and yolks, beaten separately and well, ten ounces flour, one nutmeg. Bake one hour.

Cocoanut Pound Cake.

Beat one-half pound of butter to a cream; add gradually one pound of sugar, one pound of flour sifted with two teaspoonfuls of baking powder, a pinch of salt, one teaspoonful of grated lemon peel, one-fourth pound of prepared cocoanut, four well-beaten eggs, one cup of milk; mix thoroughly; butter the tins and line them with buttered paper; pour the mixture in to the depth of one and one-half inches, and bake in a good oven; when baked, take out, spread icing over them and return to the oven to dry the icing.

Pound Cake.

One and one-half cups of flour, one cup of butter, one and one-half cups of sugar, one-half teaspoonful of baking powder. Beat butter and flour to a cream; beat four eggs and sugar very light; put all together and add the baking powder.

Plum Cake.

Beat together two cups of butter, one cup of sugar, two eggs, one cup of molasses, one cup of sweet milk, one teaspoonful each of allspice, cinnamon and mace, one gill brandy, two pounds each of currants and raisins, one-half pound citron, one-half teaspoonful soda. Flour to thicken.

Quincy Cake.

One cup of butter, three cups of powdered sugar, four cups of flour sifted with one and one-half teaspoonfuls cream of tartar, one cup of sweet milk, one teaspoonful of soda, the juice and rind of one fresh lemon, whites of ten eggs beaten to a stiff froth. Bake one and one-half or two hours in a pan.

QUEEN CAKE.

One pound of sugar, one pound of flour sifted with a heaping teaspoonful of baking powder, three-fourths of a pound of butter, five eggs, one gill of sweet cream, one teaspoonful of extract of nectarine, one tablespoonful of water, and one grated nutmeg; beat the sugar and butter to a cream, add the eggs beaten very light, then the cream and flour, and lastly the flavoring.

RAILROAD CAKE.

One cup of sugar, one cup of flour, three eggs, one teaspoonful of cream of tartar, one-half teaspoonful soda, or one and one-half teaspoonfuls of baking powder, a little salt; beat all together as for sponge cake, and spread on two square tins to bake.

RECEPTION CAKE.

Beat together two cups of butter and two cups of sugar; add ten beaten eggs, one quart of flour sifted with two teaspoonfuls of baking powder, two cups of currants, one cup of shaved citron, one-half of an orange peel cut fine, one-half cup of blanched almonds cut fine; season with allspice and cinnamon; put into a paper-lined cake tin and bake in a moderate oven.

RICE CAKE.

Beat together one-half cup of butter, two cups of sugar, and four eggs; add one-half cup of sweet cream; sift together one and one-half cups of rice flour, one and one-half cups of flour, and one heaping teaspoonful of baking powder; mix all together and season with lemon extract. Bake in patty pans in a hot oven.

ROCHESTER JELLY CAKE.

Three eggs, whites and yolks beaten separately, two cups of sugar, one-half cup of butter, one cup of sweet milk, three cups of flour, one tablespoonful of baking powder. Take one-half of the above mixture and bake in two square pans, then add to the remainder one cup of stoned and chopped raisins, one-fourth pound of citron shaved fine, one teaspoonful cinnamon, one nutmeg, one-half teaspoonful each of cloves and allspice, one tablespoonful each of molasses and flour. Bake in like pans and place in alternate layers with raspberry jam or any kind of jelly.

The same put together with frosting is called **Ribbon Cake.**

Silver Cake.

Beat to a froth the whites of six eggs; add two cups of sugar, two-thirds of a cup of butter; beat well together and add one cup of sweet milk with one teaspoonful of soda, two cups of flour and one cup corn starch sifted with two teaspoonfuls of cream of tartar; flavor with any extract.

The same made by substituting the yolks for the whites makes a nice gold cake.

Snow Cake.

One cup of sugar, one and one-half cups of flour, one heaping teaspoonful of baking powder. Sift all together through a sieve and add the whites of ten eggs beaten stiff. Bake in a quick oven.

Swiss Cake.

One-quarter cup of butter, one and a half cups of sugar, two and one-half cups of flour, one cup of sweet milk, two eggs, one teaspoonful of cream of tartar, and one-half teaspoonful of soda. Stir the butter and sugar to a cream; add the eggs, well beaten. Mix and flavor with lemon. This makes a good and inexpensive cake.

Delicious Sponge Cake.

Twelve eggs, one pound of sugar, twelve ounces of flour, a pinch of salt; flavor. Beat the whites to a very stiff froth, the yolks till the bubbles look fine. When the yolks are beaten enough add the sugar and beat till sugar is dissolved; then add the whites, and lastly the flour, and bake immediately in brick-shaped tins. This will make two loaves. You will find your cake so much nicer if baked in a paste.' Make with flour and water only; roll out on the board same as pie crust, line your greased tins all over inside with the paste and pour in the batter. Bake nearly an hour. Do not break off the paste till you want to use it. Your cake will be more moist and keep longer; indeed, the cake will be much better a day or two old.

SPONGE CAKE WITH HOT WATER.

One cup of sugar and two eggs, well beaten together, one tea-spoonful of baking powder sifted with one cup of flour; stir well together, then stir in one-third cup of boiling water or milk; bake quickly in a buttered tin. If these directions are followed the cake will be very nice.

SPONGE CAKE.

Beat together the yolks of four eggs and one cup of sugar ten minutes; add to it one cup of flour sifted with one-half teaspoonful baking powder, one teaspoonful extract of orange; then add the whites whipped to a stiff froth, and bake in a well-greased cake mould in a steady oven thirty minutes.

WHITE SPONGE CAKE.

Sift together one cup of flour, one-half cup of corn starch, one teaspoonful baking powder; add one cup of sugar, one teaspoonful extract of rose, then add the whites of eight eggs whipped to a stiff froth; mix thoroughly and bake in a well-buttered cake tin in a quick oven thirty minutes.

SULTANA CAKE.

Beat together one and one-half cups of butter and one and one-half cups of sugar; add six eggs, two at a time, beating five minutes between each addition, one and one-half pints of flour sifted with one teaspoonful baking powder, one-half cup of thick cream, four cups of Sultana raisins, one-half cup of chopped citron; mix thoroughly and put in a paper-lined cake tin well buttered. Bake in a moderate oven one and one-fourth hours. When done, spread with transparent icing.

SPICE CAKE.

Beat together one cup of butter and two cups of sugar; add two beaten eggs, one cup of milk, three cups of flour with two teaspoonfuls of baking powder, one-half cup each of seeded raisins and currants; season with nutmeg, cloves, and cinnamon.

SEED CAKE.

Beat together one cup of sugar, one-third of a cup of butter, and two eggs; add one-half cup of milk, and two cups flour sifted with two teaspoonfuls of baking powder; stir in one tablespoonful of coriander seed and season with nutmeg. Bake in a loaf or in patty tins.

TUNBRIDGE CAKE.

Bake a plain sponge cake in a cylinder-mould; when cold cut it in thin slices, lay the bottom piece on a plate, spread over any kind of fruit jelly and two tablespoonfuls of any kind of wine; repeat this until all the cake is used; prepare a meringue paste of the whites of four eggs beaten stiff, with two cups of sugar; use it to entirely cover the top and sides of the cake; sift sugar plentifully over it and place it in an oven to brown just a fawn color; when ready to serve slide it off the plate into a glass dish and pile round it one pint of whipped cream. Flavor with any extract to suit the taste. Nice for tea or for dessert.

TAYLOR CAKE.

Seven eggs beaten separately; beat with the yolks two pounds of sugar, one and one-half pounds of butter (less butter will do); then add seven coffeecups of flour sifted with two and one-half teaspoonfuls of baking powder, one pound of currants, one pound of seeded raisins, three nutmegs, a tablespoonful of cinnamon, one pint of milk, and lastly the beaten whites of the eggs.

WEDDING CAKE.

First procure the following ingredients: One pound and a half of flour, the same of butter, half a pound of candied lemon, half a pound of candied orange, half a pound of candied citron, one pound of dried cherries, one pound and a half of currants (or if the cherries cannot be readily obtained, use a pound more of currants), eight ounces of almonds, eight eggs, the rind of four oranges, or of two lemons rubbed upon sugar, half an ounce of spices, consisting of powdered cinnamon, grated nutmeg, and ground cloves in equal proportion, a teaspoonful of salt, and a small tumblerful of brandy (if objected to, the brandy may be omitted and another egg added).

Wash, pick and dry the currants, cut the cherries into moderate sized pieces, slice the candied peel into thin shreds, blanch and pound the almonds, or cut them into very small pieces, and crush the flavored sugar to powder. Put the butter into a large bowl, and beat it to cream, either with a wooden spoon or with the hand. Add very gradually the sugar, flour, and eggs, and when they are thoroughly mixed work in the rest of the ingredients. Put them in a little at a time and beat the cake between each addition. It should be beaten fully three-fourths of an hour. Line a tin hoop with double thicknesses of buttered paper, pour in the mixture, and place it on a metal baking-sheet with twelve folds of paper under it, and four or five on top, to keep it from burning. Put it into a moderately heated oven, and keep the oven at an even temperature until it is done enough. If the cake is to be iced, first prepare the almond part: Take half a pound of almonds, throw them into boiling water, and skin them. Pound them in a mortar with a few drops of orange-flower water, one pound of fine white sugar, and as much white of egg as will make a soft, stiff paste. Spread this over the top of the cake, and keep it from the edge as much as possible. Put it in a cool oven or in a warm place, till it is dry and hard. To make the sugar icing, put two pounds of icing sugar into a bowl and work it into the whites of two, or if necessary, three, or even four, eggs. The whites must not be whisked, but thrown in as they are. Work the mixture to a stiff, shiny paste, and whilst working it add occasionally a drop of lemon-juice. Be careful to obtain *icing* sugar. If a drop of liquid blue is added it will make it look whiter. The icing will need to be worked vigorously to make a paste that will not run, and the fewer eggs taken the better. The cake ought not to be iced until a short time before it is wanted, as it may get dirty. The icing should be spread evenly over with the hand wetted with cold water, then smoothed with an ivory knife, and it should be put into a gentle oven to harden. It may be ornamented with little knobs of icing placed round the edge; and on the day of the wedding a wreath of white flowers and green leaves may be placed round it by way of ornament. If anything more elaborate is required, a pretty center ornament may be made with glazed white card board, silver paper, and orange blossom; or a stand and a drum, with artificial flowers, may be hired of the confectioner. Time to bake the cake, about six hours.

WEDDING CAKE, No 2.

Six cups butter, four cups sugar, sixteen eggs, three pints flour, six cups currants, washed, dried, and picked, three cups sultana raisins, three cups citron, two cups candied lemon peel, two cups almonds, blanched and cut in shreds, one-half pint brandy, two ounces each nutmeg, mace, and cinnamon, one tablespoonful each cloves and allspice.

Prepare all these ingredients in the following manner: Place the butter and sugar in a large bowl; break the eggs into a quart measure or pitcher; cover a small waiter with a clean sheet of paper, and on it lay the sifted flour, fruit, citron, and lemon peel cut into shreds, the almonds and spices, with the brandy measured at hand; also get ready a large cake tin by papering it inside with white paper, and outside and bottom with four or five thicknesses of coarse wrapping paper, which can be tied on.

Having thus prepared everything, and the fire banked up to last, with the addition from time to time of just a shovelful of coal, by which means you will not reduce the oven heat, proceed to beat to a very light cream the butter and sugar, adding the eggs, two at a time, beating a little between each addition until all are used; then put in contents of the waiter all at once with the brandy; mix very thoroughly, and smooth; put it into the prepared cake tin, smooth over the top, put plenty of paper on to protect it, and bake eight hours, keeping the oven steadily up to a clear, moderate heat; watch it faithfully, and you will produce a cake worthy of the occasion; remove from the oven very carefully, and suffer it to stay on the tin until quite cold; the next day ice it with a thin coat of *White Icing*, both the top and the sides; and place in a cool oven to dry the icing. Now spread a second coat of icing, which will prevent any crumbs or fruit being mixed up with the icing when you are icing to finish; now with a broad knife proceed, when the first coat is dry, to ice the sides, then pour the icing on the center of the cake, in quantity sufficient to reach the edges, when stop; decorate with a vase of white, made flowers, etc., to taste.

VANILLA CAKE.

One cup of butter, two cups of pulverized sugar, one cup of sweet milk, three cups of flour, one-half cup of corn starch sifted with two teaspoonfuls of baking powder, four eggs, two teaspoonfuls extract of vanilla.

WASHINGTON CAKE.

Three-fourths pound of butter, one and one-fourth pounds of sugar beaten together; add four beaten eggs, one pint milk, one and one-fourth pounds of flour, with two teaspoonfuls baking powder, one and one-half pounds of seedless raisins, one and one-half pounds of currants, one glass brandy; spice to taste.

Wine Cake.

Beat together one and one-half cups of butter and two cups of sugar; add three beaten eggs, two cups of flour with one teaspoonful baking powder, one gill of wine; mix into a firm batter and bake in a moderate oven. Frost.

Webster Cakes.

Beat together thoroughly one cup of butter, three cups of sugar, and two eggs; add five cups of flour sifted with two teaspoonfuls of baking powder, one and one-half cups of milk, two cups of seedless raisins, one teaspoonful each of extract of bitter almonds and vanilla. Bake in a quick, steady oven forty-five minutes.

Watermelon Cake.

White part: Two cups of pulverized sugar, two-thirds cup each of butter and sweet milk, three cups of flour sifted with one tablespoonful baking powder, and the whites of five eggs; flavor.

Red part; One cup of red sugar sand, one-half cup of butter, two-thirds cup of milk, two cups of flour, one heaping teaspoonful of baking powder, whites of five eggs, and one-half pound of raisins.

In filling the cake pan put the white part outside and the red part inside; drop in the raisins here and there where they belong for seeds.

White Cake.

Whites of eight eggs well whipped, three cups of pulverized sugar, one cup of butter, one cup of milk, four cups of sifted flour with one teaspoonful cream of tartar, one-half teaspoonful of soda dissolved in the milk, juice of one lemon. Bake one hour in a moderate oven.

Yule Cake.

Rub together two and one-half cups of butter and three cups of sugar; add ten beaten eggs, four cups of flour with two teaspoonfuls baking powder, four cups of currants, two-thirds cup of chopped citron, one teaspoonful each of extract of nutmeg and cloves, one gill brandy.   Bake in a well-greased, paper-lined tin, in a moderate oven, two and one-half hours.

CRULLERS.

One-half pint of buttermilk, one cup of butter, two cups of sugar, and three eggs; beat up the eggs and add the sugar and milk.   Dissolve half a teaspoonful of saleratus in a little hot water; add to the mixture, with a teaspoonful of salt, one-half nutmeg grated and half a teaspoonful of fresh ground cinnamon. - Work in as much flour as will make a smooth dough; mix thoroughly; dredge the board, rolling-pin, and dough with flour; roll it out and cut it in rings or fingers and fry in hot fat.

CRULLERS, No. 2.

Three eggs, one cup of sugar, one-half cup of butter, one cup of milk, three teaspoonfuls of baking powder, nutmeg, cinnamon and lemon juice, or extract to taste; flour sufficient to stiffen.   Cut in strips and fry in lard.

CRULLERS, No. 3.

Six eggs, one cup of butter, two cups of sugar, one-half cup of milk, and flour to roll out easily.   They should be rolled out about one-half inch thick; cut with a jagging iron or knife in strips about one-half inch wide, and twist so as to form cakes.   The fat should boil up as the cakes are put in and they should be constantly watched while frying.   When brown on the underside, turn them; when brown on both sides they are sufficiently done.

COOKIES, JUMBLES, AND SNAPS.

ALMOND COOKIES.

Half a pound of butter, same of sugar, one-and one-fourth pounds of flour (or half corn starch), one good teaspoonful baking powder, two eggs; flavor with extract of almond, and mix into a smooth dough to roll out with a little milk; roll quarter of an inch thick, and cut in any shape; wash them over, when cut, with a little water and sprinkle with chopped almonds, and sift over a little fine sugar.

ALMOND COOKIES.

Two pounds of butter, three pounds of sugar, one pound of shelled almonds, one dozen eggs, one teaspoonful of ground cinnamon, one-half teaspoonful of soda, a cup of boiling water, one lemon grated; mix butter, sugar, yolks of eggs, lemon, cinnamon, and hot water; beat the whites, take three parts, mix also one-half of the almonds, and as much flour as it will hold; roll them, and brush with the whites of eggs. Before putting in the almonds and sugar, almonds must be scalded, dried and cut fine. Bake in a moderate oven.

COCOANUT COOKIES.

Two cups sugar, one cup butter, two eggs, one teaspoonful soda dissolved in a tablespoonful of milk, one cocoanut, and flour enough to roll.

COOKIES.

One quart flour sifted, three teaspoonfuls baking powder, two eggs, one cup of sugar, half a cup of butter, three tablespoonfuls of milk; mix soft and roll; flavor with any extract.

CREAM COOKIES.

Two cups sugar, two eggs, one cup sour cream, one cup butter, one teaspoonful soda, one teaspoonful lemon extract or one-half a nutmeg grated; flour enough to make a dough as soft as it can be rolled. Delicious.

Cookies, No. 2.

One cup sugar, one-half cup lard or butter, one-half cup sour milk, one-half teaspoonful soda, just flour enough to roll, baking quickly. Add any flavoring you wish. No eggs are required. These are very nice if grated or prepared cocoanut is added.

Cookies, No. 3.

One cup of butter, two cups sugar, four eggs, four cups flour, three tablespoonfuls milk, three teaspoonfuls baking powder. Rub the flour and butter thoroughly together, cream the butter and sugar, beat the eggs separately; add to the above, with a little nutmeg or cinnamon, or any seasoning preferred. Sift in the flour and baking powder, and add enough flour to mold and roll out. These cookies will keep fresh two weeks, and if the milk is left out, a month.

Cookies, No. 4.

One and one-half cups of white sugar, four eggs, one cup of lard, half cup of butter, three tablespoonfuls of water, one teaspoonful soda, a half grated nutmeg; roll thin; dust over with sugar and roll down lightly. Bake quickly.

Eggless Cookies.

Two cups sugar, one cup sweet milk, one cup butter, one-half teaspoonful soda. Flour enough to roll. Use vanilla, lemon or nutmeg for seasoning. They are very nice.

Ginger Cookies.

One cup sugar, one cup molasses, one cup shortening, two beaten eggs, one teaspoonful soda dissolved in four tablespoonfuls of buttermilk, one tablespoonful ginger. Stir with a spoon until stiff enough to mold with the hand; roll and bake in a quick oven.

Graham Cookies.

Two cups of sugar, one cup of sour cream, one-half teaspoonful of soda; mix quickly, roll and bake. These require less heat and more time in baking than when white flour is used.

Molasses Cookies.

Three cups of New Orleans molasses, one cup of lard, a half cup butter, four teaspoonfuls soda dissolved in ten tablespoonfuls boiling water; one tablespoonful ginger, one teaspoonful cinnamon.

Sugar Cookies.

Two cups of sugar, one cup of butter, one-half cup of milk, two eggs, two teaspoonfuls of cream of tartar, one teaspoonful soda, a tablespoonful caraway seeds. Mix soft and roll.

Hickory-nut Cookies.

Take two cups of sugar, two eggs, half a cup of melted butter, six tablespoonfuls of milk, or a little more than a third of a cup, one teaspoonful of cream of tartar, half a teaspoonful of soda and one cup of chopped meats stirred into the dough.

Sand Tarts.

Rub together two pounds of sugar, two pounds of flour, one and a quarter pounds of butter beaten with three eggs; mix smooth and roll out and cut into cakes. Place hickory-nut or almond meats over the top. Wet over with the whole of an egg beaten, and sprinkle with cinnamon and fine sugar.

Jumbles.

Three eggs, one and one-fourth cups sugar, one cup butter, three tablespoonfuls sour milk, one-quarter teaspoonful saleratus, flour to mix hard. After it is kneaded and rolled out, sift sugar over the top. Season if you like.

Jumbles, No. 2.

One cup of butter, two cups of sugar, one cup of milk, five eggs, one teaspoonful of cream of tartar, and half a teaspoonful of soda.

Ginger Snaps.

One cup of sugar, one cup of molasses, one cup of butter, one teaspoonful soda one teaspoonful ginger, one egg.

GINGER SNAPS, No. 2.

One cup molasses, one-half cup lard, one teaspoonful soda, salt and ginger to taste; mix hard.

GINGER SNAPS, No. 3.

One coffeecup New Orleans molasses, one cup butter, one cup sugar; place them on the stove, and let it come to a boil, then take off immediately, and add a teaspoonful of soda, and a tablespoonful of ginger. Roll thin and bake quickly.

DOUGHNUTS.

Two beaten eggs, one cup of sugar, four tablespoonfuls melted lard, one cup of sour milk, one teaspoonful of soda, a little salt, seasoning to the taste; flour to make a soft dough to roll out; fry in hot lard.

DOUGHNUTS WITHOUT EGGS.

Two quarts of flour, one pint of milk, one heaping cup of sugar, and a piece of butter the size of an egg. Scald the milk, and when tepid add the sugar, the butter, a half cup of yeast, and a half teaspoonful of soda. Pour this all into the center of the flour, using enough of flour to make a sponge. Let it rise all night in a warm place. In the morning sprinkle in whatever spice you want; then knead in the rest of the flour; let it rise again until light; knead again and roll them. After they are cut out let them stand five minutes. Fry in boiling lard.

DOUGHNUTS, RAISED.

Make a sponge, using one quart water and one cake yeast; let it rise until very light, then add one cup of lard, two cups of sugar, three large mashed potatoes, two eggs, season with nutmeg; let rise again until very light. Roll and cut, or pull off bits of dough and shape as you like; lay enough to fry at one time on a floured plate and set in the oven to warm; drop in boiling lard and fry longer than cakes made with baking powder.

CREAM DOUGHNUTS.

Beat one cup each of sour cream and sugar, and two eggs, together; add a level teaspoonful of soda, a little salt, and flour enough to roll.

FRIED CAKES.

Seven tablespoonfuls of sugar, three tablespoonfuls of melted lard, three tablespoonfuls of melted butter, three eggs, one cup of milk, one teaspoonful of soda, two teaspoonfuls of cream of tartar; flour enough to roll out soft. Roll in pulverized sugar when half cold.

SNOW BALLS, WHITE.

One cup of sugar, six tablespoonfuls of melted butter, two eggs, one cup of sweet milk, two teaspoonfuls of cream of tartar, one of soda, a very little nutmeg, one teaspoonful of salt; mix middling soft and roll out, and cut with a small round cutter. Your tea canister top may be just the right size. Fry in hot lard. Have ready a small bowl with a little fine white sugar in it. As you take them from the lard drop them in the sugar and roll around quickly until the surface has a very thin coat of sugar all over it, then lay carefully on a plate. Repeat with each cake separately, adding a little fresh sugar occasionally.

6

CHAPTER IV.

CREAMS AND CUSTARDS.

APPLE SNOW.

PUT twelve tart apples in cold water over a slow fire; when soft skin and core. Mix in a pint of sifted white sugar, beat the whites of twelve eggs to a stiff froth, then add to the apples and sugar. Put in a dessert dish and ornament with myrtle. It will be found much better if frozen.

ALMOND CREAM.

Take three ounces of sweet and one ounce of bitter almonds, blanch them; put them in a pan over the fire, stirring them continually. As soon as they have acquired a fine yellow color, take them off the fire, and when cold pound them into fine pieces; then add a pint of cream or rich milk, nearly boiling, and three or four heaping tablespoonfuls of sugar, and one-half package of gelatine which has been dissolved in a little water. Put it upon the ice, and when about to thicken stir it until it is very smooth, then stir in lightly a pint of whipped cream and put it into a mold.

APPLE FLOAT.

One cup of pulverized sugar, one cup of cream beaten to a stiff froth, five eggs beaten light, one lemon, four large apples grated, three tablespoonfuls of gelatine dissolved in warm water. Fills one quart bowl.

BAVAROISE.

One pint of milk; add four tablespoonfuls of ground coffee; cook until well mixed, and strain through a jelly-bag; add the beaten yolks of four eggs, a cup of sugar, and cook as for a custard; set in a cold place, and when cool add a pint of whipped cream in which has been stirred one-third of a box of dissolved gelatine, and stand in a cool place until it thickens.

BLANC MANGE.

Take four ounces of sweet almonds and one-half ounce of bitter almonds, blanched; pound them in a mortar, moistening them occasionally with orange-flower water; mix this with one quart of fresh cream; set the cream and almonds on the fire, stirring constantly; when it comes to a scald pour in one-half box of gelatine which has been previously dissolved by soaking in half a cup of cold water one hour.

CREAM A LA MODE.

Put half a pound of white sugar into a deep glass dish; the juice of one large orange and one lemon; to one ounce of isinglass or gelatine add one pint of water; let it simmer down one-half, and when cool strain it into the glass dish, and by degrees add one and one-half pints of whipped cream; stir till cool, and place it on ice to stiffen.

COFFEE CREAM.

Sweeten one pint of rich cream rather liberally; roast two ounces of coffee kernels; when they are lightly browned throw them into the cream at once, and let the dish stand an hour before using; strain, and whip the cream to a stiff froth. A teaspoonful of powdered gum arabic dissolved in a little orange-flower water, may be added to give the cream more firmness, if desired.

BAVARIAN CREAM.

Whip one pint of cream to a stiff froth, and set in a colander one minute to allow the unwhipped portion to drip away; boil one pint of milk and one-half cup of sugar; flavor with vanilla, and add one-half package of gelatine dissolved in water, remove from the fire, and cool; add the well-beaten whites of four eggs. When the mixture has become quite cold add the whipped cream gradually

until it is well mixed; put into individual molds a teaspoonful of
some bright jelly or jam, then pour the mixture and place in an
ice-chest until wanted. This cream may be flavored in any way
desired.

CHOCOLATE BAVARIAN CREAM

Can be made as the preceding by adding two cakes of sweet
chocolate, soaked and stirred smooth in two tablespoonfuls of water,
to the yolks of the eggs.

CALEDONIAN CREAM.

Two ounces of raspberry jam or jelly, two ounces of red currant
jelly, two ounces of sifted loaf sugar, the whites of two eggs put
into a bowl and beaten with a spoon for three-quarters of an hour.
This makes a very pretty cream, and is good and economical.

CHARLOTTE RUSSE ELEGANTE.

One-half package of gelatine dissolved in a very little water;
one quart of whipped cream, flavored and sweetened to taste.
Line a mold with sponge or white cake; stir the gelatine into
the cream and pour into the prepared mold. The cake may be
soaked in a little wine if preferred.

CHARLOTTE RUSSE.

One pint of cream well whipped; beat five tablespoonfuls of sugar
with the yolks of four eggs; simmer together one-half pint of milk
and one-half ounce of isinglass or gelatine till the gelatine is dissolved, then mix with the beaten yolks and the sugar, then the
whites of the eggs well beaten, then the whipped cream; flavor
with one gill of wine and set it aside to cool; pour it into a mold
which was previously lined with pieces of sponge cake. When it is
stiff and solid turn out into a dish and sift sugar over the top.

CHARLOTTE RUSSE, No. 2.

One box of gelatine soaked in milk one-half hour; while it is
soaking make a soft custard with the yolks of seven eggs, one pint
of milk, and one-half pound of crushed sugar. When the custard

begins to boil pour in the gelatine and it will dissolve; when dissolved, strain the custard through a sieve and add one gill of cold cream; then let it cool a little, but not enough to thicken; whip a good quart of thick cream, add vanilla or any flavoring to suit the taste, add this to the custard, set it in the ice chest and stir occasionally until it begins to thicken. Then beat the whites of the seven eggs to a froth, adding two tablespoonfuls of powdered sugar, and stir into the custard and cream, stirring occasionally very gently until it is thick enough to turn into the molds which have been lined with sponge fingers or slices. Set them back in the ice chest.

FRUIT CHARLOTTE.

Line a dish with sponge cake; place upon the bottom, in the centre of the dish, grated pine-apple; cover with a whipped cream blanc mange. Keep back a little of the cream to pour over the top after it is poured out of the mold.

GENOESE CREAM.

One pint of milk, one tablespoonful of flour, one tablespoonful of sugar. Boil until it thickens; add the yolks of three eggs and a piece of butter the size of an egg; flavor with lemon or vanilla. Cover the bottom of the dish with sponge cake, spreading one side of the cake with currant or other jelly. Pour on the cream and dust the top with sugar.

ITALIAN CREAM.

Put one ounce of soaked isinglass, six ounces of loaf sugar, and one pint of milk, into a sauce pan; boil slowly and stir all the time until the isinglass is dissolved; strain the mixture, and, when cool, mix it with a pint of thick cream; flavor with one teaspoonful of extract of bitter almond, and one gill of rose water. Beat thoroughly until it thickens; pour into a large or into individual molds and put into an ice box until wanted.

Manioca Cream.

Three tablespoonfuls of manioca, one pint of milk, three eggs, vanilla and sugar to taste; soak the manioca in water till soft; boil the milk; while boiling stir in the manioca and the yolks of the eggs beaten with the sugar; when cooked sufficiently pour into a dish to cool; when cold, add the vanilla; beat the whites of the eggs until stiff, sweeten and flavor them and stir part into the cream, putting the rest on top.

Russe Cream.

One-half box of gelatine soaked in a little water one hour, one quart of milk, one cup of sugar, and four eggs. Mix sugar, milk, yolks of eggs, and gelatine together; put in a pail, set in a kettle of water and boil twenty minutes. Beat the whites of the eggs stiff, and stir into the custard after taking off the fire. Flavor with vanilla and pour into molds. Serve with sugar and cream or with custard.

Rock Cream.

Boil rice until quite soft in new milk, sweeten with powdered loaf sugar. Pile it in a dish and lay on it in different places lumps of currant jelly, or any kind of preserves; beat the whites of five eggs to a stiff froth; add flavoring and a tablespoonful of thick cream; drop it over the rice forming a rock of cream.

Spanish Cream.

Make a soft custard of one quart of milk, the yolks of six eggs, six tablespoonfuls of sugar. Put one box of gelatine dissolved in one pint of water over the fire; add the custard; flavor with vanilla. Strain into molds and set in a cool place.

Tapioca Cream.

One cup of tapioca soaked for eight hours in milk enough to cover; then take one quart of milk, place on the stove, and when it boils add the beaten yolks of two eggs and the tapioca; let it boil up, then stir the beaten whites very thoroughly through it. Sweeten and flavor to taste. Eat cold.

WHIPPED CREAM.

To one quart very thick whipped cream, add powdered sugar to taste and a glass of wine. Make just before ready to use.

WHIPPED CREAM SAUCE.

Mix a plateful of whipped cream (flavored with vanilla), the beaten whites of two eggs and pulverized sugar to taste, all together; pile a bank of this mixture in the center of a platter and form a circle of little fruit puddings (steamed in cups) around it, or it is nice for corn starch, blanc manges, etc.

Single cream is cream that has stood on the milk twelve hours. It is the best for tea and coffee. Double cream stands on its milk twenty-four hours, and cream for butter frequently stands forty-eight hours. Cream that is to be whipped should not be butter cream, lest in whipping it change to butter.

ALMOND CUSTARD.

One pint of new milk, one cup of pulverized sugar, one-quarter pound of almonds (blanched and pounded), two teaspoonfuls rose water, the yolks of four eggs; stir this over a slow fire until it is of the consistency of cream, then remove it quickly and put into a dish. Beat the whites with a little sugar added to the froth, and lay on top.

APPLE CUSTARD.

One pint of mashed stewed apples, one pint of sweet milk, four eggs, one cup of sugar, and a little nutmeg. Bake slowly.

BOILED CUSTARD.

Allow five eggs to one quart of milk, a tablespoonful of sugar to each egg, set the milk in a kettle of boiling water until it scalds; then, after dipping a little of the milk on to the eggs and beating up, turn into the scalded milk, and stir until it thickens. Flavor to taste.

Baked Custard.

One quart of milk, five eggs, a pinch of salt, sugar and flavor to taste, boil the milk; when cool, stir in the beaten eggs and sugar, pour into cups, set them in pans of water, and bake; if baked too long, will become watery.

Chocolate Custard.

Make a boiled custard with one quart of milk, the yolks of six eggs, six tablespoonfuls of sugar, and one-half cup of grated vanilla chocolate. Boil until thick enough, stirring all the time. When nearly cold, flavor with vanilla. Pour into cups, and put the whites of the eggs beaten with some powdered sugar on the top.

Coffee Custard.

One-half pint of rich cream, one-half cup cold coffee, four eggs, sugar to taste.

Corn Starch Custard.

Most persons know how to make a corn starch custard. A rich one can be made as follows: One quart of milk with five beaten eggs in it; sweeten and flavor to choice, adding one-fourth pound of corn starch; place over the fire, stirring quickly to avoid burning to the bottom, until it begins to thicken. Or, can take less egg by using more corn starch, as follows: One quart of milk, two eggs, sugar and flavor to taste, one-half pound of corn starch. If this is too much starch and it becomes too thick, take it off the fire, add a a little milk, stirring till smooth. A custard is best made in a vessel placed in boiling water, as there is no risk of burning. Custards require to be stiffer for filling cream puffs, chocolate eclares, charlotte russes, etc. The above receipts are thick enough for any of the purposes, and, if required for simple custard, less starch will do.

Cocoanut Custard.

To one pound of grated cocoanut, allow one pint of scalding milk and six ounces of sugar. Beat well the yolks of six eggs and stir them alternately into the milk with the cocoanut and sugar. Pour this into a dish lined with paste and bake twenty minutes; or, if preferred, treat the milk, cocoanut, eggs, and sugar as for boiled custard, and serve in cups.

Cold Cup Custard.

One quart of new milk, one pint of cream, one-fourth pound of fine white sugar, three large tablespoonfuls of wine, in which rennet has been soaked. Mix the milk, cream and sugar together, stir the wine into it, pour the mixture into custard cups, and set them away until the milk becomes a curd. Grate nutmeg on top and eat them with cream that has been kept on ice.

Caramel Custard.

Put two dessert-spoonfuls of crushed sugar into a tin pan; let it stand on the stove till it begins to brown, then stir constantly till it is a thick, black syrup. Pour it into a quart of scalding milk; add six ounces of white sugar and the yolks of six eggs. Beat and pour into cups, set in a pan of hot water in the oven and bake twenty minutes.

Lemon Custard.

Four eggs (leave out the white of one), one cup of sugar, one cup of cold water, one grated lemon, a small piece of butter, one tablespoonful of corn starch; bake as custard; after it is baked, cover it with the beaten white and pulverized sugar; return to the oven; bake a light brown.

Moonshine.

Beat the whites of six eggs into a very stiff froth, then add gradually six tablespoonfuls of powdered sugar, beating for not less than fifteen minutes; then beat in one heaping tablespoonful of preserved peaches cut in tiny bits. In serving, pour in each saucer some rich cream sweetened and flavored with vanilla, and on the cream place a liberal portion of the moonshine. This quantity is enough for seven or eight persons.

FLOATING ISLAND.

Set a quart of milk to boil, then stir into it the beaten yolks of six eggs; flavor with any extract liked and sweeten to taste; whip whites of eggs to a stiff froth. When the custard is thick, put into a deep dish, and heap the frothed eggs upon it. Place pieces of currant jelly on top and serve cold.

FLOATING ISLAND, No. 2.

Into three-quarters of a pint of cream, put sugar to make it very sweet, and the juice and rind of a lemon grated. Beat it for ten minutes. Cut French rolls into thin slices, and lay them on a round dish on the top of the cream. On this put a layer of apricot or currant jam, and some more slices of roll. Pile upon this, very high, a whip made of damson jam, and the whites of four eggs. It should be rough to imitate a rock. Garnish with fruits or sweetmeats.

IRISH MOSS.

Soak a scant handful of Irish moss in strong soda water until it swells; then squeeze the moss until it is free from water, and put it in a tin bucket which contains six pints of sweet milk. Set the bucket in a large iron pot which holds several pints of hot water; stir seldom, and let it remain until it will jell slightly by dropping on a cold plate. Strain through a sieve, sweeten and flavor to taste. Rinse a mold or a crock with tepid water; pour in the mixture, and set it away to cool. In a few hours it will be palatable. Eat with cream and sugar—some add jelly.

QUAKING CUSTARD.

Three cups of milk; yolks of four eggs, reserving the whites for the meringue ; one-half package gelatine; six tablespoonfuls of sugar; vanilla flavoring; juice of one lemon for meringue. Soak the gelatine two hours in a cup of the cold milk. Then add to the rest of the milk, which must be boiling hot, and stir until dissolved. Let it stand a few minutes, and strain through muslin over the beaten yolks and sugar. Put over the fire and stir five minutes, or until you can feel it thickening. Stir up well when nearly cold, flavor, and let it alone until it congeals around the edges of the bowl into which you have poured it; then stir again, and put into a wet mold. Set upon ice, or in cold water until firm Turn it, when you are ready for it, into a glass bowl. Have a meringue made by whipping the whites stiff with three tablespoonfuls of powdered sugar, and the lemon juice.

ORANGE SNOW.

Peel sweet oranges, slice and lay them in a glass dish with alternate layers of grated cocoanut and powdered loaf sugar, leaving a layer of cocoanut on top. Pour over the whole a glass of orange and lemon juice mixed. Place on ice until ready to serve.

CHAPTER V.

CONFECTIONERY.

GENERAL DIRECTIONS.

GRANULATED sugar is preferable. Candy should not be stirred while boiling. Cream of tartar should not be added until the syrup begins to boil. Butter should be put in when the candy is almost done. Flavors are more delicate when not boiled in the candy.

ALMOND CANDY.

Proceed in the same way as for cocoanut candy. Let the almonds be perfectly dry and do not throw them into the sugar until it approaches the candying point.

ALMOND CREAMS.

Three cups of sugar, one and one-half cups of water, one-half teaspoonful of cream of tartar, flavor with vanilla. Boil until drops will almost keep their shape in water, and add a cup of blanched almonds chopped fine, then pour into a bowl set in cold water; stir steadily with a silver or wooden spoon until cool enough to bear the hand; then place on a platter and knead to a fine even texture. If too hard, a few drops of warm water may be stirred in. If too soft, it must be boiled again. When well molded, cut in squares or bars. Almond cream is very nice flavored with chocolate.

BON BONS.

Take some fine fresh candied orange rind or citron, clear off the sugar that adheres to it, cut it into inch squares, stick these singly on the prong of a fork or ozier twigs, and dip them into a solution of sugar boiled to the consistency of candy, and place them on a dish rubbed with the smallest possible quantity of salad oil. When perfectly cold put them into dry tin boxes with paper between each layer.

BUTTER SCOTCH.

One cup of molasses, one cup of sugar, one-half cup of butter. Boil until done.

BOSTON CARAMELS.

One pint bowl of grated chocolate, two bowls of yellow sugar, one bowl of New Orleans molasses, one-half cup of milk, a piece of butter the size of a small egg, and vanilla flavor; boil about twenty-five minutes; this should not be so brittle as other candies. Pour in buttered tins and mark deeply with a knife.

CREAM COCOANUT CANDY.

One and a half pounds of sugar, one-half cup of milk; boil ten minutes; one grated cocoanut added; boil until thick; put on greased pans quite thick; when partially cold cut in strips.

COCOANUT CARAMELS.

Two cups of grated cocoanut, one cup of sugar, two tablespoonfuls of flour, the whites of three eggs beaten stiff; bake on a buttered paper in a quick oven.

COCOANUT CANDY.

One cup of water, two and a half cups of fine white sugar, four spoonfuls of vinegar, a piece of butter as large as an egg; boil till thick about three-quarters of an hour. Just before removing stir in one cup desiccated cocoanut and lay in small flat cakes on buttered plates to cool and harden,

CHOCOLATE CARAMELS.

One cup sweet milk, one cup of molasses, half a cup of sugar, half a cup of grated chocolate, a piece of butter the size of a walnut; stir constantly, and let it boil until it is thick; then turn it out on to buttered plates, and when it begins to stiffen mark it in squares, so that it will break readily when cold.

CHOCOLATE CREAM DROPS.

Mix one-half cup of cream with two of white sugar, boil and stir full five minutes; set the dish into another of cold water and stir until it becomes hard. Then make into small balls about the size of marbles, and with a fork roll each one separately in the chocolate, which has in the meantime been put in a bowl over the boiling tea kettle and melted; put on brown paper to cool; flavor with vanilla if desired. This amount makes about fifty drops.

CHOCOLATE KISSES.

One pound of sugar and two ounces of chocolate pounded together and finely sifted; mix with the whites of eggs well beaten to a froth; drop on buttered paper and bake slowly.

FRUIT CANDY.

One and one-half pounds of granulated sugar, wet with the milk of a cocoanut; put into a sauce-pan and let it heat slowly; boil rapidly five minutes, then add one cocoanut grated very fine, and boil ten minutes longer, stirring constantly. Try a little on a cold plate, and if it forms a firm paste when cool, take from the fire. Pour part of it out on to a large tin lined with greased paper; then add to the remaining cream one-fourth pound of stoned raisins, one-half pound of blanched almonds, one pint of pecans, one-half cup of chopped walnuts. Pour over the other cream, and when cool cut into bars and squares.

HICKORY-NUT CANDY.

Boil two cups of sugar, one-half cup of water, without stirring, until thick enough to spin a thread; flavor; set the dish off into cold water; stir quickly until white, then stir in one cup of hickory-nut meats; turn into a flat tin, and when cool cut into squares.

HOREHOUND CANDY.

Prepare a strong decoction, by boiling two ounces of the dried herb in a pint and a half of water for about half an hour; strain this, and add three and one-half pounds of brown sugar; boil over a hot fire until it reaches the requisite degree of hardness, when it may be poured out in flat tin trays, previously well greased, and marked into sticks or squares with a knife, as it becomes cool enough to retain its shape.

LEMON-CREAM CANDY.

Six pounds best white sugar, strained juice of two lemons, grated peel of one lemon, one teaspoonful of soda, three cups clear water. Steep the grated peel of the lemon in the juice for an hour; strain, squeezing the cloth hard to get out all the strength. Pour the water over the sugar, and, when nearly dissolved, set it over the fire and bring to a boil. Stew steadily until it hardens in cold water; stir in the lemon; boil one minute; add the dry soda, stirring in well; and, instantly, turn out upon broad, shallow dishes. Pull as soon as you can handle it, into long white ropes, and cut into lengths when brittle.

Vanilla cream candy is made in the same way, with the substitution of vanilla flavoring for the lemon-juice and peel.

LEMON AND PEPPERMINT DROPS.

Take of dry granulated sugar a convenient quantity; place it in a saucepan having a lip from which the contents may be poured or dropped. Add a very little water, just enough to make, with the sugar, a stiff paste; two ounces of water to a pound of sugar is about the right proportion. Set it over the fire and allow it to nearly boil, keeping it continually stirred. It must not actually come to a full boil, but must be removed from the fire just as soon as the bubbles, denoting that the boiling point is reached, begin to rise. Allow the syrup to cool a little, stirring all the time; add strong essence of peppermint or lemon to suit the taste, and drop on tins or sheets of smooth white paper. The dropping is performed by tilting the vessel slightly, so that the contents will run out, and with a small piece of stiff wire the drops may be stroked off on to the tins or paper. They should be kept in a warm place for a few hours to dry. In the season of fruits, delicious drops may be made by substituting the juice of fresh fruits, as strawberry, raspberry, lemon, pineapple or banana, or any of these essences may be used.

MOLASSES CANDY.

Into a kettle holding at least four times the amount of molasses to be used, pour a convenient quantity of Porto Rico molasses; place over a slow fire and boil for a half hour, stirring all the time to diminish as much as possible the increase of bulk caused by boiling, and checking the fire or removing the kettle if there is any danger of the contents running over. Be very careful not to let the candy burn, especially near the close of the boiling. When a little, dropped in cold water, becomes quickly hard and snaps apart like a pipestem, add a teaspoonful of carbonate of soda, free from lumps, to every two quarts; stir quickly to mix, and pour on greased platters to cool. When the candy is sufficiently cool to handle without burning the hands, it is pulled back and forth, the hands being rubbed with a little butter (do not use flour) to prevent the candy from sticking to them. The more the candy is worked, the lighter it will be in color.

WHITE MOLASSES CANDY.

Take two pounds of refined sugar (termed by grocers "Coffee C"), one pint of pure sugar-house syrup, and one pint best Porto Rico or New Orleans molasses. Boil together until it hardens, as above described, add one teaspoonful of carbonate of soda, and work in the usual manner.

PEANUT CANDY.

One scant pint of molasses, four quarts of peanuts, measured before they are shelled, two tablespoonfuls of vanilla, one teaspoonful of soda. Boil the molasses until it hardens in cold water, when dropped from the spoon. Stir in the vanilla, then the soda, dry. Lastly, the shelled peanuts. Turn out into shallow pans well buttered, and press it down smooth with a wooden spoon.

We can heartily recommend the candy made according to this receipt as being unrivaled of its kind.

The molasses should be good in quality, and the peanuts freshly roasted.

Pop-Corn Balls.

Add one ounce of white gum arabic to a half pint of water, and let it stand until dissolved. Strain, add one pound of refined sugar and boil until when cooled it becomes very thick, so much so as to be stirred with difficulty. To ascertain when it has reached this point, a little may be cooled in a saucer. A convenient quantity of the freshly popped corn having been placed in a milk pan, enough of the warm syrupy candy is poured on and mixed by stirring, to cause the kernels to adhere in a mass, portions of which may be formed into balls by pressing them into the proper shape with the hands. Ordinary molasses, or sugar-house syrup may be used as well, by being boiled to the same degree, no gum being necessary with these materials. Corn cake is prepared in a similar manner. This mass, while warm, is put into tins and pressed by rollers into thin sheets, which are afterwards divided into small, square cakes.

Taffy.

Either of the two kinds of molasses candy, if poured from the kettle into tin trays without working, will produce a fine plain taffy. It may be left in one sheet the size of the tray, or, when slightly cold, may be marked off in squares.

Efferton Taffy.

This is a favorite English confection. To make it take three pounds of the best brown sugar and boil with one and one-half pints of water, until the candy hardens in cold water. Then add one-half pound of sweet-flavored, fresh butter, which will soften the candy. Boil a few minutes until it again hardens and pour it into trays. Flavor with lemon if desired.

7

VINEGAR CANDY.

Three cups white sugar; one and one-half cups clear vinegar; stir the sugar into the vinegar until thoroughly dissolved; heat to a gentle boil, and stew uncovered until it ropes from the tip of the spoon. Turn out upon broad dishes, well buttered, and cool, and, as soon as it can be handled, pull. It can be pulled beautifully white and porous.

VINEGAR CANDY, No. 2.

To one quart of good New Orleans molasses, add one cup of good cider vinegar; boil until it reaches the point where a little dropped into cold water becomes very hard and brittle. Pour into shallow platters until cool enough to be handled, and form into a large roll, which may be drawn down to any size and cut off in sticks.

WALNUT CANDY.

The meats of hickory-nuts, English walnuts, or black walnuts may be used according to preference in that regard. After removal from the shells in as large pieces as practicable, they are to be placed on the bottoms of tins, previously greased, to the depth of about a half inch. Next, boil two pounds of brown sugar, a half pint of water, and one gill of good molasses until a portion of the mass hardens when cooled. Pour the hot candy on the meats and allow it to remain until hard.

MERINGUES.

Take one pound of powdered sugar, and add to it the beaten whites of eight eggs (slowly), until it forms a stiff froth; fill a tablespoon with the paste, and smooth it over with another spoon to the desired shape; sift a little sugar over a sheet of paper, drop the meringues about two inches apart; dust a little sugar over them, and bake in a quick oven with the door left open part way, so they can be continually watched; when fawn colored, take them out; remove them from the paper with a thin knife; scrape out of each a little of the soft part. They may be neatly arranged around a dish of whipped cream, or filled with ice cream. If whipped cream is used, they would be improved by the addition of a little bright jelly inside each meringue.

CREAM MERINGUES.

Four eggs (the whites only), whipped stiff, with one pound powdered sugar, lemon or vanilla flavoring. When very stiff, heap in the shape of half an egg upon stiff letter-paper lining the bottom of your baking pan. Have them half an inch apart. Do not shut the oven door closely, but leave space through which you can watch them. When they are a light yellow-brown, take them out and cool quickly. Slip a thin bladed knife under each; scoop out the soft inside and fill with cream whipped as for charlotte russe. They are very fine. The oven should be very hot.

MACAROON.

Pound in a mortar one pound of blanched sweet almonds and one and one-fourth pounds of lump sugar until they are fine; then add one-half pound of corn starch, one-fourth pound of rice or wheat flour; mix into a fine smooth batter with the whites of about eight eggs. Drop the mixture in small quantities through a cornucopia on a sheet of paper, dust with sugar, and bake in a steady oven. They should be baked a fawn color.

BACHELOR BUTTONS.

Rub two ounces of butter into five ounces of flour; add five ounces of white sugar; add one beaten egg; flavor; roll into small balls with the hands; sprinkle with sugar. Bake on tins covered with buttered paper.

CORN STARCH RATEFFES.

One-fourth pound sweet and the same of bitter almonds, one-half pound corn starch, one-fourth pound of rice flour, one and one-fourth pounds of pulverized sugar, the whites of eight eggs. Proceed the same as for macaroons, only drop one-fourth the size. Do not dust with sugar, and bake in a hotter oven.

CHAPTER VI.

CATSUPS.

OOD home-made catsup is a most valuable addition to the store-room, and a good housekeeper will always look with pride upon it as it stands upon the shelves in closely-corked bottles, neatly labeled, feeling, as she may, that she possesses close at hand the means of imparting a delicious flavor to her sauces and gravies without at the same time placing any deleterious compound before her friends. Though excellent preparations are no doubt sold by respectable dealers, the superiority of catsup when made at home is undisputed, and the comfortable certainty attending its use is so great, that we would earnestly recommend every lady who has the time and opportunity to do so, to superintend personally the manufacture of that which is used in the kitchen. It is not well, however, to make a very large quantity, as it is rarely improved by being long kept. Catsup should be stored in a cool, dry place; the corks should be covered with resin, and the liquid should be examined frequently, and if there are the slightest signs of fermentation or mold, it should be re-boiled with a few pepper-corns, and put into fresh, dry bottles. Always select perfect fruit, and cook in a porcelain-lined kettle.

Currant Catsup.

Boil five pints of ripe currants in one pint of vinegar until soft; strain all through a sieve, then add three pints of sugar, and one tablespoonful each of cinnamon and allspice; boil about one hour.

100

Cucumber Catsup.

Take one-half bushel of full-grown cucumbers, peel and chop them, sprinkle them with salt, and put them in a sieve and let them stand over night; add two dozen onions, cut up small, one-half pound white mustard seed, one-half pound of black mustard seed, two ounces of black pepper, ground. Mix well with the best cider vinegar, making it the consistency of thick catsup, and fill your jars, tying up closely. It requires no cooking.

Gooseberry Catsup.

Ten pounds of gooseberries, six pounds of sugar, one quart of vinegar, three tablespoonfuls cinnamon, one tablespoonful each of allspice and cloves. Mash the gooseberries thoroughly; scald and put through the colander; add the sugar and spices, and boil fifteen minutes, then add the vinegar; bottle immediately. Ripe grapes may be prepared in the same manner.

Plum Catsup.

To three pounds of fruit put one and three-fourths pounds of sugar, one tablespoonful of cloves, one tablespoonful of cinnamon, one tablespoonful of pepper, a very little salt; scald the plums and put them through a colander; then add sugar and spices, and boil to the right consistency.

Tomato Catsup.

Take sound ripe tomatoes, slice and cook until done enough to put through a sieve; then to every gallon of the pulp and juice add one cup of chopped onion, one-half cup of black pepper, four pods of red pepper, cut fine, one-half cup of ground ginger and mustard mixed, one ounce celery seed, one-half cup of allspice, nutmeg and cinnamon, mixed, one-half teaspoonful cloves, two cups of sugar, and sufficient salt to taste distinctly, one pint strong cider vinegar; put all together and cook two hours, or longer if not thick enough. It must not be thin or watery. Bottle and seal while hot, and in a good cellar it will keep two years.

Tomato Catsup, No. 2.

One bushel of good ripe tomatoes, one-half gallon of cider vine-gar, one-fourth pound of allspice, two ounces of cloves, three tablespoonfuls of black pepper, six large onions or two heads of garlic, one pint of salt, four large red peppers; cook thoroughly, and strain through a sieve, then boil till it is thick enough, and add the vinegar.

CHAPTER VII.

DESSERTS.

PUDDINGS.

WITHOUT pretending to make a skillful cook by book, we believe that any intelligent beginner may compound a good pudding by attending to the following simple rules and plain directions: Attention is all that is required, and a little manual dexterity in turning the pudding out of the mold or cloth. Let the several ingredients be each good and fresh of its kind, as one bad article, particularly eggs, will taint the whole composition Have the molds and pudding cloths carefully washed when used the cloths with wood ashes, and dried in the open air. Lay them aside sweet and thoroughly dry. Pudding ought to be put into plenty of boiling water, which must be kept on a quick boil; or, baked, in general in a sharp but not scorching oven. A pudding in which there is much bread must be tied loosely, to allow room for swelling. A batter pudding should be tied up firmly. Molds should be quite full, well buttered and covered with a fold or two of paper floured and buttered. Eggs for puddings must be used in greater quantities when of small size. The yolks and whites, if the pudding is wanted particularly white and nice, should be strained after being separately well beaten. A little salt is necessary for all potato, bean, or pease puddings, and all puddings in which there is suet or meat, as it improves the flavor. The several ingredients, after being well stirred together, should in general have a little time to stand, that the flavors may blend. A frequent fault of boiled puddings, which are often solid bodies, is being underdone. Baked puddings are as often scorched. Puddings may be steamed with advantage, placing the mold or basin in the steamer and keeping the water boiling under it. When the pudding-cloths are to be used, dip them in hot water, and dredge them with flour; the molds must be buttered. When a pudding begins to set, stir it up in the dish, if it is desired that the fruit, etc., should not settle to the bottom; and, if boiled, turn over the cloth in the pot for the same reason, and also to prevent it sticking to the bottom, on which a plate may be laid as a preventive. The time of boiling must be according to size and solidity. When the pudding is taken out of the pot, dip it quickly into cold water. Set it in a basin of its size; it will then more readily separate from the cloth without breaking. Remember that sugar, butter, and suet become liquids in boiling; it is from their excess that puddings often break. Be, therefore, rather sparing of sugar; for if you have much syrup you must have more eggs and flour, which make puddings heavy. It is often the quantity of sugar that makes tapioca and arrowroot, boiled plain, troublesome to keep in shape when molded. Rice or other grain puddings must not be allowed to boil in the oven before setting, or the ingredients will separate and never set; so never put them in a very hot oven. As a rule, we may assume that such flavoring ingredients as lemon—grate or juice, vanilla and cocoanut, are more admired in modern puddings than cinnamon, cloves and nutmeg. Care must be taken to mix batter puddings smoothly. Let the dried flour be gradually mixed with a little of the milk, as in making starch, and afterwards, in nice cookery, strain it through a coarse sieve. Puddings are lighter boiled than baked. Raisins, prunes, and damsons, for puddings must be carefully stoned; or, Sultanas may be used in place of other raisins; currants must be picked and plunged in hot water, rubbed in a floured cloth, and plumped and dried before the fire; almonds must be blanched and sliced; and in mixing grated bread, pounded biscuit, etc., with milk, pour the milk on them while hot, and cover the vessel for an hour, which is both better and easier

than boiling. Suet must be quite fresh and free from fiber. Mutton suet for puddings is lighter than beef; but marrow, when it.
can be obtained, is richer than either. A baked pudding, for company, has often a paste border, or a garnishing of blanched and
sliced almonds about it, but these borders are merely matters of
ornament; if molded, puddings may also be garnished in various
ways, as with bits of currant jelly. The best seasoning for plain
batter puddings are extracts of orange or lemon, or orange-flower
water. The sweetness and flavor of pudding must, in most cases,
be determined by individual tastes. Sugar can be added at table.

To Young Housekeepers.

All young housekeepers should learn as soon as possible how to
prepare dishes for dessert which can be made on very short notice.
that they may not be annoyed in the event of unexpected company
to dinner. In summer, fruit answers every purpose, but at other
seasons, and particularly if the first course is not very elaborate.
she will need to have something more substantial. A delicious
pudding can be made in a few minutes by taking one pint of milk
and stirring into it half a cup of cassava, half a cup of cocoanut, two
eggs, a little butter, salt and sugar to taste; flavor with vanilla.
Cook this as you would boiled custard. When cooked and put in
the dish in which it is to be served, pour over the top the white of
one egg beaten to a stiff froth, with a tablespoonful of pulverized
sugar added. Set it in the oven for a short time to brown. This
may be eaten warm or cold, with jelly or preserves or without.
Another dish which is easily made and which is economical as well
as palatable, is to take slices of cake which are a little dry and pour
over them while hot some boiled custard; cover the dish quickly,
and the hot custard will steam the cake sufficiently. Raisin cake
steamed and served with some pudding sauce is good. Velvet
cream, to be eaten with cake, is made in this way: Beat the whites
of four eggs to a stiff froth; add two tablespoonfuls of sugar, two
tablespoonfuls of currant jelly, two tablespoonfuls of raspberry

jam; beat all well together; cream may be added or not, as you choose.   Oranges cut up, with sugar and grated cocoanut sprinkled over them are also nice for cake.

ARROWROOT PUDDING.

One quart milk, three and one-half tablespoonfuls arrowroot, four eggs, one cup sugar, one teaspoonful each of extract nutmeg and cinnamon.

Boil the milk, add the arrowroot dissolved in a little water, and the sugar; let reboil; take from the fire; beat in the eggs, whipped a little, and the extracts; pour in a well-buttered earthenware dish, and bake in a quick oven one-half an hour; a few minutes before taking from the oven, sift two tablespoonfuls sugar over it, and set back to glaze.   This pudding is generally eaten cold.

ALMOND PUDDING.

Two egg muffins, one cup almonds, blanched—pouring boiling water on them till the skin slips easily off—and pounded to a fine paste, one and one-half cups sugar, four eggs, one and one-half pints milk, one teaspoonful each of extract bitter almonds and rose. Cut off the top crust from muffins very thin; steep them in the milk; beat the yolks of the eggs and sugar with the almonds, then add the steeped muffins squeezed a little dry; dilute with the milk, add the extract, and put it thus prepared into a well-buttered earthenware dish; then stir gently in the whites beaten to a dry froth, and bake in a moderately quick oven about one-half hour.

PIE-PLANT CHARLOTTE.

Wash and cut the pie-plant into small pieces, cover the bottom of a pudding dish with a layer of pie-plant and sugar, then a layer of bread crumbs and bits of butter, or thin slices of bread nicely buttered, and so on until the dish is full.   Bake three-quarters of an hour in a moderate oven.   Allow a pound of sugar to a pound of fruit.   If preferred, turn over the charlotte a boiled custard when ready for the table.

CROQUETTES OF RICE.

Put a quarter of a pound of rice, one pint of milk, three table-spoonfuls of finely-sifted sugar, a piece of butter the size of a small nut and the thin rind of a lemon, into a saucepan. Any other flavoring may be used if preferred. Simmer gently until the rice is tender and the milk absorbed. It must be boiled until thick and dry, or it will be difficult to mould into croquettes. Beat it thoroughly for three or four minutes, then turn it out, and when it is cold and still, form it into small balls; dip these in egg, sprinkle a few bread crumbs over them, and fry them in clar-ified fat till they are lightly and equally browned. Put them on a piece of clean blotting paper, to drain the fat from them, and serve them piled high on the dish. If it can be done without breaking them, it is an improvement to introduce a little jam into the middle of each one; or jam may be served with them. Time, about one hour to boil the rice, ten minutes to fry the croquettes.

BOMBES AU RIZ.

Take half a pint of rice, put in three pints of boiling water, and salt. Let it boil fifteen minutes. At the end of that time drain the rice, pour on milk enough to cover it; put it on the back part of the stove, where it will not burn, and let it absorb the milk; put in enough milk to make the rice soft. While the milk is being absorbed add four tablespoonfuls of sweetening and one teaspoonful of flavoring. When the rice is thoroughly tender take it from the fire and add the yolks of three eggs. If the rice is not hot enough to thicken the eggs, put it back on the fire; stir constantly and let it remain just long enough to thicken, but don't let it burn. As soon as it thickens put it on a dish and rub with salad oil; then put it where it will get very cold. As soon as cold it is ready to use for rice croquets or bombes. Take a tablespoonful of rice in your hand and flatten it; put a plum or any sweetmeat in the center, roll the rice round the sweetmeat, roll in cracker dust, dip in egg, then roll in the cracker dust again. Fry in smoking hot lard and, serve hot or cold.

GREEN CORN PUDDING.

A most delicious accompaniment to a meat course. Take one quart of milk, five eggs, two tablespoonfuls melted butter, one tablespoonful white sugar, and a dozen large ears green corn; grate the corn from the cob; beat the whites and the yolks of the eggs separately; put the corn and yolks together, stir hard and add the butter, then the milk gradually, beating all the while, next the sugar, and a little salt, lastly the whites. Bake slow at first, covering the dish for an hour; remove the cover and brown nicely.

COTTAGE PUDDING.

One cup milk, two of flour, three teaspoonfuls baking powder, two tablespoonfuls melted butter, one egg, one cup of sugar. Steam three-quarters, or bake one hour. Serve with sauce.

CRANBERRY ROLL.

Stew a quart of cranberries in just water enough to keep them from burning. Make very sweet, strain, and cool. Make a paste, and when the cranberry is cold, spread it on the paste about an inch thick. Roll it, tie it close in a flannel cloth, boil two hours and serve with a sweet sauce. Stewed apples or other fruit may be used in the same way.

DELMONICO PUDDING.

One quart scalded milk, three tablespoonfuls corn starch, moistened with a little cold milk; stir into the boiling milk the yolks of six eggs well beaten, four tablespoonfuls sugar; stir all together. Take it off the fire, flavor it, and put into a pudding dish. Then beat the whites of the eggs to a stiff froth, spread over the top, and brown in the oven.

EVE'S PUDDING.

Take equal quantities of flour, fresh butter, and sugar, six ounces of each; beat the butter to a cream, and beat the sugar and flour into it. Separate the yolks from the whites of four eggs, beat them until light, and add the yolks first, then the whites, to the batter, and lastly half a dozen almonds, blanched and pounded, and the grated rind of a lemon. Beat well, and fill small cups to about half; then set before the fire to rise. In five minutes put them into the oven and bake for half an hour.

FIG PUDDING.

Half a pound figs, half cup suet, half a pound bread crumbs, one tablespoonful sugar, three eggs, one cup milk; chop the suet and figs fine, add some cinnamon and nutmeg, and a glass of wine, if you choose, or leave it out if you prefer. Boil it three hours— sauce.

FRUIT PUDDING.

Take one cup each sweet milk, suet (minced), raisins, currants, and molasses. Stiffen with bread crumbs and a little flour, having added three teaspoonfuls baking powder to the flour and crumbs; boil or steam till done. This pudding is equally as good the second day as the first.

BAKED FARINA PUDDING.

Stir into a quart of milk when boiling one-half pound farina, cook it five minutes and set it aside to cool, meanwhile stir four ounces of butter to a cream, grate the rind of a lemon and add the yolk of six eggs, one cup each of sugar, raisins, and currants, and mix all well together with the cooked farina. Beat the whites of the eggs to a froth, stir it into the batter, and bake slowly for an hour.

PLAIN FRUIT PUDDING.

Take one and a half cups of flour, one cup of bread crumbs, one cup of raisins, half a cup of currants, two nutmegs, one cup of suet chopped fine, two tablespoonfuls of sugar, four eggs, a wine glass of brandy, a wine glass of syrup, and a little milk if necessary. Mix very thoroughly; tie it in a cloth as tight as possible, and boil fast for five or six hours. Serve with wine sauce.

FLORENTINE PUDDING.

Put a quart of milk into your pan, let it come to a boil; mix smoothly three tablespoonfuls of corn starch and a little cold milk; add the yolks of three eggs beaten, half a cup of sugar, flavor with vanilla, lemon, or anything your fancy suggests; stir into the scalding milk, continue stirring till of the consistency of starch (ready for use), then put into the pan or dish you wish to serve it in; beat the whites of the eggs with a cup of pulverized sugar, and spread over the top; place in the oven a few minutes, till the frosting is a pretty brown. Can be eaten with cream, or is good enough without. For a change, you can bake in cups.

GELATINE PUDDING.

One ounce gelatine, one pint cold milk; set on range, and let come slowly to a boil, stirring occasionally; separate the yolks and whites of six fresh eggs; beat the yolks well and stir slowly into hot milk; add half a pound of granulated sugar; when quite cold, stir in a quart of whipped cream; flavor with vanilla and lemon extract mixed; have the whites of the eggs beaten very stiff, and stir in the last thing; pack on ice.

GINGER PUDDING.

One egg, one cup of molasses, half a cup butter, half a cup of fruit, half a cup of hot water, one tablespoonful of ginger, one teaspoonful of soda. Stir stiff and steam one hour.

Sauce for Ginger Pudding.—One egg, one cup sugar, one-third of a cup of butter, one tablespoonful of flour, one and one-half tablespoonfuls of lemon. Pour boiling water in and make like thin starch.

HONEY COMB PUDDING.

Three cups flour, one cup beef suet, one cup milk, one cup

molasses, one cup raisins, currants or whortleberries in the season, one teaspoonful soda, a little salt. Boil or steam three hours— sauce.

HUCKLEBERRY PUDDING.

One cup sugar, one-half cup butter, two of milk, two eggs, two cups of berries, one teaspoonful of soda, two of cream of tartar, salt. Mix stiff as gingerbread. Boil two hours in a tin pail. Serve with sauce.

HEN'S NEST.

Make blanc mange, pour in egg shells and set to cool; when cold, break the egg shells, place in glass dish, cut strips of lemon peel and let boil in syrup of sugar and water till tender, and sprinkle on the egg shapes, and make custard and pour over the nest.

INDIAN PUDDING.

Stir a pint of corn meal into a quart of boiling milk; melt four ounces of butter; mix it first with a pint of molasses, and then, very gradually, with the meal. Flavor with nutmeg and grated lemon peel, or cinnamon, and as soon as the mixture has cooled, add, stirring briskly, six well-beaten eggs. Butter a dish and bake at once.

APPLE PUDDING.

A loaf of stale bread, steamed twenty minutes before dinner, sliced, spread with stewed apple, and a little butter, strewn with sugar and browned lightly in a quick oven, makes as good a pudding as any one would like, with either hard or liquid sauce.

APPLE BATTER PUDDING.

Six or eight fine juicy apples, pared and cored, one quart of milk, ten tablespoonfuls of flour, six eggs, beaten very light, one tablespoonful butter—melted, one saltspoonful of salt, one-half teaspoonful soda, one teaspoonful cream of tartar. Set the apples close together, in the baking dish; put in enough cold water to half cover them, and bake closely covered, until the edges are clear, but

not until they begin to break. Drain off the water, and let the
fruit get cold before pouring over them a batter made of the ingredients enumerated above. Bake in a quick oven. Serve in the
baking dish, and eat with sauce.

APPLE FLOAT.

To one quart of apples partially stewed and well mashed, put the
whites of three eggs well beaten, and four heaping tablespoonfuls
loaf sugar; beat them together fifteen minutes, and eat with rich
milk and nutmeg.

APPLE SLUMP.

One quart flour sifted with three teaspoonfuls baking powder;
shorten with one teaspoonful butter rubbed into the flour. Mix
with cold milk or water, the same as for biscuit. Put two
quarts of pared, sliced or quartered apples with one pint of water
into the dish in which the slump is to be cooked. Roll the crust
about an inch thick, cut into quarters and with it cover the apples
in the dish; then cover the whole with a close fitting cover, and
boil or steam till done. Take out on a platter and grate nutmeg
over the apple. Serve with a sweet sauce or sugar and cream.

BAKED APPLE DUMPLINGS.

To one quart flour add two heaping teaspoonfuls baking powder,
and the usual quantity of salt. Thoroughly mix while dry and
sift. Then take one tablespoonful lard and one tablespoonful butter and chop them into the flour prepared as above. Then mix
with sweet milk to a thin dough, just stiff enough to handle.
Roll it out half an inch thick and cut into squares.

APPLES SURPRISED.

Peel, core, and slice about five nice cooking apples, sprinkle the
slices with a spoonful of flour, one of grated bread, and a little
sugar. Have some lard quite hot in a small stew-pan, put the slices
of apple in it, and fry of a light yellow; when all are done, take
a piece of butter the size of a walnut, and a good spoonful of grated

bread, a spoonful of sugar, and a cup of milk; put into the pan, and when they boil up throw in the apple slices, hold the whole over the fire for two minutes, when it will be ready to serve.

AMBER PUDDING.

Six eggs beaten light, one cup of cream, creamed with one-half cup of butter, juice of a lemon, and half the grated peel, a good pinch of nutmeg, puff paste. Mix sugar, butter, eggs, together; put into a custard kettle, set in hot water, and stir until it thickens. Stir in lemon and nutmeg, and let it get cold. Put a strip of paste around the edge of a pie plate; print it prettily; pour in the cold mixture, and bake in a steady, not too hot oven. Eat cold.

AMBROSIA.

Eight fine oranges, peeled and sliced, one-half grated cocoanut, one-half cup of powdered sugar. Arrange slices of orange in a glass dish; scatter grated cocoanut thickly over them; sprinkle this lightly with sugar, and cover with another layer of orange. Fill the dish in this order, having a double quantity of cocoanut and sugar at top. Serve soon after it is prepared.

APPLE OMELETTE.

Six large pippins or other large tart apples, one tablespoonful of butter, three eggs, six tablespoonfuls of white sugar, nutmeg to the taste, and one teaspoonful of rosewater; pare, core, and stew the apples, as for sauce; beat them very smooth while hot, adding butter, sugar, and flavoring; when quite cold, add the eggs, beaten separately very light; put in the whites last and pour into a deep bake-dish previously warmed and well buttered. Bake in a moderate oven until it is delicately browned. Eat warm—not hot. A wholesome dish for children.

APPLE CHARLOTTE.

Butter your pudding dish, line it with bread buttered on both sides; put a thick layer of apples, cut in thin slices, sugar, a little cinnamon and butter on top, then another layer of bread, apples, sugar, cinnamon and butter last. Bake slowly one and a half hours, keeping the pan covered until half an hour before serving; let the apples brown on top.

BANCROFT PUDDING.

One tablespoonful melted butter, one cup sugar, one egg well beaten, one pint flour, two teaspoonfuls cream of tartar, one of soda, one cup sweet milk; beat well and bake thirty minutes.

BREAD PUDDING.

One pint fine bread crumbs to one quart of milk, one cup sugar, yolks of four eggs, well beaten,. grated rind of lemon, piece of butter size of an egg. Don't let it bake till watery. Whip the whites of the eggs with one cup sugar to a stiff froth, and put into this the juice of the lemon; spread over the pudding a layer of jelly or other sweemeat; then spread the whites of eggs over this, and replace in the oven and bake lightly.

BANANA AND APPLE TART.

Make crust of fine flour and fresh butter. Make little crust, but make it good. Slice apples fine and put in dish with three or four bananas sliced, only adding sugar and perhaps a little syrup, if you have got it. Cover crust over fruit; brush a little melted butter over top, strew white sugar on and bake twenty minutes or more, as required.

BIRD'S NEST PUDDING.

Pare, quarter and core nice tart apples; butter a pie tin and slice the apples in it; make a batter of one cup cream (sour and not very rich), one teaspoonful soda, one egg, a little salt, and flour enough to make a stiff batter. Pour this over the apples and bake; when done turn bottom side up and spread thickly with good sweet butter and sugar. To be eaten warm.

BIRD'S NEST PUDDING, No. 2.

Take eight or ten nice apples, pare whole and core; place in a pudding dish; fill the cores with sugar and nutmeg. Make a custard of five eggs to one quart of milk, sweeten to taste; pour this over the apples and bake half an hour.

CABINET PUDDING.

In making it use one pint of milk, six eggs, and a quantity of stale cake—stale bread could be used. The tin must be carefully greased with butter, and around the inside place bits of fruit. For this, citron, cherries, currants, or any kind of dried fruit, could be used. Over this is put a layer of light colored cake, sponge cake perhaps, and the center is filled to near the top of the dish with broken up pieces. Upon this is poured the custard made of the eggs and milk thoroughly beaten up and flavored to suit the taste. The dish is then placed in a kettle of boiling water, the water coming up within about two-thirds of the way to the top. The pot is covered and boiled until done thoroughly.

CREAM BATTER PUDDING.

Take one cup of sour cream and rub with one cup of flour until smooth; then pour in one cup of sweet milk, three eggs—the yolks and whites beaten separately, a little salt and two-thirds of a teaspoonful of soda. Bake in a quick oven. To be eaten with cream and sugar.

CRACKER PUDDING.

Four crackers pounded and sifted, small piece of butter, one and one-half pints milk, scalded and poured on the cracker and butter, four eggs, sugar to sweeten, nutmeg.

CHOCOLATE PUDDING.

One quart of sweet milk, three ounces grated chocolate. Scald the milk and chocolate together; when cool, add the yolks of five eggs and one cup sugar. Bake about twenty-five minutes; beat the whites from the top; brown in the oven; eat cold.

CHARLOTTE PUDDING.

Remove the crust from a loaf of bread, dip in milk, and spread the slices with butter. Pare and cut apples very thin. Lay the bread in a buttered dish, spread over the apples, sweeten and flavor with the juice and grated rind of a lemon. Bake till the apples are tender.

COTTAGE PUDDING.

Warm two and one-half tablespoonfuls butter, stir in a cup of sugar and two eggs well beaten, two teaspoonfuls cream of tartar in one pint flour, one teaspoonful soda dissolved in one cup milk, flavor with nutmeg or lemon. Bake three-quarters of an hour and serve hot with sauce.

CUSTARD BREAD PUDDING.

Two cups fine dry crumbs; one quart of milk; five eggs, beaten light; one tablespoonful corn starch; one teaspoonful of salt, and one-half teaspoonful of soda, dissolved in milk; flavor to taste. Soak the crumbs in the milk, and heat in a custard kettle to a boil. Add the corn starch wet with cold milk, cook one minute, turn out and beat hard. When smooth and almost cold, whip in the yolks, the flavoring, lastly, the whites. Boil in a buttered mold an hour and a half. Eat hot with sweet sauce. It is excellent.

COCOANUT PUDDING.

Take sufficient stale bread to make a pudding, the size you require; pour boiling water over it. After it is soaked well, take a fork and see that no lumps of bread remain; then add half a cup of grated cocoanut, make a custard of one quart of milk, and four eggs, flavor with nutmeg (of course you will sweeten it with white sugar); pour over and bake immediately.

CREAM PUDDING.

One quart of milk; one cup of hot boiled rice well cooked but not broken; one cup of sugar; one heaping tablespoonful of corn starch; five eggs; one-fourth teaspoonful of cinnamon and the same of grated lemon peel. Heat the milk, stir in the corn starch wet up with cold milk; then the beaten yolks and sugar. Add to these the heaping cup of boiled rice. Stir until it begins to thicken, add the seasoning, and pour into a buttered bake-dish. Bake until well "set;" spread with a meringue of the whites and a little sugar, made very stiff. When this has colored lightly, take from the oven. Make on Saturday, and set on ice until Sunday. The colder it is the better.

CRUMB PUDDING.

Three egg yolks, one ounce of sugar, one ounce of bread crumbs, half a teaspoonful of cinnamon. Beat the egg-yolks, sugar, crumbs, and spice in a basin for five minutes. Add the three egg-whites beaten to a white snow (not too firm), bake in a buttered shallow tin or dish, and when quite cooled turn into a flat dish with the lower side upward, pour over it a glassful of wine boiled with a little sugar and spice, and serve while hot.

IRISH ROCK.

A sweet for dessert. Wash the salt from half a pound of butter, and beat into it a quarter of a pound of finely powdered sugar; blanch a pound of sweet almonds and an ounce of bitter; pound these in a mortar, reserving enough of the sweet almonds to spike for ornamenting the dish when sent to table; add the butter and sugar, with a quarter of a glass of brandy, and pound until smooth and white; when, after having become firm, it may be molded into a large egg-like shape, and stuck full of almond meats. It should be placed high on a glass dish, with a decoration of green sweetmeats and a sprig of myrtle, or garnish with any green fruits or sweetmeats.

JELLY RICE.

Mix four ounces of rice flour smoothly and gradually with a quart of cold milk; put them into a sauce pan, with a quarter of an ounce of clarified isinglass, the thin rind of half a lemon, four bitter almonds, blanched and pounded, and four ounces of sugar. Boil and stir briskly until quite thick; take out the lemon rind and pour the mixture into a damp mold. When it is firmly set, turn it on a glass dish, pour melted currant jelly, or any fruit syrup, round it, and send a dish of cream to table with it.

JELLY CUSTARD.

One quart of milk, six eggs—whites and yolks, one cup sugar, flavoring to taste, some red and yellow jelly,—raspberry is good for one, orange jelly for the other. Make a custard of the eggs, milk and sugar; boil gently until it thickens well; flavor when cold; fill your custard glasses two-thirds full and heap up with the two kinds of jelly—the red upon some, the yellow upon others.

JELLY TARTLETS.

Make the paste the same as for pies; line small patty pans, pricking the paste in the bottom to keep it from puffing too high; bake in a quick oven and fill with jelly or jam.

KISS PUDDING.

Beat the yolks of three eggs and half a cup of sugar till light, add one and a half tablespoonfuls of corn starch, stir in one pint of boiling milk, stir on the stove till thick, pour in a pudding dish; beat the whites of the eggs with half a cup of sugar, spread over the top and brown.

LEMON PUDDING.

One lemon grated, rind and pulp, one cup of sugar, one cup of water or sweet milk, four eggs, three tablespoonfuls of melted butter, two tablespoonfuls of flour. Line a deep dish with pastry crusts, pour the custard in, bake thirty minutes. Beat the whites of three or four eggs to a stiff froth, sweeten, spread over the top of the pudding, and let brown slightly.

LEMON TRIFLE.

Two lemons—juice of both and grated rind of one, one cup sherry, one large cup of sugar, one pint cream well sweetened and whipped stiff, a little nutmeg. Strain the lemon juice before adding the wine and nutmeg. Strain again and whip gradually into the frothed cream. Serve in jelly glasses and send around cake with it. It should be eaten soon after it is made.

Lemon Pudding.

Two eggs, four tablespoonfuls of flour, one-half cup sweet cream, one cup sweet milk, one tablespoonful butter, one cup sugar, grated rind and juice of one-half lemon. Bake in a moderate over.

Meringue Rice Pudding.

Take a cup of rice to one pint of water; when the rice is boiled dry add one pint milk, a piece of butter size of an egg, and five eggs. Beat the yolks, and grated rind of a lemon, and mix with the rice. Butter a dish; pour in the mixture, and bake lightly. Beat the whites to a stiff froth; add a cup of sugar and the juice of a lemon. When the pudding is nearly done, spread on this frosting, and bake in a slow oven till the top is light brown.

Malagan Pudding.

One-third cup rice, one cup sugar, two eggs, one pint milk, half a lemon and salt. Soak the rice over night. Beat the yolks of the eggs with one tablespoonful of the sugar, and grate in the lemon rind; add the rice and milk. Bake one hour. Take the whites of the eggs and beat to a stiff froth with the rest of the sugar, then add the lemon juice. Pour it over the pudding after it is baked, and brown it in the oven two or three minutes. To be eaten cold.

Mitchell Pudding.

One cup raisins, one cup chopped suet or butter, one cup molasses —some like one cup sugar with two spoonfuls molasses better—one cup sour milk, one teaspoonful soda, salt, flour to make a stiff batter. Steam three or four hours. Sauce.

Maud's Pudding.

Six eggs, ten tablespoonfuls flour, butter the size of an egg, salt; mix to a light batter with sweet milk and baking powder in flour— it will rise high, bake in ten minutes in a quick oven—put into the oven just as dinner is being served so it will not fall before coming to the table. Serve with cream flavored with lemon or other extract to taste.

Orange Pudding.

Soak the crumbs of a French roll in milk, let it drain in a colander for half an hour, break it with a spoon in a basin, add two ounces of sugar, grated, one ounce of butter, warmed, the yolks of four eggs, the juice of four oranges, the grated rind of one, and finally the four egg-whites beaten (not too stiffly) on a plate with a knife, and bake in a buttered dish in a quick oven. The pudding will be equally good boiled in a mold for an hour and a half, and served with a sweet sauce.

Christmas Plum Pudding.

Shred finely three-quarters of a pound of beef suet, and add to it a pinch of salt, one pound and a half of bread crumbs, half a pound of flour, three-quarters of a pound of raisins, three-quarters of a pound of currants, picked and dried, two ounces of candied lemon and citron together, and half a large nutmeg. Mix these thoroughly, then add four eggs and milk enough to moisten it, but not too much or the pudding will be heavy. Tie in a pudding cloth, well floured, and boil for five or six hours; or, we think better when boiled in a mold, which should be well buttered before the mixture is put in. The mold should not be quite full and should be covered with one or two folds of paper, buttered and floured, and then with a floured pudding cloth.

Plum Pudding.

One pound of raisins, one of currants, one of suet chopped fine, and add three-quarters of a pound of stale bread crumbs, one-quarter pound of flour, one-quarter pound of brown sugar, rind of one lemon (chopped fine), one-half nutmeg grated, five eggs, one-half pound mixed candied peel, one-half pint of brandy; mix well the dry ingredients; beat the eggs with the brandy; pour this over the other things and thoroughly mix; to be boiled in a basin or mold for six hours at the time of making, and six hours when wanted for use.

English Plum Pudding.

One pound beef suet, three-quarters pound bread crumbs (not flour), three-quarters pound raisins, three-quarters pound currants, two ounces sweet almonds, with two or three bitter ones, eight eggs, well beaten, one quarter pound citron, a glass of brandy and one of sherry wine; grate in one-half of a nutmeg, and sweeten to your taste; mix all these ingredients well; boil six hours in a bowl or cloth. When turned out and ready for the table, pour over brandy, set on fire and carry to table surrounded by blue flame. This quantity will be dessert for six persons. Two or three times the quantity may be made, boiled five hours, and set away for use New Year's, Easter, or any intervening birthday. It will be good at the end of twelve months. When wanted to use, boil two hours longer.

Plum Pudding.

One coffeecup of molasses, one coffeecup of milk, one coffeecup of chopped suet, one coffeecup of chopped raisins, four coffeecups of flour, one teaspoonful of salt, three teaspoonfuls of baking powder, and one egg. Boil or steam three hours. Flavor with wine, or extract of orange, on sauce.

Rich Plum Pudding.

Beat up eight eggs, yolks and whites separately, and strain; mix them with a pint of thick cream; stir in half a pound of flour and half a pound of bread crumbs rubbed through the colander; when well mixed beat in one pound of beef suet, chopped very fine, one pound of currants, one pound of finely chopped raisins, one pound of powdered sugar, two ounces of candied lemon, and two of citron, and a nutmeg grated; mix up all with half a pint of brandy or of wine; boil in a cloth for six or seven hours. Any of these Christmas puddings may be kept for a month after boiling, if the cloth in which they are made be replaced by a clean one, and the puddings be hung to the ceiling of a kitchen or any warm store-room; they will then be ready for use, and will require only one hour's boiling to heat them thoroughly.

BAKED PLUM PUDDING.

One and a half cups of suet, chopped fine, one cup of raisins, stoned, one-half cup of milk, one cup of currants, one teaspoonful of saleratus, one-half cup of citron, chopped, one-half teaspoonful each of spice and salt, one-half cup sugar, one-half cup of molasses, two eggs, flour enough for a stiff batter. Bake two hours and serve with sauce.

POOR MAN'S PUDDING.

Take one quart of milk, six eggs, six tablespoonfuls of flour, and a little salt. Bake half an hour. Use butter and sugar dip.

RAISIN PUFFS.

Two eggs, one-half cup butter, three teaspoonfuls baking powder, two tablespoonfuls sugar, two cups of flour, one of milk, one of raisins, chopped very fine. Steam one-half hour in small cups.

ROLY POLY PUDDING.

The pastry for this favorite pudding may be made in several different ways, according to the degree of richness required. For a superior pudding, mix a pound of flour with half a pound of very finely shred suet, freed from skin and fibre; add a good pinch of salt, an egg, and nearly half a pint of milk; roll it out to a long thin form, a quarter of an inch thick, and of a width to suit the size of the saucepan in which it is to be boiled; spread over it a layer of any kind of jam, berries, or fruit, and be careful that the sauce does not reach the edges of the pastry. Begin at one end and roll it up, to fasten the fruit inside, moisten the edges and press them securely together; dip a cloth in boiling water, flour it well, and tie the pudding tightly in it; put it into a saucepan of boiling water, at the bottom of which a plate has been laid to keep the pudding from burning, and boil quickly until done. If it is necessary to add more water, let it be boiling when put in, or the pudding may be steamed. Marmalade, sliced lemon or orange and sugar, chopped apples, or currants, may be used for filling. If boiled, it will require from an hour and a half to two hours to boil.

RICE PUDDING.

One quart of milk, one cup of rice (boiled), three eggs, two tablespoonfuls of sugar, and one teaspoonful of extract of lemon, vanilla, or orange.

SAGO PUDDING.

One quart rich, sweet milk, four tablespoonfuls of sago, four eggs, one cup sugar, and flavoring; soak sago over night in water; then beat yolks of eggs, sugar, and sago together; add milk and flavoring; set a basin in the steamer, pour in the mixture and steam one hour; beat whites with one tablespoonful of sugar to a stiff froth; spread over pudding and brown in oven five minutes; stir while steaming or the sago will settle to the bottom.

SUET PUDDING.

One small cup of suet cut fine, one cup of molasses, one cup chopped raisins, one cup sour milk, half a teaspoonful each of cloves, cinnamon and nutmeg, and one teaspoonful of soda. Stir thick with flour, and put in pudding bag, leaving room to rise, and boil three hours.

STEAMED PUDDING.

One cup of sugar, one-half cup of butter, three eggs, one cup of milk, three heaping teaspoonfuls of baking powder, and three cups of flour; steam one hour.

SNOW PUDDING.

Pour one pint of boiling water on half a box of gelatine; add juice of one lemon and two cups sugar; when nearly cold, strain it, add the whites of three eggs beaten to a stiff froth, then beat all well together again, put it into a mold to shape it, and let it cool. Take the yolks of these eggs, one pint milk, and one teaspoonful corn starch, flavor with vanilla; cook this like any soft custard, put the hard part of the pudding into a dish, when you want to serve it, with the custard round it.

STEAMED PUDDING.

One cup sweet milk, two-thirds cup butter, one cup molasses, one cup chopped raisins, three cups flour, two-thirds teaspoonful soda. Put into a covered pail and steam three hours.

STRAWBERRY SHORT CAKE.

Rub into one quart of flour five ounces of lard, a pinch of salt, and three tablespoonfuls of baking powder; add gradually enough milk to make a soft dough; divide into four parts; roll one part out lightly; cover a straight-sided Vienna cake tin with it. Roll out another part and lay it on top of the first. Proceed in the same way with the other two parts, using another baking tin. Bake quickly, and when done, while hot, lift the upper part from each pan, butter the inner surfaces, and place between the two crusts a layer, an inch thick, of fresh berries, mashed and sweetened. Serve immediately, with cream. A raspberry shortcake may be made with the same pastry.

Custard to pour over Strawberry Shortcake.—One cup sugar, one tablespoonful corn starch, one egg, and one pint of milk. Flavor and cook as custard.

STRAWBERRY SHORTCAKE, No. 2.

Mix a saltspoonful of salt with a pound of flour; chop in three tablespoonfuls of butter; dissolve a teaspoonful of soda in a little hot water, and add with a well-beaten egg to a large cup of sour cream or rich "lobbered" milk, and a tablespoonful of sugar. Put all together, handling as little as possible, and mix as soft as can be rolled. Roll lightly and quickly into two sheets, and bake in round tins, well greased, laying one sheet on the other. When done, separate, they will part where they were joined. Lay on the lower sheet a thick layer of strawberries, and dust with powdered sugar. If desired, strawberries can be placed on top and sugared as before. Serve with sweet cream. If the strawberries are just heated a little and crushed lightly with a spoon and then put between the crusts, it is much improved.

TAPIOCA PUDDING.

Put a cup of tapioca and a teaspoonful of salt into a pint and a half of water and let it stand a couple of hours where it will be quite warm and not cook. Peel six tart apples, take out their cores and fill them with sugar in which is grated a little nutmeg and lemon peel, and put them in a pudding dish. Over these pour the tapioca, first mixing with it a tablespoonful of melted butter and a little cold milk. Bake one hour. Eat with sauce.

TAPIOCA PUDDING, No. 2.

One cup tapioca, soaked in water an hour, one quart milk, three eggs, one cup sugar. Bake.

TO COOK RICE.

To cook rice so that the grains will be whole and tender, wash it in cold water until the water looks clear, then cook it rapidly in boiling water for fifteen minutes, after which drain and place the covered saucepan on the back of the stove to steam until the grains crack open and are tender, which will be about fifteen minutes longer.

VEGETABLE PUDDING.

Half a pound of carrots, half a pound of cold, mashed potatoes, the same of flour, suet, sugar, four ounces candied lemon peel, one-quarter of a pound of currants. Boil slowly for two hours.

WHIPPED SYLLABUBS.

One pint of cream, rich and sweet, one-half cup sugar, powdered, one glass of wine, vanilla, or other extract one large teaspoonful.

Sweeten the cream, and, when the sugar is thoroughly dissolved, stir in the wine carefully with the flavoring extract, and churn to a strong froth. Heap in glasses and eat with cake.

Yankee Pudding.

One cup of molasses, one cup of sour milk or buttermilk, one-half cup sugar, two teaspoonfuls of butter, two teaspoonfuls of saleratus, one teaspoonful of ginger, same of cinnamon, five of flour, one egg; bake in a shallow pan.

Sauce.—One pint of milk or cream, half cup sugar, white of one egg, beaten lightly, one teaspoonful of corn starch; flavor with nutmeg. Boil one minute.

Pudding Sauce.

A nice and easily made sauce for plum and all kinds of rich puddings may be made as follows: Beat the yolks of two eggs, and add four ounces of powdered sugar and half a pint of Madeira, and set it upon a slow fire and stir until it becomes smooth, and thickens. Serve in a sauce-tureen.

Sweet Sauce.

Sweeten a little good, melted butter, and flavor it with grated lemon rind, nutmeg, or powdered cinnamon, strew a little of the grate over the top, and serve in a tureen. A little wine or brandy may be added at pleasure. This sauce is suitable for almost all ordinary boiled puddings.

Fruit Sauce.

Boil fruit (almost any kind may be used) with a little water until it is quite soft; rub it through a fine sieve; sweeten to taste; make it hot, and pour over boiled or steamed puddings.

Fruit Pudding Sauce.

One-half cup butter, two and one-half cups sugar, one dessert-spoonful corn starch wet in a little cold milk, one lemon—juice and half the grated peel, one glass of wine, one cup boiling water.

Cream the butter and sugar well; pour the corn starch into the boiling water, and stir over a clear fire until it is well thickened; put all together in a bowl and beat five minutes before returning to the saucepan. Heat once, almost to the boiling point, add the wine, and serve.

ARROWROOT SAUCE.

Mix a tablespoonful of arrowroot smoothly with a little cold water; add a third of a pint of water, a glass of wine, the juice of a lemon, and sugar and flavoring; stir the sauce over the fire till it boils. This sauce may be varied by omitting the wine, and using milk with the arrowroot. The juice of almost any fruit, too, may be boiled with the arrowroot.

GERMAN CUSTARD SAUCE.

Four yolks eggs, two ounces powdered sugar, grated rind of a lemon, a glass of sherry, and a little salt. Beat it sharply over a slow fire, until it assumes the appearance of a light, frothy custard. It is a good sauce.

PUDDING SAUCE.

Two eggs, two cups sugar, and one cup butter, one glass of wine; beat all well together till creamy, and set over the fire a few minutes to scald through once, or set it in the tea kettle top to heat through.

PUFF PASTE.

Use for each pound of butter one pound of flour. First the butter should be worked or kneaded with the hand until all the buttermilk or water which may be in it is squeezed out. Wet the hand and the molding board with cold water. The butter must not be put in with the cracks in it, which you will see on breaking it, for these make the pastry full of flakes. By working with the hand a smooth even paste can be made without melting the butter. After working, wrap in a towel dusted with flour and put in a cool place. Mix one pound of flour, the yolk of one egg, one teaspoonful of butter, the juice of a lemon, and a saltspoonful of salt, with cold water enough to make a paste as soft as bread dough. The lemon juice is for making the dough tender, and the egg is used simply to give a yellowish appearance to the crust. This is the French method of preparing paste. The pastry is worked to mix the gluten with the water to make, first, a slightly tough dough to hold the butter; the lemon juice afterward makes it tender. It should be kneaded about five minutes. You can always tell when it is kneaded enough, because it will then pull away from the hand and not stick. Roll it out about the size of a large dinner plate, lay in it the butter, fold the sides over, turn it over and roll into a strip three times as long as it is wide, square at the corners, and one-quarter of an inch thick. Fold one-third over the middle and the other third over that, making three layers; roll again into a strip three times as long as it is wide. Fold a second time and roll out again in the same way. Fold again and wrap in a cloth, place it in a pan and set where it will get very cold. This is called giving the pastry "one turn." When it is made by fine confectioners it usually has six "turns."

PIE CRUST.

Into one quart sifted flour, thoroughly mix two heaping teaspoonfuls baking powder, and sift again. Weigh out three-quarters of a pound good butter. Take half of it and chop into the flour until it is very fine. Then add enough cold water (ice water is the best) to make a stiff dough. Roll out into a thin sheet and baste with one-third the remaining butter, then roll it up closely into a long roll, flatten and re-roll, then baste again. Repeat this operation until the butter is gone. Then make out your crust. Do it all as quickly as possible. The quantity of butter may be increased or decreased to suit the taste, following the other directions as stated.

GOOD AND CHEAP PIE CRUST.

One quart sifted flour, one teaspoonful salt, two heaping teaspoonfuls baking powder; mix thoroughly together while dry, and sift. Then add cold sweet milk enough to make a stiff dough, and roll out as usual. Use the "Pie Crust Glaze" on both the bottom and top crusts, as per following recipe. Some prefer less of the baking powder in the pie crust. A trial will determine what quantity best suits your taste.

Pie Crust Glaze.

To prevent the juice soaking through into the crust and making it soggy, wet the crust with a beaten egg just before you put in the pie mixture. If the top of the pie is wet with the egg it gives it a beautiful brown.

Pie Crust for Four Small Pies.

One and a half cups lard, one cup cold water, three and a half cups flour, mix lard and flour together; add water last.

Tart Crust.

One cup of lard, one-half teaspoonful of salt, the white of an egg, one-quarter teaspoonful of cream of tartar, one tablespoonful of sugar, one-eighth teaspoonful of saleratus, three tablespoonfuls of ice water; flour to roll; mix lard with one cup of flour; add salt, sugar, and cream of tartar; beat egg; mix with water and saleratus, all together; keep the dough cold; add flour to roll, one-quarter of an inch thick. The above makes eighteen tarts.

Icing Pastry.

When nearly baked enough, take the pastry out of the oven and sift fine powdered sugar over it. Replace it in the oven, and hold over it a hot salamander or shovel till the sugar is melted. The above method is preferred for pastry to be eaten hot; for cold, beat up the whites of two eggs well, wash over the tops of the pies with a brush, and sift over this a good coating of sugar; cause it to adhere to the egg and pie crust; trundle over it a clean brush, dipped in water, till the sugar is all moistened. Bake again for about ten minutes.

9

Puff Paste with Beef Suet.

When you cannot obtain good butter for making paste, the following is an excellent substitute: Skin and chop one pound of kidney beef suet very fine, put it into a mortar and pound it well, moistening with a little oil, till it become as it were one piece, about the consistency of butter.

Apricot Pie.

Pare, stone, and half the apricots; place them in a pie dish, piling them high in the center, strew over them a little sifted sugar, and a few of the kernels, blanched and chopped fine. Cover them with a good, light crust and bake in a moderate oven.

Apple Pie.

Fill the pie crust with sour, juicy apples, pared and sliced thin, put on the upper crust and bake until the apples are soft, then remove the upper crust, adding sugar to taste, a small piece of butter, and a little grated nutmeg; stir this well through the apple and replace the crust.

Apple Custard Pie.

Peel sour apples and stew until soft and not much water left in them, then rub them through a colander, beat three eggs for each pie to be baked, and put in at the rate of one cup of butter and one of sugar for three pies. Line the pie tins with paste, put in the apples first, spread the beaten eggs, butter and sugar, flavored with nutmeg over it. Bake as pumpkin pie.

Boiled Cider Pie.

A boiled cider pie may be a novelty to some one. Take four tablespoonfuls of boiled cider, three tablespoonfuls each of sugar and water, two tablespoonfuls of flour, and one egg; beat all together. Bake in a deep plate and with upper and under crusts.

Banana Pie.

Slice raw bananas, add butter, sugar, allspice, and vinegar, or boiled cider or diluted jelly. Bake with two crusts.

CRACKER PIE.

Soak ten crackers in one and one-half cups of boiling water, add one cup of molasses, one cup sugar, one cup butter, one cup raisins, two-thirds cup of vinegar, one-half nutmeg, one-half teaspoonful ground cloves, one teaspoonful cinnamon.   Bake with two crusts.

CHOCOLATE PIE.

One coffeecup milk, two tablespoonfuls grated chocolate, three-fourths cup sugar, yolks of three eggs. Heat chocolate and milk together; add the sugar and yolks together, beaten to cream. Flavor with vanilla. Bake with under crust. Spread meringue of the whites over the top.

COCOANUT PIE.

Open the eyes of a cocoanut with a pointed knife or gimlet, and pour out the milk into a cup; then break the shell and take out the meat and grate it fine. Take the same weight of sugar and the grated nut and stir together; beat four eggs, the whites and yolks separately, to a stiff foam; mix one cup of cream and the milk of the cocoanut with the sugar and nut, then add the eggs and a few drops of orange or lemon extract. Line deep pie-tins with a nice crust, fill them with the custard, and bake carefully one-half an hour.

JELLY CUSTARD.

To one cup of any sort of jelly, add one egg and beat well together with three teaspoonfuls cream or milk. After mixing thoroughly, bake in a good crust.

CUSTARD PIE.

Line a deep plate with pie crust and fill with a custard made of one pint of milk, three eggs, three tablespoonfuls of white sugar and a pinch of salt; flavor with nutmeg; bake until firm in the center; this you can tell by inserting the handle of a teaspoon; do not let the oven get hot enough to boil it.

CREAM PIE.

Pour a pint of cream upon a cup and a half of powdered sugar; let it stand till the whites of three eggs have been beaten to a stiff froth; add this to the cream, and beat up thoroughly, grate a little nutmeg over the mixture and bake as custard pies.

CREAM PIE, No. 2.

Three eggs, one cup sugar, one and one-fourth cups flour, juice and grated rind of lemon, half teaspoonful soda dissolved, and one tablespoonful cold water, stirred in the last thing. Bake in round sheets.

CUSTARD FOR CREAM PIE.

A little more than half pint milk, half cup flour, one cup sugar, two eggs. Boil, when cold, spread on the cakes and lay them together. This receipt makes two pies.

DELICATE PIE.

To stewed apples sufficient for four pies, one-half pound of butter, six eggs, beaten separately, one pound of sugar; flavor with lemon, the apples being quite cold before adding the eggs. Bake as a tart pie.

LEMON PIE.

One cup of hot water, one tablespoonful of corn starch, one cup of white sugar, one tablespoonful of butter, the juice and grated rind of one lemon. Cook for a few minutes, add one egg, and bake with a top and bottom crust.

FRUIT PIE.

Line a soup plate with a rich paste, and spread with a layer of strawberry or raspberry preserves; over which sprinkle two table-spoonfuls of finely-chopped almonds (blanched of course), and one-half ounce of candied lemon peel cut into shreds. Then mix the following ingredients: One-half pound white sugar, one-quarter pound butter, melted, four yolks and two whites of eggs, and a few drops of almond essence. Beat well together and pour the mixture into the soup plate over the preserves, etc. Bake in a moderately warm oven. When cold, sprinkle or sift a little powdered sugar over the top. A little cream eaten with it is a great addition.

Lemon Pie, No. 2.

The juice and grated rind of one lemon, one cup of white sugar, the yolks of two eggs, three tablespoonfuls of sifted flour, and sufficient milk to fill a plate. Make with undercrust, but not the uppercrust. Bake till nearly done and then add a frosting made of the beaten whites of two eggs, and two tablespoonfuls of powdered sugar, and set back in the oven and brown slightly.

Mince Meat.

One pint of chopped meat, two pints of chopped apples, one pint each of molasses and vinegar, two pints of sugar, one tablespoonful each of cinnamon, cloves, and allspice, a cup of chopped suet or butter, a little salt, and a little brandy if liked. Add raisins when the pies are baked.

Mince Meat.

Two pounds of lean beef boiled; when cold chop fine; one pound of suet minced to a powder, five pounds of juicy apples, pared and chopped, two pounds of raisins, seeded, two pounds of sultanas or seedless raisins, two pounds of currants, one-half pound of citron, chopped, three tablespoonfuls of cinnamon, two tablespoonfuls of mace, one tablespoonful of allspice, one tablespoonful of fine salt, one grated nutmeg, three pounds of brown sugar, one-half gallon of sweet cider. Mince meat made by this recipe will keep till spring.

Mince Pie.

It is supposed you have your meat ready for the paste. Make the paste by rubbing into a quart of your best flour one-third of a pound of sweet lard; chop it in with a broad knife, if you have time; wet up with ice water; roll out very thin and cover with dabs of butter, also of the best; fold into a tight roll; flatten with a few strokes of the rolling-pin, and roll out into a sheet as thin as the first; baste again with the butter; roll up and out into a third sheet hardly thicker than drawing paper; a third time dot with butter and fold up closely. Having used as much butter for this purpose as you have lard, set aside your roll for an hour on ice, or in a very cold place; then roll out, line your pie plates with the paste, fill with mince meat, put strips across them in squares or triangles and bake in a steady and not dull heat.

MINCE PIE, No. 2.

Boil a piece of beef weighing six pounds, and a beef's tongue weighing six pounds, six hours. Then skin the tongue, chop it and the beef fine; add five pounds beef suet chopped fine, five pounds raisins stoned, three pounds dried currants, one and one-half pound citron, four pounds brown sugar, one pint good molasses, one quart brandy, one quart wine, or, omit these, and add in their place boiled cider; half a cup each of salt, cinnamon, allspice and cloves, three nutmegs and a tablespoonful of mace. Mix all well together, and let it stand over night. Mix apples stewed when you make the pies, as the meat keeps better without apple. Keep it in a stone jar. You should have about a third as much apple as you have of the mince meat for a batch of pies.

MINCE MEAT WITHOUT MEAT.

Take nine lemons, squeeze out the juice, boil the rinds and pulp (remove seed) in three or four waters till bitterness is out and rinds quite tender; beat them to a pulp; two and one-half pounds beef suet after it is picked from the skins, two pounds currants after they are picked and washed, one and one-half pounds raisins after they are stoned, two ounces almonds, two pounds sugar, one-half pound citron, a glass of brandy, and one of any kind of sweet wine; mix all these ingredients well together with the juice from the lemons, and as many sweetmeats as you please.

MARLBOROUGH PIE.

Grate six apples, one cup sugar, three tablespoonfuls melted

butter, four eggs, juice and grated rind of a lemon, two tablespoonfuls brandy or wine, if you choose; if not, omit it. Bake in an
under, but without top crust.

ORANGE PIE.

Take four good-sized oranges, peel, seed, and cut in very small
pieces. Add a cup of sugar, and let stand. Into a quart of nearly
boiling milk stir two tablespoonfuls of corn starch mixed with a
little water, and the yolks of three eggs. When this is done,
let it cool, then mix with the oranges. Put it in simply a lower
crust. Make a frosting of the whites of the eggs and one-half cup
sugar. Spread it over top of pies, and place for a few seconds in
the oven to brown.

CREAM PEACH PIE.

Pare ripe peaches and remove the stones; have your pie dishes
ready lined with a good paste, fill with the peaches; stew these
with sugar; lay the upper crust on lightly, slightly buttering the
lower at the point of contact. When the pie is done, lift the cover
and pour in a cream made thus: One cup (small) of rich milk,
heated; whites of two eggs, whipped and stirred into the milk;
one tablespoonful of sugar; one-half teaspoonful of corn starch wet
up in milk. Boil three minutes. The cream must be cold when it
goes into the hot pie. Replace the crust, and set by to cool. Eat
fresh.

PINE-APPLE PIE.

One granted pine-apple, its weight in sugar, half its weight in
butter, five eggs, the whites beaten to a stiff froth, one cup of
cream; cream the butter and beat it with the sugar and yolks until
very light; add the cream, the pine-apple and the whites of the
eggs. Bake with an under crust. To be eaten cold.

PUMPKIN PIE.

Pare the pumpkin and take out the seeds without scraping the
inside; stew and strain through a sieve. To every quart of milk
add five eggs, and stir the pumpkin into the milk and eggs until

the proper consistency; sweeten with sugar or the best syrup; molasses makes it too strong. Add some salt, powdered cinnamon, powdered ginger and the grated peel of lemon. Bake in either deep or shallow dishes in a hot oven.

POTATO PIE.

One pound mashed potato, rubbed through a colander; one-fourth pound of butter, creamed with the sugar; six eggs, whites and yolks beaten separately; one lemon, squeezed into the potato while hot; one teaspoonful of nutmeg and the same of mace; two cups of white sugar. Cream the butter and sugar; add the yolks, the spice, and beat in the potato gradually until it is very light. At last, whip in the whites. Bake in open shells of paste. Eat cold.

SWEET POTATO PIE.

A plate deeper than the common pie plate is necessary. Bake medium-sized potatoes, not quite done. Yams are best. Line the plate with good paste; slice the potatoes; place a layer upon the bottom of the plate; over this sprinkle thickly a layer of good brown sugar; over this place thin slices of butter and sprinkle with flour, seasoning with spices to the taste. A heaped tablespoonful of butter and a heaped teaspoonful of flour will be sufficient for one pie. Put on another layer of potatoes, piled a little in the middle. Mix together equal quantities lemon juice and water, or vinegar and water and pour in enough to half fill the pie; sprinkle over the potato a little flour and place on the upper crust, pinching the edges carefully together. Cut a slit in the center and bake slowly an hour.

SWEET POTATO PIE, No. 2.

Boil potatoes until tender, pare and put through a colander or sieve. To one pint of potato add one pint of milk, three eggs, and from one to two cups sugar, to suit taste; flavor with ginger or lemon.

APPLE OR PEACH MERINGUE PIE.

Stew the apples or peaches and sweeten to taste. Mash smooth and season with nutmeg. Fill the crusts and bake until just done. Put on no top crusts. Take the whites of three eggs for each pie and whip to a stiff froth, and sweeten with three tablespoonfuls powdered sugar. Flavor with rose water or vanilla. Beat until it will stand alone, then spread it on the pie one-half to one inch thick, and set back into the oven until the meringue is well "set." Eat cold.

PEACH PIE.

Peel, stone and slice the peaches; line a pie plate with crust and lay in your fruit, sprinkling sugar liberally over them in proportion to their sweetness. Allow three peach kernels chopped fine to each pie; pour in a very little water and bake with an upper crust, or with cross-bars of paste across the top.

QUINCE PIE.

Pare, slice, and stew six quinces till soft; press them through a sieve; add to them one pint milk and four well-beaten eggs. Sweeten to taste, and bake in a bottom crust three-fourths of an hour in a moderate oven.

CREAM RASPBERRY PIE.

Line a pie-dish with puff paste, and fill with raspberries, sweetened bountifully. Cover with a paste crust, but do not pinch this down at the edges. Also rub the edge of the lower crust with butter to prevent adhesion. Bake in a good oven. While it is cooking, heat a small cup of rich milk, putting in a pinch of soda; stir into it half a teaspoonful of corn starch, wet in cold milk, one tablespoonful of white sugar, and cook three minutes. Take it off, and beat in the frothed whites of two eggs. Whip to a cream, and let it get cold. When the pie comes out of the oven, lift the top crust and pour in the mixture; replace the crust and set aside to cool; sift sugar upon the top before serving.

RAISIN PIE.

One lemon—juice and yellow rind, one cup of raisins, one cup of water, one cup of rolled crackers; stone the raisins, and boil in water to soften them.

RHUBARB PIE.

One and one-half bunches rhubard, one and one-quarter cups sugar. Cut the fruit in small pieces after stripping off the skin, and cook it very fast in a shallow stewpan, with sugar. Line a pie plate with the paste; wet the rim; add the rhubarb, cold; lay three bars of paste across, fastening the ends; lay three more across, forming diamond-shaped spaces; lay round a rim, wash over with egg, and bake in a quick oven fifteen minutes.

RICE PIE.

For two pies, take two tablespoonfuls of rice; wash and put it into a farina boiler with a quart of milk; cook until perfectly soft. Let it cool; add three eggs, well beaten, with three tablespoonfuls of sugar and one of butter, a little salt, cinnamon and a few stoned raisins. Bake with undercrust.

SQUASH PIE.

Pare the squash and remove the seeds; stew until soft and dry; then pulp it through a colander; stir into the pulp enough sweet milk to make it thick as batter; spice with ginger, cinnamon, nutmeg, or other seasoning to taste; sweeten with sugar and add four beaten eggs for each quart of milk. Fill a pie plate lined with crust and bake one hour.

VINEGAR PIES.

One and one-half cups good vinegar, one cup of water, lump of butter size of an egg, sugar enough to sweeten to the taste; flavor with lemon; put in stewpan on stove; take five eggs, beat the yolks with one cup of water and two heaping teaspoonfuls of flour; when the vinegar comes to a boil, put in the eggs and flour, stirring till well cooked; have ready crust for four pies, put in the filling and bake. Beat the whites with two teaspoonfuls of white sugar to a froth, spread on the pies when done, and color in the oven. These are excellent.

TARTS.

Use the best of puff paste; roll it out a little thicker than the pie crust, and cut with a large biscuit-cutter twice as many as you intend to have of tarts; then cut out of half of them a small round, in the center, which will leave a circular rim of crust; lift this up carefully, and lay on the large pieces. Bake in pans, and fill with any kind of preserves, jam, or jelly.

CHAPTER VIII.

DRINKS.

COFFEE.

SINCE Pasquet Rossee opened the first coffee-house in Europe in Newman's Court, Cornhill, London, in 1652, its popularity has constantly increased until to-day those who use it embrace the whole world, and its annual consumption is measured by millions of pounds. But as common as is its use, it has not been a common occurrence in our experience to have set before us a really good cup of coffee. This fact convinces us that there is still much need of information on this subject.

The following, by H. K. & F. B. Thurber & Co., is so appropriate that we quote it in full :

"Nothing is more generally desired or appreciated, nothing harder to find than a uniformly good cup of coffee. Its production is usually considered an easy matter, but it involves the observance of a considerable number of conditions by a considerable number of persons, and a volume might be written about these and still leave much to be said. We will, however, briefly state the most important requisites.

"The wholesale dealer must exercise care and judgment in his selections, as there is almost as much difference in the flavor of coffee as there is of tea; this is especially true of Mocha, Java, Maracaibo, and other fancy coffees, of which frequently the brightest and handsomest looking lots are greatly lacking in the flavor and aroma which constitute the chief value of coffee, and which can be ascertained only by testing carefully each invoice purchased. It should be roasted by a professional roaster, as this is a very important part of the programme, and requires skill, experience and constant practice. Expert roasters are usually experienced men and command high salaries. A bad coffee roaster is dear at any price, as the coffee may be ruined or its value greatly injured by an error in judgment or an instant's inattention. Owing to these circumstances, in addition to the fact that in order to do good work it is necessary to roast a considerable quantity at a time, none of the small hand machines produce uniformly good results, and they are only to be tolerated where distance makes it impossible for the retail merchants to obtain regular and (when not in air-tight packages) frequent supplies of the roasted article. *How much* it should be roasted is also an important part of the question. For making "black" or "French" coffee it should be roasted higher than usual (the French, also, often add a little chicory), and some sections are accustomed to a higher roast than others, but as a whole the customary New York standard will best suit the average American palate. Retail dealers should buy their roasted coffee of a reliable house that has a reputation to sustain, and that cannot be induced to cut down prices below what they can afford to furnish an article that will do them credit. Do not buy much at a time (unless in air-tight packages), a week or ten day's supply is enough, and if you are situated so you can buy it twice a week, so much the better. Keep it in a dry place and, if possible, in a tin can which shuts tightly, never in a pine box or bin, for the smell of the wood is quickly absorbed by the coffee. Get your customers in the habit of buying it in the berry, or, if they have no mill at home and want you to grind it for them (every grocer should have a mill), grind it pretty fine, so that when used the strength is readily extracted, but do not sell them much at a time, as it is a necessity to have it freshly ground.

"Consumers should adopt the above suggestions to retail dealers —buy of a reliable dealer who will not represent an inferior article as 'Java;' buy in small quantities and buy often; keep it dry in a tightly closed tin can or in a glass or earthen jar. Have a small hand coffee mill and grind only when ready to use it, and if, during rainy weather, the kernels become damp and tough warm them up in a clean pot or skillet but do not scorch them; this drives off the moisture, restores the flavor and makes it grind better. The grinding is an important feature; if ground too coarse you lose much of the strength and aroma of the coffee; if too fine it is hard to make it clear, but of the two the latter is the least objectionable; both the strength and the flavor of the coffee, however, is a necessity, and if a little of the finely powdered coffee flows out with the liquid extract it is clean and will hurt nobody. It is better, however, to grind it just right, which is that the largest pieces will be no larger than pin heads."

We now come to the important part of making coffee. For this there are many receipts and formulas, including a large number of new and so-called improved coffee-pots, but we have never seen any of the new methods which, in the long run, gave as satisfactory results as the following old-fashioned receipt:

Grind moderately fine a large cup of coffee; break into it one egg with shell; mix well, adding just enough cold water to thoroughly wet the grounds; upon this pour one pint boiling water; let it boil slowly for ten to fifteen minutes, and then stand three minutes to settle; pour through a fine wire sieve into coffee-pot, which should be first rinsed with hot water; this will make enough for four persons. Coffee should be served as soon as made. At table, first rinse the cup with hot water, put in the sugar, then fill half full of hot milk, add your coffee, and you have a delicious beverage that will be a revelation to many poor mortals who have an indistinct remembrance of and an intense longing for an ideal cup of coffee. If you have cream so much the better; and in that case boiling water can be added either in the pot or cup to make up for the space occupied by milk, as above; or condensed milk will be found a good substitute for cream.

General Remarks.—We have thus briefly indicated the points necessary to be observed in obtaining uniformly good coffee, whether made from Rio, or Java, and other mild flavored coffees. In the Eastern and Middle States, Mocha, Java, Maracaibo, Ceylon, etc., are most highly esteemed and generally used; but at the west and south more Rio coffee is consumed. The coffee par excellence, however, is a mixture of Mocha and Java together, and thus thoroughly blended. Mocha alone is too rough and acrid, but, blended as above, it is certainly delicious. In all varieties, however, there is a considerable range as to quality and flavor, and, as before stated, the best guide for the consumer is to buy of a reliable dealer and throw upon his shoulders the responsibility of furnishing a satisfactory article.

Hotels and restaurants that desire good coffee, should make in small quantities and more frequently. It is impossible for coffee to be good when it is kept simmering for hours after it is made.

COFFEE SUBSTITUTES.

French cooks, who are celebrated for making good coffee, mix three or four different kinds, and recommend as a good proportion, to add to one pound of Java about four ounces of Mocha and four ounces of one or two other kinds. It is said that from three parts of Rio, with two parts of Old Government Java, a coffee can be made quite as good, if not superior, to that made of Java alone.

Wheat coffee, made of a mixture of eight quarts of wheat to one pound of real coffee, is said to afford a beverage quite as agreeable as the unadulterated Rio, besides being much more wholesome. It is probably known to many that a very large per cent. of the ground coffee sold at the stores is common field pease, roasted and ground with genuine coffee. There are hundreds of thousands of bushels of peas annually used for that purpose. Those who are in the habit of purchasing ground coffee can do better to buy their own pease, burn and grind them, and mix to suit themselves.

NOVEL MODE OF MAKING COFFEE.

Put two ounces of ground coffee into a stewpan, which set upon the fire, stirring the powder around with a spoon until quite hot, when pour over a pint of boiling water; cover over closely for five minutes, when strain it through a cloth, rinse out the stewpan, pour the coffee, which will be quite clear, back into it, place it on the fire, and when near boiling, serve with hot milk.

TEA.

We find the following eminently sensible lines in *Household Hints:*

One of the most surprising things one constantly meets is to find that the people who have the same duties to perform, day after day, or year after year, do not improve in their method or even once blunder into the right way of doing them. Nothing is more easily made than good tea, and yet how seldom, away from home, does one enjoy delicately fragrant tea which Hawthorne calls "an angel's gift" and which Miss Mitford said she could be awake all night drinking. The first thing needed is a clean tea-pot; it is useless to try to make good tea in a rusty pot, or one in which the leaves have been allowed to remain all night. The water should be boiling but the tea itself should never boil. I wish these words could be painted on the wall of every hotel and restaurant kitchen in the United States. After the boiling water has been poured over the tea set the tea-pot on an extra griddle on the back of the stove. All that is good in the tea will be gradually extracted from it; then when brought to the table one may well echo De Quincey's wish for an "eternal tea-pot," though not inclined to follow his example of drinking it from eight o'clock in the evening until four o'clock in the morning.

The most satisfactory steeper I ever used is an old-fashioned brown earthern tea-pot. This may be kept perfectly clean with almost no trouble. Whatever may be said of the hurtfulness of tea, when immoderately used, a cup of the afternoon tea so frequently mentioned in novels and essays is an unpurchasable luxury. Hamerton says in "The Intellectual Life:" "If tea is a safe stimulant it is certainly an agreeable one; there seems to be no valid reason why brain workers should refuse themselves this solace."

Iced Tea.

The tea should be made in the morning, very strong, and not allowed to steep long. Keep in the ice-box till the meal is ready and then put in a small quantity of cracked ice. Very few understand the art of making iced tea, but pour the scalding hot tea on a goblet of ice lumped in, and as the ice melts the tea is weak, insipid, and a libel on its name. Iced coffee is very nice made in the same way. Too much ice is detrimental to health and often causes gastric fever; so beware of it when in a heated state, or do not drink of it in large quantities.

A Good Summer Drink.

Two pounds Catawba grapes, three tablespoonfuls loaf sugar, one cup of cold water. Squeeze the grapes hard in a coarse cloth, when you have picked them from the stems. Wring out every drop of juice; add the sugar, and when it is dissolved, the water, surround with ice until very cold; put a lump of ice into a pitcher, pour out the mixture upon it, and drink at once. You can add more sugar if you like, or if the grapes are not quite ripe.

Cottage Beer.

Take a peck of good wheat bran and put it into ten gallons of water with three handfuls of good hops, and boil the whole together until the bran and hops sink to the bottom. Then strain it through a hair sieve or a thin cloth into a cooler, and when it is about lukewarm add two quarts of molasses. As soon as the molasses is melted, pour the whole into a ten-gallon cask, with two tablespoonfuls of yeast. When the fermentation has subsided, bung up the cask, and in four days it will be fit to use.

Ginger Beer.

Boil six ounces of bruised ginger in three quarts of water, for half an hour; then add five pounds of loaf sugar, a gill of lemon juice, quarter pound of honey, and seventeen quarts more of water,

10

and strain it through a cloth. When it is cold put in the whole of an egg, and two drachms of essence of lemon. After standing three or four days, it may be bottled.

SPRUCE BEER.

Take four ounces of hops, boil half an hour in one gallon of water; strain it; add sixteen gallons of warm water, two gallons of molasses, eight ounces of essence of spruce dissolved in one quart of water; put it in a clean cask, shake it well together, add half pint of yeast, let it stand and work one week; if warm weather, less time will do. When drawn off, add one teaspoonful of molasses to each bottle.

ICED BUTTERMILK.

There is no healthier drink than buttermilk, but it must be the creamy, rich buttermilk to be good. It should stand on the ice to cool, though if very rich and thick a little ice in it is an improvement.

CLARET CUP.

Put into a bowl three bottles of soda water, and one bottle of claret. Pare a lemon very thin and grate a nutmeg; add to these, in a jug, one pound of loaf sugar, and pour over them one pint of boiling water; when cold, strain and mix with the wine and soda water; a little lemon juice may be added.

FRUIT CUP.

Pare the yellow rind very thinly from twelve lemons; squeeze the juice over it in an earthern bowl, and let it stand over night if possible. Pare and slice thinly a very ripe pine-apple, and let it lay over night in half a pound of powdered sugar. Crush one quart of berries, and let them lay over night in half a pound of powdered sugar. If all these ingredient cannot be prepared the day before they are used, they must be done very early in the morning, because the juices of the fruit need to be incorporated with the sugar at least twelve hours before the beverage is used. After all the ingredients have been properly prepared, as above, strain off the juice, carefully pressing all of it out of the fruit; mix it with two pounds of powdered sugar and three quarts of ice water, and stir it until all the sugar is dissolved. Then strain it again through a muslin or bolting-cloth sieve, and put it on the ice or in a very cool place until it is wanted for use.

CREAM OF TARTAR DRINK.

Two teaspoonfuls of cream of tartar, the grated rind of a lemon, half a cup of loaf sugar, and one pint of boiling water. This is a good summer drink for invalids, and is cleansing to the blood.

JELLY DRINKS.

A little jelly or fruit syrup dissolved in a goblet of water with a little sugar is a refreshing drink. Lime juice squeezed into lemonade gives it a tart but pleasing flavor. A little orange juice is also an improvement in nearly all summer drinks.

SIMON PURE LEMONADE.

Take thin-skinned lemons; roll them on the table until very soft; slice very thin with a sharp knife into a large pitcher, averaging one lemon to a person, thus allowing them two glasses apiece. Put in the pitcher with the sliced lemon a cup of white sugar to five lemons (or more if you want it sweeter) and pound all well together with a potato masher; put in a lump of ice; let it stand a few minutes and fill the pitcher with ice water. This makes lemonade that is lemonade, and the peel in the pitcher is delicious.

JELLY LEMONADE.

Pare the yellow rind thinly from two oranges and six lemons and steep it four hours in a quart of hot water. Boil a pound and a half of loaf sugar in three pints of water, skimming it until it is clear. Pour these two mixtures together. Add to them the juice of six oranges and twelve lemons, mix and strain through a jelly-bag until clear; keep cool until wanted for use. If the beverage is to be kept several days, it should be put into clean glass bottles and corked tightly. If for a small party, half of the quantity will be sufficient.

GINGER LEMONADE.

Take a half cup of vinegar, one cup of sugar, two teaspoonfuls ginger; stir well together, put in a quart pitcher and fill with ice water. If one wants it sweeter or sourer than these quantities will make it, more of the needed ingredients may be put in. It is a cooling drink and almost as good as lemonade, some preferring it.

BERRY SHERBET.

Crush one pound of berries, add them to one quart of water, one lemon sliced, and one teaspoonful of orange flavor, if you have it. Let these ingredients stand in an earthen bowl for three hours; then strain, squeezing all the juice out of the fruit. Dissolve one pound of powdered sugar in it, strain again, and put on the ice until ready to serve.

EXCELLENT MEAD.

Three pounds brown sugar, one pint of molasses, one-fourth pound tartaric acid; mix, pour over them two quarts boiling water, stir till dissolved. When cold, add half ounce essence sassafras and bottle. When you wish to drink it, put three tablespoonfuls of it in a tumbler, fill half full with ice water, add a little more than one-fourth teaspoonful soda. An excellent summer beverage.

CHAPTER IX.

EGGS AND OMELETTES.

EGGS of various kinds are largely used as food for man, and it is scarcely possible to exaggerate their value in this capacity, so simple and convenient are they in their form and so manifold may be their transformations. They are exceedingly delicious, highly nutritious and easy of digestion, and when the shell is included they may be said to contain in themselves all that is required for the construction of the body. It has been claimed for them that they may be served in about six hundred ways, although it is generally found that the more simply they are prepared the more they are approved. Although other eggs besides birds' eggs are eaten it is generally agreed that the eggs of the common fowl and of the plover possess the sweetest and richest flavor. The eggs of ducks and geese are frequently used in cookery, but they are of too coarse a nature to be eaten alone. The eggs of the turkey and of the peahen are highly esteemed for some purposes· The weight of an ordinary new-laid hen's egg is from one and a half to two and a half ounces avoirdupois, and the quantity of solid matter contained in it amounts to two hundred grains. In one hundred parts about ten parts consist of shell, sixty of white and thirty of yolk. The white of the egg contains more water than the yolk. It contains no fatty matter but consists chiefly of albumen in a dissolved state. All the fatty matter of the egg is accumulated in the yolk, which contains relatively a smaller proportion of nitrogenous matter and a larger proportion of solid matter than the white. Therefore, in an alimentary point of view the white and the yolk differ considerably from each other, the former being, mainly a simple solution of albumen, the latter being a solution of a modified form of albumen together with a quantity of fat.

Raw and lightly boiled eggs are easy of digestion. It is said that raw eggs are more easily digested than cooked ones; but this may be doubted if the egg is not over-cooked. A hard-boiled egg presents a decided resistance to gastric solution, and has constipatory action on the bowels.

BREADED EGGS.

Boil hard and cut in round, thick slices; pepper and salt and dip each in beaten raw egg, then in fine bread crumbs or powdered cracker crumbs and fry in butter, hissing hot. Drain off every drop of grease and serve hot.

EGG A LA MODE.

Remove the skin from a dozen tomatoes, medium size, cut them up in a saucepan, add a little butter, pepper and salt; when sufficiently boiled, beat up five or six eggs, and just before you serve, turn them into the saucepan with the tomato, and stir one way for two minutes, allowing them time to be well done.

HOW TO BAKE EGGS.

Butter a clean, smooth saucepan, break as many eggs as will be needed into a saucer, one by one. If found good, slip it into the dish. No broken yolk allowed, nor must they crowd so as to risk breaking the yolk after being put in. Put a small piece of butter on each, and sprinkle with pepper and salt. Set into a well-heated oven, and bake till the whites are set. If the oven is rightly heated, it will take but a few minutes, and is far more delicate than fried eggs.

EGG BASKETS.

Boil quite hard as many eggs as will be needed. Put into cold water till cold, then cut neatly into halves with a thin, sharp knife; remove the yolk and rub to a paste with some melted butter, adding pepper and salt. Cover up this paste and set aside till the filling is ready. Take cold roast duck, chicken, or turkey which may be on hand, chop fine and pound smooth, and while pounding mix in the paste prepared from the yolks. As you pound moisten with melted butter and some gravy which may have been left over from the fowls; set this paste when done over hot water till well heated. Cut off a small slice from the end of the empty halves of the whites so they will stand firm, then fill them with this paste; place them close together on a flat, round dish, and pour over the rest of the gravy, if any remains, or make a little fresh. A few spoonfuls of cream or rich milk improves this dressing.

To Pickle Eggs.

Sixteen eggs, one quart of vinegar, one-half ounce of black pepper, one-half ounce Jamaica pepper, one-half ounce of ginger; boil the eggs twelve minutes; dip in cold water and take off the shell; put the vinegar with the pepper and ginger into a stew pan and simmer ten minutes; place the eggs in a jar, pour over the seasoned vinegar boiling hot, and when cold tie them down with a bladder to exclude the air; ready for use in a month.

Scrambled Eggs.

Heat the spider and put in a little butter; have the eggs broken into a dish, salt and pepper them; add a small piece of butter; beat up just enough to break the eggs, then pour into the buttered spider; scrape them up from the bottom with a thin knife to prevent their cooking fast. Do not cook too dry.

To Poach Eggs.

Have the water well salted, and do not let it boil hard. Break the eggs separately into a saucer, and slip gently into the water; when nicely done, remove with a skimmer, trim neatly, and lay each egg upon a small thin square of buttered toast, then sprinkle with salt and pepper. Some persons prefer them poached, rather than fried, with ham; in which case substitute the ham for toast.

STUFFED EGGS.

Boil the eggs hard, remove the shells, and then cut in two either way, as preferred. Remove the yolks, and mix with them pepper, salt, and a little dry mustard—some like cold chicken, ham, or tongue chopped very fine—and then stuff the cavities, smooth them, and put the halves together again. For picnics they can simply be wrapped in tissue paper to keep them together. If for home use, they can be egged, and bread-crumbed, and browned in boiling lard; drain and garnish with parsley.

OMELETTE.

First have fresh eggs, not omelette eggs (in restaurants all eggs that will not in any way do to boil, are put aside for omelettes), break the eggs in a bowl and to every egg add a tablespoonful of milk and whip the whole as thoroughly as you would for sponge cake. The omelette pan must be so hot that butter will melt almost brown in it but not quite. Then run the whipped egg and milk into the pan and put it directly over the fire. Take a thin-bladed knife and run it carefully under the bottom of the omelette so as to let that which is cooked get above. If the fire is right the whole mass will swell and puff and cook in just about one minute. Watch carefully that it does not burn. It is not necessary to wait till the whole mass is solid as its own heat will cook it after it has left the pan, but begin at one side and carefully roll the edge over and over till it is all rolled up, then let it stand a moment to brown. Turn out on a hot plate and serve immediately.

OMELETTE, No. 2.

Six eggs, one tablespoonful of flour, one cup of milk, a pinch of salt; beat the whites and yolks separately: mix the flour, milk and salt, add the yolks, then add beaten whites. Have a buttered spider very hot; put in. Bake in a quick oven five minutes.

Apple Omelette.

Eight large apples, four eggs, one cup of sugar, one tablespoonful of butter, nutmeg or cinnamon to taste. Stew the apples and mash fine; add butter and sugar; when cold, add the eggs, well beaten. Bake until brown, and eat while warm.

, Baked Omelette.

Set one-half pint of milk on the fire and stir in one-half cup of flour mixed with a little cold milk and salt; when scalding hot, beat the yolks of six eggs and add them; stir in whites and set immediately in the oven. Bake twenty minutes and serve as soon as done.

Oyster Omelette.

Allow for every six large oysters or twelve small ones, one egg; remove the hard part and mince the rest very fine; take the yolks of eight eggs and whites of four, beat till very light; then mix in the oysters, season and beat all up thoroughly; put into a skillet a gill of butter, let it melt; when the butter boils, skim it and turn in the omelette; stir until it stiffens, fry light brown; when the under side is brown, turn on to a hot platter. If wanted the upper side brown, hold a red-hot shovel over it.

Omelette Souffle.

Stir five tablespoonfuls of sifted flour into three pints of milk. strain through a sieve; add **the yolks** of eight eggs, beaten very light, and, just as it goes into **the oven**, the whites beaten stiff. Bake quickly.

French Omelette.

One quart of milk, one pint of bread crumbs, five eggs, one tablespoonful of flour, one onion chopped fine, chopped parsley, season with pepper and salt. Have butter melted in a spider; when the omelette is brown, turn it over. Double when served.

Omelette with Ham.

Make a plain omelette, and just before turning one-half over the other, sprinkle over it some finely chopped ham. Garnish with small slices of ham. Jelly or marmalade may be added in the same manner.

Eggs a la Bonne Femme.

Take six large eggs, boil them ten minutes; when cool, remove the shells carefully; divide them equally in halves, take out the yolks, and cut off from each the pointed tip of the white, that they may stand flatly. Make tiny dice of some cold chicken, ham, boiled beet root, and the eggs. Fill the hollows with these up to the brim, and pile the dice high in the center—two of ham and chicken, two of boiled beetroot, and two with the hard yolks. Arrange some neatly cut lettuce on a dish and place the eggs amongst it.

CHAPTER X.

FRESH FRUITS.

PINE APPLES.

SLICE on a slaw cutter, or very thin with a knife; mix with finely-powdered sugar. Set on ice till ready to serve.

A NICE WAY TO PREPARE APPLES.

Pare a dozen tart apples, take out the core, place sugar, with a small lump of butter, in the center of each apple, put them in a pan with half a pint of water, bake until tender, basting occasionally with the syrup while baking; when done, serve with cream.

TO STEW APPLES.

One pound sugar boiled in one quart of spring water and skimmed, one pound of the largest pippins, cut in quarters and the cores taken out. Have the syrup boiling; when you put them in let them stew till they are quite tender, then add the juice of two large lemons, and the peel cut small; give them a few more boils after the lemons are put in. If you want them to keep all the year, the syrup must be well boiled after the apples are taken out. As you peel the apples fling them into cold water.

BANANAS AND CREAM.

Peel, slice, and heap up in a glass dessert-dish, and serve raw, with fine sugar and cream.

TO CRYSTALLIZE FRUIT.

Pick out the finest of any kind of fruit—leave in the stones; beat the whites of three eggs to a stiff froth; lay the fruit in the beaten egg, with the stems upward; drain them and beat the part that drips off again; select them out, one by one, and dip them into a cup of finely-powdered sugar; cover a pan with a sheet of fine paper, place the fruit on it, and set it in a cool oven; when the icing on the fruit becomes firm, pile them on a dish, and set them in a cold place.

To Keep Grapes.

Select nice fresh clusters, and cut the end of the stem smooth and dip it into melted sealing wax; then put it in cotton batting; pack them away in wooden boxes; keep them in a dry cool place. In this way they will keep fresh all winter. Another way—Take full bunches, ripe and perfect; seal the end that is cut from the vine so that no air can get in, or the juice of the stem run out, and let them stand one day after sealed, so as to be perfectly sure they are sealed (if not they will shrivel up); then pack in boxes of dry sawdust and keep in a cool place; they will keep nicely all winter without losing their flavor; in packing, do not crowd the bunches; sprinkle the sawdust over the bottom of the box, then lay the grapes carefully, a bunch at a time, all over the box, then sawdust and grapes alternately until the box is full.

Melons.

Melons are much nicer if kept on ice until time for serving. Cut off a slice at each end of the water-melon, then cut through the center; stand on end on platter. Cantaloupe melons should have the seeds removed before sending to the table. Eat with a spoonful of strained honey in each half of melon.

Oranges.

Slice, mix with powdered sugar, and strew grated cocoa-nut over the top. Are also nice served whole, the skins quartered and turned down. Form in a pyramid with bananas and white grapes.

Candied Cherries.

Two quarts large, ripe, red cherries, stoned carefully; two pounds loaf sugar, one cup water. Make a syrup of the sugar and water and boil until it is thick enough to "pull," as for candy. Remove to the side of the range, and stir until it shows signs of granulation. It is well to stir frequently while it is cooking, to secure this end. When there are grains or crystals on the spoon, drop in the cherries, a few at a time. Let each supply lie in the boiling syrup two minutes, when remove to a sieve set over a dish. Shake gently but long, then turn the cherries out upon a cool, broad dish, and dry in a sunny window.

STEWED PEARS.

Peel pears. Place them in a little water, with sugar, cloves, cinnamon and lemon peel. Stew gently, and add one glass of cider. Dish up cold.

GLACÉ CHERRIES.

Make as above, but do not let the syrup granulate. It should not be stirred at all, but when it "ropes" pour it over the cherries, which should be spread out upon a large flat dish. When the syrup is almost cold, take these out, one by one, with a teaspoon, and spread upon a dish to dry in the open air. If nicely managed. these are nearly as good as those put up by professional confectioners. Keep in a dry, cool place.

CANDIED LEMON-PEEL.

Twelve fresh, thick-skinned lemons, four pounds loaf sugar, a little powdered alum, three cups clear water. Cut the peel from the lemons in long, thin strips, and lay in strong salt and water all night. Wash them in three waters next morning, and boil them until tender in soft water. They should be almost translucent, but not so soft as to break. Dissolve a little alum—about half a teaspoonful, when powdered—in enough cold water to cover the peel, and let it lie in it for two hours. By this time the syrup should be ready. Stir the sugar into three cups of water, add the strained juice of three lemons and boil it until it "ropes" from the end of the spoon. Put the lemon-peels into this, simmer gently half an hour; take them out and spread upon a sieve. Shake, not hard, but often, tossing up the peels now and then, until they are almost dry. Sift granulated sugar over them and lay out upon a table spread with a clean cloth. Admit the air freely, and, when perfectly dry, pack in a glass jar.

CHAPTER XI.

CANNING FRUIT.

FOR the benefit of those thrifty housewives who have fruit of their own which they wish to save, or who think that any preparation of food made outside of the home kitchen, and branded "factory make," should be considered "common and unclean," we append a few recipes which will be found in every way satisfactory.

The canning industry has grown within the few years of its existence to such enormous dimensions and includes so great a variety of articles, and competition is so sharp among the different firms who make it a specialty, that in point of expense it is cheaper to buy on the market than to purchase the fruit and be to the trouble and further expense of canning it at home.

There is, probably, no one thing which has done more to drive stern winter beyond the threshold than this simple but late-discovered process of keeping fruit fresh by excluding the air, and there is genuine satisfaction in contemplating the rows of cans filled with the different kinds of fruit, showing clear and distinct through the glass, and we are conservative enough to hope that the time will not come when the business of canning fruit shall be relegated, entirely, into the hands of the mercenary factory owner with his tin can with its overdrawn label.

GENERAL DIRECTIONS.

First. See that the cans and elastics are perfect and that the screw fits properly. Second. Have fruit boiling hot when sealed.

Have pan on stove in which each empty can is set to be filled after it is rolled in hot water. Fill can to overflowing, put on the top quickly, screw tightly; as contents cool, screw again and again, to keep tight. Third. Use glass cans, and keep in a cool, dark, but dry place. Light spoils them.

TABLE FOR CANNING FRUIT.

	Time for boiling fruit.	Quantity of sugar per qt.
Apricots	10 min.	8 oz.
Sour Apples	10 "	6 "
Crab Apples	25 "	8 "
Blackberries	6 "	6 "
Gooseberries	8 "	8 "
Raspberries	6 "	4 "
Huckleberries	5 "	4 "
Strawberries	8 "	8 "
Cherries	5 "	6 "
Currants	6 "	8 '
Wild Grapes	10 "	8 "
Sour Pears, whole	30 "	8 "
Bartlett Pears	20 "	6 "
Peaches, in halves	8 "	4 "
Plums	10 "	8 "
Peaches, whole	15 "	4 "
Pine-apple, sliced	15 "	6 "
Tomatoes	30 "	0 "
Quinces	30 "	10 "
Rhubarb	10 "	10 "

APPLE SAUCE.

Ready for table use or for pies may be kept till apples are out of the market by putting it into hot jars and sealing at once.

CANNED PINE-APPLE.

Pare the fruit and be very particular to cut out the eyes; chop fine and weigh it; add to it the same weight of sugar; mix thoroughly in a large crock; let it stand twenty-four hours, then put into cans, filling them full, and seal tight. After leaving them about two weeks it is well to see if there are any signs of working; if so, pour into a kettle and heat through and replace in the cans.

CANNED PINE-APPLE, No. 2.

Three-fourths pound of sugar to one pound of fruit, allowing one cup of water to a pound of sugar. Pick the pine-apple to pieces with a silver fork; scald and can hot.

CANNED BERRIES.

Heat slowly to boiling in a porcelain kettle; when they begin to boil, add sugar according to table above.' Before doing this, however, if there is much juice in the kettle, dip out the surplus and save for jelly; it will only increase the number of cans. Leave the berries almost dry before putting in the sugar, this will make syrup enough. Boil all together and can.

CANNED PEARS.

Prepare a syrup, allowing a pint of water and one-fourth pound of sugar to one quart of fruit. While this is heating peel the pears, dropping each as it is pared into a pan of clear water. When the syrup has come to a fast boil, put in the pears carefully and boil until they look clear and can be easily pierced by a fork. Have the cans ready rolled in hot water; pack with the pears and fill to overflowing with the scalding syrup, which must be kept on the fire all the while, and seal. The tougher and more common pears must be boiled in water until tender, and thrown while warm into the hot syrup, then allowed to boil ten minutes before they are canned.

CANNED PEACHES.

Pare, cut in half and stone, taking care not to break the fruit; drop each piece in cold water as soon as it is pared. Allow a heaping tablespoonful of sugar to each quart of fruit, scattering it between the layers. Fill your kettle and heat slowly to a boil. Boil three minutes, until every piece of fruit is heated through.

11

Can and seal. Put a cup of water in the bottom of the kettle before packing it with fruit, lest the lower layer should burn.

Dried Peaches.

Peaches, as usually dried, are a very good fruit; but can be made vastly better if treated the right way. Last season, the recipe which had quite a circulation in the papers, of drying the fruit by a stove after halving it, and sprinkling a little sugar into the cavity left by the extracted pits, was tried in our family. The fruit was found to be most excellent; better to the taste of nine out of ten persons, than any other peach preserves, by far. The peaches, however, were good ones before drying; for it is doubtful whether poor fruit can be made good by that process or any other.

CHAPTER XII.

ICES AND ICE-CREAMS.

SE only the best materials for making and flavoring if good ice-cream is desired, and avoid using milk thickened with arrow-root, corn starch or any other farinaceous substance. Pure cream, ripe natural fruits, or the extracts of the same, and sugar of the purest quality, combine to make a perfect ice-cream. In the first place secure a good ice-cream freezer. Of these several are made. Without recommending any particular make, we would suggest one be secured working with a crank and revolving dashers. Next secure an ice tub not less than eight inches greater in diameter than the freezer. See that it has a hole in the side near the bottom, with a plug, which can be drawn at pleasure, to let off water accumulating from melting ice. Get a spatula of hard wood —not metal—with a blade about twelve inches long and four or five inches wide and oval shaped at the end. This is used to scrape off cream which may adhere to the sides of the freezer in the process of freezing, also for working fruits and flavorings into the cream. A smaller spade is also necessary for mixing ice and salt together, and for depositing this mixture in the intervening space between can and ice tub. Ice must be pounded fine in a coarse, strong bag. To freeze the cream after it has been flavored, first pound up ice and mix with it a quantity of coarse salt, in the proportion of one-third the quantity of salt to the amount of ice used. Put freezing can in center of tub, taking care that the lid is securely fastened on, and pile the mixed ice and salt around it on inside of tub to within three inches of top. First turn the crank slowly, and as the cream hardens increase the speed until the mixture is thoroughly con-gealed and the revolving dashers are frozen in. Remove the lid, take out the dashers, cut away the cream which has adhered to the sides and proceed to work the mixture with the spatula until it is smooth and soft to the tongue. Re-insert the dashers, cover the can again, and work the crank until the entire contents are hard and well set. It is now ready to be served.

BERRY CREAM.

Any kind of berries may be used for this, strawberries being the nicest. Mash with a potato masher in an earthen bowl, one quart of berries with one pound of sugar; rub it through the colander; add one quart sweet cream and freeze. Very ripe peaches or mashed apples may be used instead of the berries.

BURNT SUGAR ICE-CREAM.

Take one-half pound of sugar, burn half of it in a sauce-pan or skillet; stir in sufficient water to bring to a liquid state; add the other sugar with one pint of milk containing four eggs well beaten. Flavor strongly with lemon, proceed as with other ices.

CHOCOLATE ICE-CREAM.

Use three or four ounces of the common unsweetened chocolate to a gallon of cream, or boiled custard. Boil the chocolate in some milk and sweeten to taste; strain it into the cream and flavor with vanilla. Beat the ice-cream to make it bright and rich colored. Melted chocolate cannot be mixed at once in cold cream as it sets and makes trouble. It must be considerably diluted first.

COFFEE ICE-CREAM.

To three quarts of pure, sweet cream add one pint of a decoction of very strong clear coffee. Sugar as usual—eight ounces to the quart.

LEMON ICE-CREAM.

This is made with the same proportion of cream and sugar and one lemon; grate the lemon rind into the sugar; this extracts the oil; then add the juice and the raw cream; strain and freeze immediately. Lemon cream sours more quickly than any other.

PEACH ICE-CREAM.

Take one quart of milk, two eggs, sugar to taste, one quart of peaches pared and stoned—mash and add to the custard. Proceed as usual.

PINE-APPLE ICE-CREAM.

Take two cans of pine-apples, two pounds of sugar, two quarts of cream (the cream must be nearly frozen, else the pine-apple pulp or syrup, upon being added, will immediately curdle it). Beat all thoroughly and finish freezing.

ORANGE ICE-CREAM.

Make a custard same as for vanilla; add orange pulp, or simply flavor with orange, if preferred.

STRAWBERRY AND RASPBERRY ICE-CREAM.

Bruise a pint of strawberries or raspberries with two large spoonfuls of fine sugar; add a quart of cream and strain through a sieve and freeze it. If you have no cream, boil a teaspoonful of arrowroot in a quart of milk, and if you like, beat up one egg and stir into it.

VANILLA ICE-CREAM.

One quart of cream, half a pound of sugar, granulated, half a vanilla bean. Boil half the cream with the sugar and bean, then add the rest of the cream; cool and strain it. If extract of vanilla, or any other extract is used, do not boil it, but put it in the cream with the sugar and freeze. Make it strong with the flavoring, as it loses strength with freezing.

COCOANUT ICE-CREAM.

Same as vanilla, omitting vanilla flavoring, and adding chopped cocoanut.

FROZEN TAPIOCA CUSTARD.

Soak six or seven ounces of tapioca in one quart of milk; when soft, boil two quarts of milk sweetened with one and one-fourth pounds of sugar; then add the tapioca and let it cook fifteen minutes; then stir in two ounces of butter and eight beaten eggs and take the custard immediately off the fire; cool and flavor with vanilla or lemon and freeze like ice-cream; when nearly finished, add one cup of whipped cream and beat well.

FROZEN RICE CUSTARD.

Wash six ounces of rice in several waters and cook it in milk; then proceed as in tapioca custard, using cinnamon or any other flavoring desired.

FROZEN SAGO CUSTARD.

Soak the sago in cold milk first, it will then cook in a few minutes; then proceed as in tapioca custard.

WATER-ICES.

These are made with the juices of ripe fruits, sweetened and frozen like ice-cream; but it must be remembered that if the juices are sweetened excessively they will not freeze. It is therefore generally necessary to test them with an instrument called a saccharometer. This applies equally to ice-creams and all drinks to be frozen; and for water-ices clarified sugar should be used, which may be prepared in the following manner: To a quart of water add three pounds of sugar and half of the white of an egg well beaten up. This should be boiled ten minutes and skimmed.

CHERRY WATER-ICE WITH NUT CREAM.

Two freezers will be required. For the cherry ice take two quarts of sweet cherries, one quart of water, one and one-half pounds of sugar. Pound the raw fruit in a mortar so as to break the stones and strain the juice through a fine strainer into the freezer. Boil the cherry pulp with some of the sugar and water to extract the flavor from the kernels, and mash that also through the strainer; add to the remainder of water and sugar and freeze. No eggs are needed and only beat the ice enough to make it even and smooth.

For the nut cream, use one pound of either pecan or hickory-nut meats, three-fourths of a pound of sugar, one quart of rich milk or cream, one tablespoonful of burnt sugar for coloring. Pick over the kernels carefully, that there be no fragments of shells to make the cream gritty, then pound them in a mortar with part of the sugar and a few spoonfuls of milk. Only a few can be pounded effectually at a time. Mix the milk with the pulp thus obtained, the rest of the sugar and caramel coloring, enough to make it like coffee and cream, and run it through a strainer into a freezer. Freeze it as usual and beat smooth with a spatula, then pack down with more ice to freeze firm. Line the moulds with cherry ice and fill the middle with the cream, or dish the ice as a border in shallow glasses with the cream piled in the center.

Strawberry Water-Ice.

To a pound of ripe strawberries and half a pound of currants add a pint of clarified sugar. If desired, a little coloring may be used. The whole must then be strained through a hair sieve and frozen.

Raspberry Water-Ice.

This may be made the same as strawberry water-ice by merely substituting raspberries for strawberries.

Burnt Almond Ice Cream and Orange-Ice.

First make the almond candy as follows: Take one pound of sugar, three-fourths pound of sweet almonds, two ounces of bitter almonds. Blanch the almonds, split them and put them in a slow oven to dry and acquire a light yellow color; put the sugar in a kettle on the fire, without any water, and stir it until it is all melted and of the color of golden syrup; then put in the hot almonds, stir gently to mix and pour the candy on a platter. When cold, pound the candy quite fine, put it into three pints of rich milk, set it on the fire, and when it boils add the beaten yolks of ten eggs. Strain the burnt almond custard thus made into a freezer, and freeze as usual and beat well.

For the orange ice: Take three pints of water, one pound of sugar, five or six oranges, according to size, juice of one lemon, if the oranges are sweet, whites of four eggs. Make a thick syrup of the sugar and a very little water. Peel half the oranges, divide them by their natural divisions and drop the pieces of oranges into the boiling syrup. Grate the yellow peel of the other three oranges into a bowl and squeeze in the juice, then pour the syrup from the scalded orange slices also into the bowl through a strainer and keep the slices on ice to be mixed in at the last. Add the water and lemon juice to the orange syrup in the bowl, strain and freeze. Beat in the whipped whites as usual, and when finished stir in the sugared fruit. Use the burnt almond cream and fill with the orange ice.

BISCUIT GLACES.

To half a pound of powdered sugar add the yolks of four eggs; flavor with vanilla; beat well, then take two quarts of whipped cream and mix with the sugar and yolks; color some of it red and spread on the bottom of paper capsules and fill up with fresh cream. Then put them in a tin box with cover and pack well up on all sides with pounded ice and salt and let stand for two hours; it is then ready for use.

RATEFFE BISCUIT CREAM.

Make the same as vanilla; when nearly frozen add one-half pound of rateffe biscuit and finish freezing.

TUTTI FRUTTI.

When a rich vanilla cream is partly frozen, candied cherries, chopped raisins, chopped citron or any other candied fruit chopped rather fine are added; add about half the quantity of fruit that there is of ice-cream; mold and imbed in ice and salt; or make also two quarts of orange ice in another freezer, add the white of eggs in the usual manner and beat it up white and smooth, then spread it evenly over the insides of two or three melon molds to coat them. Imbed the molds in the freezing mixture, and when the coating of orange ice is frozen firm fill up with the tutti frutti. Spread the orange ice also on top, put on the lids, secure with a number of rubber bands, close all spaces securely with butter and place the molds in the freezing mixture to remain two or three hours. When to be served wash the outsides with a cloth dipped in tepid water, carefully turn out the tutti frutti on to a folded napkin on a dish, lay a decoration of gelatine paste upon the white surface and serve.

Gelatine Paste for Ornamenting Ices.

Make clear jelly in the usual manner, then reduce it by slow boiling to little more than half, color it as desired, filter again. flavor, and cool it on large platters. Stamp out leaves, fern leaves, flower shapes, etc., and have them ready to place on the molded ices as soon as they are turned out.

Pine-Apple Sherbet.

Take two cans of pine-apples or the same amount of ripe pine-apples, two pounds of sugar, two quarts of water, whites of six eggs. Strain the juice from the cans into the freezer. Make a boiling syrup of the sugar and one quart of water. Chop the pine-apples small, scald it in the boiling syrup, then rub it through a colander with the syrup and the remaining quart of water into the freezer. Freeze and add the whites of four eggs, and beat it perfectly white.

To Color Ice Cream or Water Ices.

For Green, use juice of spinach or beet leaves. Vegetable green, already prepared, can be bought at the druggists.

For Yellow, saffron soaked in warm water.

For Red, take cochineal, which can be had at any druggists, or made as follows: One-quarter ounce cochineal, pound finely and add one-half pint boiling water, one-half ounce cream of tartar, one-quarter ounce alum, and one-quarter ounce salt of tartar. Let it stand until the color is extracted, then strain and bottle.

For Purple, mix a small quantity of cochineal and ultramarine blue.

For Brown, use powdered chocolate.

Other colors can be used, but these are all good, showy and quite harmless.

CHAPTER XIII.

ICINGS.

OR icing cakes use only fresh eggs and sift your pulverized sugar.

ALMOND ICING.

Whites of three eggs, whisked to a standing froth, three-quarters pound of powdered sugar, one-half pound of sweet almonds, blanched and pounded to a paste. When beaten fine and smooth, work gradually into the icing; flavor with lemon juice and rose water. This frosting is delicious. Dry in the open air when this is practicable.

BOILED ICING.

One and one-half cups of sugar; put to this two tablespoonfuls of water; let it boil on the back of the stove until it is waxy, or stringy; then add whites of two eggs.

BOILED ICING, No. 2.

Whites of four eggs, beaten stiff; one pint of sugar, melted in water and then boiled; add to it the eggs, and beat until cold.

CHOCOLATE ICING.

Take the whites of two eggs, one and one-half cups powdered sugar, and six large tablespoonfuls of chocolate.

CHOCOLATE ICING, No. 2.

One-half cake of chocolate grated fine, two-thirds of a cup of sugar, one-half cup of milk or cream; boiled and stirred to a paste.

Chocolate Icing, No. 3.

One-half cake chocolate; warm in the oven ten minutes; add one heaping cup of sugar, one teaspoonful cinnamon, one-half teaspoonful cloves, the same of ginger, two teaspoonfuls of vanilla; pour a little water on the sugar, put it on the chocolate, heat on the stove, melt it to a smooth paste, stir in the spices.

Clear Icing, for Cake.

Put one cup sugar into a bowl with a tablespoonful lemon juice and whites of two eggs. Just mix together smooth and pour over the cake; if the cake is not hot enough to dry it, place it in the mouth of a moderately warm oven.

Icing for Cakes.

Whites of four eggs, one pound of pulverized sugar, flavor with lemon; break the whites into a broad, cool, clean dish; throw a small handful of sugar upon them and begin to whip it in with long, even strokes of the beater. A few minutes later throw in more sugar and keep adding it at intervals until it is all used up. Beat until the icing is of a smooth, fine and firm texture; if not stiff enough, put in more sugar; use at least a quarter of a pound of sugar for each egg. To spread it, use a broad-bladed knife dipped in cold water.

Tutti Frutti Frosting.

One-half cup of water, three cups of sugar, whites of two eggs; boil sugar and water until very thick and waxy; beat the whites of eggs to a stiff froth, and pour the syrup over them, beating all till cool; then add one-half pound of almonds, chopped fine; one small half cup of large white raisins, and a little citron, sliced thin. Very nice for sponge cake.

Lemon Icing.

Whites of two eggs, two cups of sugar, juice and a part of the rind of two lemons.

ORNAMENTAL ICING.

Fill a paper cone with the icing, and work upon the cake, by slightly pressing the cone, any design you may choose.

YELLOW ICING.

Yolk of one egg to nine heaping teaspoonfuls of pulverized sugar and flavor with vanilla, or lemon.

ROSE COLORING.

Mix together one-fourth ounce each of powdered alum and cream of tartar, one ounce cochineal, four ounces loaf sugar, a saltspoonful of soda. Boil ten minutes in a pint of clear, soft water; when cool, bottle and cork for use. This is used for jellies, cakes, ice-cream, etc.

CHAPTER XIV.

JAMS AND JELLIES.

N making jam, the first thing to be looked after is the fruit. As a general rule, this should be fully ripe, fresh, sound, and scrupulously clean and dry. It should be gathered in the morning of a sunny day, as it will then possess its finest flavor. The best sugar is the cheapest; indeed, there is no economy in stinting the sugar either as to quality or necessary quantity, for inferior sugar is wasted in scum, and the jam will not keep unless a sufficient proportion of sugar is boiled with the fruit. At the same time too large a proportion of sugar will destroy the natural flavor of the fruit, and in all probability make the jam candy. The sugar should be dried and broken up into small pieces before it is mixed with the fruit. If it is left in large lumps it will be a long time in dissolving, and if it is crushed to powder it will make the jam look thick instead of clear and bright. The quantity to be used must depend in every instance on the nature of the fruit. Fruit is generally boiled in a brass or copper kettle uncovered, and this should be kept perfectly bright and clean. Great care should be taken not to place the kettle flat upon the fire, as this will be likely to make the jam burn to the bottom. Glass jars or cans are much the best for jams, as through them the condition of the fruit can be observed. Whatever jars are used, however, the jam should be examined every three weeks for the first two months, and if there are any signs of mold or fermentation it should be boiled over again. If you do not use the patent glass jar, the best way to cover jam is to lay a piece of paper the size of the jar upon the jam, to stretch over the top a piece of writing paper or tissue paper which has been dipped in white of egg, and to press the sides closely down. When dry, this paper will be stiff and tight like a drum. The strict economist may use gum Arabic dissolved in water instead of white of egg. The object aimed at is to exclude the air entirely. Jam should be stored in a cool, dry place, but not in one into which fresh air never enters. Damp has a tendency to make the fruit mold, and heat to make it ferment. Some cooks cover the jam as soon as possible after it is poured out, but the generally-approved plan is to let the fruit grow cool before covering it. In making jam continual watchfulness is required, as the result of five minutes' inattention may be loss and disappointment.

APRICOT JAM.

Pare three pounds of fresh, sound apricots, halve them, and take out the stones. They should be ripe enough to halve with the fingers. Place them in a deep dish, and strew over them one pound of finely sifted sugar. Let them remain for eight hours. Then place them with the syrup that will have oozed from them in ? preserving-pan; add a few of the kernels blanched and sliced, and another pound and a half of sugar. Let them boil very gently, and, when done, put them into glasses or jars and cover closely with gummed paper.

MARMALADES AND JAMS.

In making marmalades, jams, etc.—If put up in small quantities and for immediate use, three-quarters of a pound of sugar to one pound of fruit is sufficient; but if desirable to keep them longer, a pound of sugar to a pound of fruit is a better proportion. As in preserves, the best sugar should be used.

APPLE JAM.

Peel and core the apples, cut in thin slices and put them in a preserving kettle with three-quarters of a pound of white sugar to every pound of fruit; add (tied up in a piece of muslin) a few cloves, a small piece of ginger and a thin rind of lemon; stir with a wooden spoon on a quick fire for half an hour.

Blackberry, Raspberry, Currant or Strawberry Jam,

May be made by putting into a preserving kettle and boiling fifteen or twenty minutes, stirring often and skimming off any scum that may rise; then add sugar in the proportion of three-fourths pound of sugar to one pound of fruit. Boil thirty minutes longer stirring continually; when done pour into small jars or jelly glasses. A good way is to mix raspberries and currants in the proportion of two-thirds of the former to one-third of the latter.

Grape, Gooseberry, or Plum Jam.

Stew the berries in a little water, press through a coarse sieve or colander; then return to the kettle and add three-fourths pound of sugar to one pound of the pulped fruit. Boil three-fourths of an hour, stirring constantly. Pour in jars or bowls and cover as directed for other jams.

Apple Marmalade.

Peel and slice the apples; weigh and put into a kettle and stew until tender; wash fine and add sugar in proportion of pound to pound; let them cook slowly, stirring very frequently; be careful not to allow it to scorch; when the mass has a jellied appearance it is done. About half an hour will generally be found sufficient for making the marmalades after adding the sugar.

Orange Marmalade.

Eighteen sweet, ripe oranges, six pounds best white sugar. Grate the peel from four oranges, and reserve it for the marmalade. The rinds of the rest will not be needed. Pare the fruit carefully, removing the inner white skin as well as the yellow; slice the orange; remove the seeds; put the fruit and grated peel in a porcelain or enamel saucepan and boil steadily until the pulp is reduced to a smooth mass; take from the fire and rub quickly through a clean, bright colander, as the color is easily injured. Stir in the sugar, return to the fire, and boil fast, stirring constantly half an hour, or until thick. Put while warm into small jars, but do not cover until cold. This is a handsome and delicious sweetmeat.

PINE-APPLE MARMALADE.

Pare, slice, core, and weigh the pine-apple; then cut into small bits; make a syrup of a cup of water to two pounds of sugar; melt and heat to a boil; heat the chopped pine-apple in a vessel set within one of boiling water, covering it closely to keep in the flavor; when it is smoking hot all through, and begins to look clear, add to the syrup; boil together half an hour, stirring all the while, or until it is a clear, bright paste.

PEACH MARMALADE.

Pare, stone, and weigh the fruit; heat slowly to draw out the juice, stirring up often from the bottom with a wooden spoon; after it is hot, boil quickly, still stirring, three-quarters of an hour; add, then, the sugar, allowing three-quarters of a pound to each pound of the fruit; boil up well for five minutes, taking off every particle of scum; add the juice of a lemon for every three pounds of fruit, and the water in which one-fourth of the kernels have been boiled and steeped; stew all together ten minutes, stirring to a smooth paste, and take from the fire; put up hot in air-tight cans, or, when cold, in small stone or glass jars, with brandied tissue-paper fitted neatly to the surface of the marmalade. A large ripe pine-apple, pared and cut up fine, and stirred with the peaches, is a fine addition to the flavor.

QUINCE MARMALADE.

Such quinces as are too knotty and defective to make good preserves may be pared and cored, cut into small pieces and put into the kettle with three-quarters of a pound of sugar to each pound of fruit; put a small cup of cold water in first to prevent burning. When the quince begins to soften, take a potato masher and mash it

12

to a pulp, without taking it from the fire; let it boil gently from fifteen to twenty minutes, not longer than twenty. Take from the fire and put into jars.

Strawberries, raspberries, blackberries and grapes all make nice marmalades.

PLUM MARMALADE.

Choose plums that are fully ripe; scald them till the skins peel off, and take out the stones. Allow a pound and a half of sugar to a pound of fruit; let them lie in the sugar a few hours, then boil to a smooth mass.

PUMPKIN MARMALADE.

Take ripe, yellow pumpkins, pare and cut them into large pieces, scraping out the seeds with an iron spoon; weigh the pieces, and to every pound allow one pound of white sugar, and a small orange or lemon; grate pieces of pumpkin on a coarse grater, and put, together with the sugar, into a preserving pan, the yellow rind of the orange, grated, and the juice, strained. Let all boil slowly, stirring it frequently and skimming it well till it is a smooth, thick marmalade; put it warm into small glass jars or tumblers and lay a double round of tissue paper with a bladder or waxed paper.

JELLIES.

APPLE JELLY.

Slice the apples, skins, cores and all; put them in a stone jar with a small quantity of water to keep them from sticking; then place the jar in water and let them remain boiling until perfectly soft; then strain and to one pint of the liquor add three-quarters of a pound of loaf sugar; boil and clear with the whites of two or three eggs beaten to a froth. When it jellies pour into the glasses to cool and seal them.

BLACKBERRY JELLY.

Take blackberries before they are ripe, when they are turned red, put them into a porcelain kettle and cook until reduced to a pulp; then strain them and to a pint of juice add one pound of sugar. Boil to a jelly.

CRANBERRY JELLY.

Stew the cranberries until they are tender, then pour into a jelly-bag and let drip over night; take one pound of sugar to each pint of juice; let the juice boil five minutes, then pour in the sugar and stir until thoroughly dissolved.

CRAB-APPLE JELLY.

Boil the fruit whole in water enough to cover it until perfectly soft, then pour into a coarse linen bag and let it drip until it ceases, then press it a little. Allow one pound of sugar to each pint of juice. If you choose add the juice of a lemon to each quart of syrup. Boil the juice first, then skim it; heat the sugar in a dish in the oven and add it as the juice boils up. Boil gently twenty minutes and pour in tumblers or molds.

CURRANT JELLY.

From the *Home Messenger* we copy the following: This recipe is the only one which we will warrant to make good jelly against odds. We have made jelly by it on the fifth of July and on the fifteenth, and each time it was a perfect success. While we recommend all persons to make their jelly from fresh fruit, early in the season, we can still assure those who are behindhand that they need not despair of jelly that will set firm and hard later in the season. Run the currants through your hand picking out the leaves and any stray thing that may adhere to them but leaving the currants on their stems. Weigh the fruit, being accurate in remembering the number of pounds. Put a pint of water into your preserving kettle and add a bowl or two of currants, mashing and pressing them till you have sufficient juice to cover the bottom of the kettle; then

180

add the remainder of the currants; let them come to a boil and boil at least twenty minutes, of course stirring and pressing them from time to time that they may not burn. Have a three-cornered bag of thin but strong unbleached cotton that has been well scalded and wrung till almost dry; hang it up and pour the boiled currants into it. Let it drip into a stone crock all night, but by no means squeeze it, the currants will drain perfectly dry. In the morning pour the strained juice into the preserving kettle without measuring; let it come to a boil and boil thoroughly for three or four minutes, then pour in half as many pounds of sugar as you had pounds of currants. For instance, a peck of currants will probably weigh twelve pounds; therefore use six pounds of sugar. The moment the sugar is entirely dissolved the jelly is done. To make sure of the sugar being entirely dissolved see that it begins to jelly on the ladle. It will look thick and drop thick and a little stringy, but if let heat beyond this point it will loose its thickness and not jelly nearly so well and always disappoint you if you lose faith in your instructions and insist upon 'letting it come to a boil.' All the boiling is done before you put in the sugar.

CURRANT JELLY.

One pound of granulated sugar to each pint of juice. Squeeze the currants and boil twenty minutes, then add the sugar, which should be heating while the juice boils; stir well together until the sugar is well dissolved.

GRAPE JELLY.

Put the grapes into a preserving kettle and heat, bruising them meantime with a potato masher, until the juice runs freely, then strain through a sieve or thin cloth and measure one pint of juice for one pound of sugar. Boil the juice fifteen or twenty minutes before putting in the sugar; after adding the sugar let it boil from three to five minutes. All fruit will form more readily into a jelly if not quite ripe.

PEACH JELLY.

Crack one-third of the kernels and put them into the jar with the peaches, which have been wiped, stoned and sliced. Heat in a pot of boiling water, stirring occasionally until the fruit is well broken; strain, and to every pint of peach juice add the juice of a lemon; measure again and to every pint of juice allow one pound of sugar. Heat the sugar very hot and add when the juice has boiled twenty minutes. Let it come to a boil and take instantly from the fire.

PIE-PLANT JELLY.

Stew the stalks until tender in a preserving kettle; strain through a jelly-bag; flavor with extract of lemon. To each pint of juice add a pound of sugar; boil until it jellies on the skimmer; remove it from the fire and put into jars.

QUINCE JELLY.

Peel, cut up and core some fine, ripe quinces; put them in sufficient cold water to cover them and stew gently till soft, but not red; strain the juice without pressure, weigh, and to every pound of juice allow one pound of crushed sugar; boil the juice twenty minutes, add the sugar and boil again until it jellies—about a quarter of an hour; stir and skim well all the time; strain through thin cloth into your jelly glasses, and when cold, cover it. The remainder of the fruit can be made into marmalade with three-quarters of a pound of sugar and a quarter of a pound of juicy apples to every pound of quinces, or it can be made into compotes or tarts.

QUINCE JELLY, No. 2.

Take the cores and parings of the quinces, put them in enough cold water to cover them, and boil until they are soft; squeeze, and add the juice to the water, and any syrup which may be left from the quince preserve, and strain it; to each pint of juice allow a pound of sugar; spread the sugar in pans, put it in the oven to heat, it must be watched and stirred to prevent burning. Let the juice boil for five minutes, then pour in the hot sugar, stirring until it is entirely dissolved, and skimming any scum that may rise. There will be very little. Let it come to a boil, then take from the fire and put in jars or glasses; the jelly will be clear, of a good color and keep well. All kinds of jellies can be made in this way, and it saves much labor in the time of boiling the juices and the trouble of skimming.

GELATINE JELLIES.

COFFEE JELLY.

One box gelatine soaked for an hour in just water enough to cover; take one quart of strong coffee, made as for table use; sweeten it to taste; have the coffee hot and add the dissolved gelatine; stir well and strain into a mold that has just been rinsed in cold water. Set on ice or in a cool place, and when cold, serve with whipped cream.

LEMON SNOW JELLY.

Dissolve one box of gelatine in nearly a quart of boiling water, then add the juice of five lemons and enough of sugar to sweeten to taste; strain and set aside until nearly cool. Beat the whites of five eggs and whip into the jelly; turn into a dish and let it set until cool. After it becomes solid, decorate with pieces of red jelly.

LEMON JELLY.

One ounce of gelatine, red is the best, one pound of sugar, one quart of boiling water, and four lemons; cut the lemons into slices and bruise them, then add the sugar and gelatine, and pour upon the whole boiling water; set the vessel containing them upon the stove and stir until the gelatine is thoroughly dissolved; then pour into molds and set to cool.

ORANGE JELLY.

Take two ounces of gelatine and pour on hot water enough to cover it, and let soak until it is dissolved; boil together one quart of water and one-half pound of sugar, and add the dissolved gelatine; add the juice of five oranges and one lemon and the whites of two eggs, well beaten. Boil a few minutes and strain through a jelly-bag; turn into molds and set to cool.

Any jellies may be colored by using fruit coloring, which may be obtained at the bakeries.

WINE JELLY.

One box of gelatine dissolved in just water enough to cover it, one pint of wine, one pint of boiling water, one pint of granulated sugar, and juice of three lemons.

MOULDINESS.

Fruit jellies may be preserved from mouldiness by covering the surface one-fourth of an inch deep with finely pulverized loaf sugar. Thus protected, they will keep in good condition for years.

CHAPTER XV.

MUSHROOMS.

HE peasants of a great portion of Europe eat mushrooms raw with salt and dry bread, and wholesome and good they are. The true flavor of mushrooms, nevertheless, is greatly heightened by cooking; and cook them how you may—a broil, a stew, or a fry, with the simple addition of butter, salt, and pepper, and they are excellent. There is one rule that should always be observed in whatever mode they are cooked, and that is that they should be served up quickly and hot. The following modes of cooking mushrooms may prove useful:

MUSHROOMS AU GRATIN.

Take twelve large mushrooms about two inches in diameter, pare the stalks, wash, and drain the mushrooms on a cloth; cut off and chop the stalks. Put in a quart stewpan an ounce of butter and half an ounce of flour; stir over the fire for two minutes; then add one pint of broth; stir till reduced to half the quantity. Drain the chopped stalks of the mushrooms thoroughly in a cloth; put them in the sauce with three tablespoonfuls of chopped and washed parsley, one tablespoonful of chopped and washed shalot, two pinches of salt, a small pinch of pepper; reduce on a brisk fire for eight minutes, put two tablespoonfuls of oil in a *saute* pan; set the mushrooms in, the hollow part upwards; fill them with the fine herbs, and sprinkle over them lightly a tablespoonful of raspings; put in a brisk oven for ten minutes and serve.

Mushrooms a la Provencale.

Take mushrooms of good size; remove the stems and soak them in olive oil; cut up the stems with a clove of garlic and some parsley; add meat of sausages, and two yolks of eggs to unite them; dish the mushrooms, and garnish them with the forcemeat; sprinkle them with fine oil, and dress them in an oven, or in a *four de campagne.*

Mushrooms a la Creme.

Trim and rub half a pint of button mushrooms, dissolve two ounces of butter rolled in flour in a stewpan, then put in the mushrooms, a bunch of parsley, a teaspoonful of salt, half a teaspoonful each of white pepper and of powdered sugar, shake the pan round for ten minutes, then beat up the yolks of two eggs, with two tablespoonfuls of cream, and add by degrees to the mushrooms; in two or three minutes you can serve them in the sauce.

Baked Mushrooms.

Peel the tops of twenty mushrooms; cut off a portion of the stalks, and wipe them carefully with a piece of flannel, dipped in salt; lay the mushrooms in a tin dish, put a small piece of butter on the top of each, and season them with pepper and salt. Set the dish in the oven, and bake from twenty minutes to half an hour. When done, arrange them high in the centre of a very hot dish, pour the sauce round them and serve quickly and as hot as you possibly can.

Breakfast Mushrooms.

Clean a dozen or so of medium size; place two or three ounces of nice, clean beef-dripping in the frying pan, and with it a tablespoonful or more of nice beef gravy. Set the pan on a gentle fire, and as the dripping melts place in the mushrooms, adding salt and pepper to taste. In a few minutes they will be cooked, and being soaked in the gravy and served upon a hot plate, will form a capital dish. In the absence of gravy, a *soupcon* of "extractum carnis " may be substituted.

CURRIED MUSHROOMS.

Peel and remove the stems from a dish of full-grown mushrooms, sprinkle with salt, and add a very little butter; stew them gently in a little good gravy or stock. Add four tablespoonfuls of cream, and one teaspoonful of curry powder, previously well mixed with two teaspoonfuls of wheat flour; mix carefully, and serve on a hot dish, with hot toast and hot plates attendant. Mind the "curry stuff " is good, says an Indian friend, and not too much of it. The word "curry," by itself, it seems, being merely the Tamul word for "meat." The large horse mushroom, when half or three parts grown, and curried in this fashion, will be found to be delicious.

MUSHROOMS EN CAISSE.

Peel the mushrooms lightly, and cut them into pieces. Put them into cases of buttered paper, with a bit of butter, parsley, green onions, and shalots chopped up, salt and pepper. Dress them on the gridiron over a gentle fire, and serve in the cases.

MUSHROOM CATSUP.

Mushroom catsup is more highly esteemed and more generally useful than any other. It is best when made of large mushroom flaps, fully ripe, fresh, and perfectly dry—that is, gathered during dry weather. If this point is not attended to the catsup will not keep. Do not wash nor skin the mushrooms, but carefully remove any decayed, dirty, or worm-eaten portions; cut off about half an inch from the end of the stalks, then break the rest into small pieces, put them into an earthen jar, and strew three-fourths of a pound of salt amongst two gallons of mushrooms, scattering the larger portions on top. Let them remain all night, and the next day stir them gently with a wooden spoon, and repeat this three times a day for two days. At the end of that time put the jar into a cool oven for half an hour, then strain the liquid which flows from them through a coarse cloth, and let it boil for a quarter of an hour. Do not squeeze the mushrooms. To every quart of the liquid put a quarter of an ounce each of Jamaica ginger and black pepper, and a drachm of mace. Boil again till the quantity is reduced one-half. Pour it out, and let it stand until cool, then put it into perfectly dry bottles, being careful to leave the sediment, which will have settled to the bottom, undisturbed. Seal the corks and keep in a cool, dry place.

Mushrooms en Ragout.

Put into a stew-pan a little stock, a small quantity of vinegar, parsley, and green onions chopped up, salt and spices. When this is about to boil, the mushrooms being cleaned, put them in. When done, remove them from the fire, and thicken with yolks of eggs.

Mushrooms with Bacon.

Take some full-grown mushrooms, and having cleaned them, procure a few rashers of nice streaky bacon, and fry it in the usual manner. When nearly done, add a dozen or so of mushrooms, and fry them slowly until they are cooked. In this process they will absorb all the fat of the bacon, and with the addition of a little salt and pepper, will form a most appetizing breakfast relish.

Mushroom Stems.

If young and fresh, make a capital dish when the supply of mushrooms is limited. Rub them quite clean, and after washing them in salt and water, slice them to the thickness of a shilling, then place them in a sauce-pan with sufficient milk to stew them tender; throw in a piece of butter and some flour for thickening, and salt and pepper to taste. Serve upon a toast of bread, in a hot dish, and add sippets of toasted bread. This makes a light and very delicate supper dish, and is not bad sauce to a boiled fowl.

To Stew Mushrooms.

Trim and rub clean a half pint large button mushrooms; put into a stew-pan two ounces of butter; shake over the fire until thoroughly melted; put in the mushrooms, a teaspoonful of salt, half as much pepper, and a small piece of mace pounded; stew till the mushrooms are tender, then serve them on a hot dish. They are usually sent in as a breakfast dish, thus prepared in butter.

To Pot Mushrooms.

The small open mushrooms suit best for potting. Trim and rub them; put into a stew-pan a quart of mushrooms, three ounces of butter, two teaspoonfuls of salt, and half a teaspoonful of Cayenne and mace mixed, and stew for ten or fifteen minutes, or till the mushrooms are tender; take them carefully out and drain them perfectly on a sloping dish, and when cold press them into small pots, and pour clarified butter over them, in which state they will keep for a week or two. If required to be longer preserved, put writing paper over the butter, and over that melted suet, which will effectually preserve them for many weeks, if kept in a dry, cool place.

Mushrooms and Toast.

Peel the mushrooms, and take out the stems. Fry them over a quick fire. When the butter is melted take off the pan. Squeeze the juice of a lemon into it. Let the mushrooms fry again for some minutes. Add salt, pepper, spices, and a spoonful of water, in which a clove of garlic, having been cut into pieces, has soaked for half an hour; let it stew. When the mushrooms are done make a thickening of yolks of eggs. Pour the mushrooms on bread fried in butter, and laid in a dish ready for them.

Mushrooms on Toast.

Put a pint of mushrooms into a stew-pan, with two ounces of butter rolled in flour; add a teaspoonful of salt, half a teaspoonful of white pepper, a blade of mace powdered, and half a teaspoonful grated lemon; stew till the butter is all absorbed, then add as much white *roux* as will moisten the mushrooms; fry a slice of bread in butter, to fit the dish, and as soon as the mushrooms are tender serve them on the toast.

To Pickle Mushrooms.

Select a number of small, sound, pasture mushrooms, as nearly as possible alike in size; throw them for a few minutes into cold water; then drain them; cut off the stalks, and gently rub off the outer skin with a moist flannel dipped in salt; then boil the vinegar, adding to each quart two ounces of salt, half a nutmeg sliced, a drachm of mace, and an ounce of white pepper-corns; put the mushrooms into the vinegar for ten minutes over the fire; then pour the whole into small jars, taking care that the spices are equally divided; let them stand a day, then cover them.

Another Method.

In pickling mushrooms, take the buttons only, and while they are quite close, cut the stem off even with the gills, and rub them quite clean. Lay them in salt and water for forty-eight hours, and then add pepper and vinegar, in which black pepper and a little mace have been boiled. The vinegar must be applied cold. So pickled they will keep for years.

CHAPTER XVI.

PICKLES.

PICKLES are made of fruit or vegetables preserved in vinegar, and may be used as accompaniments to cold meat, to garnish dishes, and to flavor hashes and sauces. It is generally understood that they can be bought cheaper than they can be made. Nevertheless, there is always a certain amount of satisfaction in using home-made preparations, as by this means the quality of the article can be assured beyond all question, and many ladies take great pride in their store of home-made pickles. A great outcry was raised some years ago about the unwholesomeness of pickles, and attention was called to the fact that most of those ordinarily sold were positively pernicious, because the vinegar used in making them was boiled in copper vessels. This evil has now been, to a great extent, remedied; and it may be reasonably assumed that pickles which are sold by respectable dealers have been properly prepared. At the same time, for safety's sake, the rule should be laid down that all pickles which are beautiful and brilliant in color and appearance should be avoided, as this is a certain sign that the vinegar used has been boiled in a metal pan. In making pickles, care must be taken that the vegetables and fruit used for the purpose are procured at the right season, that they are perfectly sound, not overripe, and have been gathered on a dry day. They should be trimmed and wiped before they are used, and not washed, unless they are afterwards to be partially boiled or soaked. The vinegar must be of the best quality. White wine vinegar is generally recommended, for the sake of the appearance, but it is not as wholesome as the best cider vinegar. Metal utensils should never be used in making pickles, as the vinegar acting upon the metal produces a poison. Enameled or stone vessels and wooden spoons should therefore be used; and the best method that can be adopted is to put the vinegar into a stone jar, and heat it on a stone or hot hearth. Pickles should be kept in glass bottles, or unglazed earthen jars, and should be closely corked, and the corks sealed down, or covered with wet bladder. They should be stored in a dry place. As the vinegar becomes absorbed more should be added, as it is important that the vegetables should be covered at least two inches above the surface with vinegar. If any of the vinegar is left after the pickle is used, it should be boiled up with fresh spices, and bottled for flavoring sauces, etc. It should be remembered that to boil vinegar is to decrease its strength. If it is wished to hasten the preparation of the pickles, partially boil the vegetables in brine and let them cool and get quite dry before the vinegar is poured over them.

PICKLED ARTICHOKES.

Boil your artichokes in strong salt and water for two or three minutes; lay on a hair sieve to drain; when cold, lay in narrow-topped jars. Take as much white wine vinegar as will cover the artichokes, and boil it with a blade or two of mace, some root ginger, and a nutmeg grated fine. Pour it on hot, seal and put away for use.

PICKLED BUTTERNUTS AND WALNUTS.

Gather them when soft enough to be pierced by a pin; lay them in brine five days, changing this twice in the meantime; drain, and wipe them with a coarse cloth; pierce each by running a large needle through it, and lay in cold water for six hours. To each gallon of vinegar allow a cup of sugar, three dozen each of cloves and black peppers, half as much allspice, and a dozen blades of mace. Boil five minutes; pack the nuts in small jars and pour over them scalding hot. Repeat this twice within a week; tie up and set away. They will be good to eat in a month.

PICKLED BEANS.

The beans should be gathered young. Place them in a strong brine of salt and water; when turning yellow, which will be in a day or two, remove them and wipe them dry. Boil the vinegar with a little mace, whole pepper, and ginger (two ounces of pepper and one ounce each of ginger and mace to each quart of vinegar); pour this over the beans. A small bit of alum, or a teaspoonful of soda will bring back the color. Cover them to keep in the steam and reboil the vinegar the next day; throw over hot as before. Cover, but do not tie down till cold.

PICKLED BEETS.

Take the beets, cleanse and boil two hours. When cold peel and slice, put into a jar and cover with vinegar prepared in the following manner: Boil half an ounce each of cloves, pepper-corns, mace and ginger in a pint of vinegar, when cold add another pint.

PICKLED BROCOLI.

Choose the finest, whitest and closest vegetables before they are quite ripe. Pare off all green leaves and the outsides of the stalks. Parboil them in well-salted water. When drained and dry pull off the branches in convenient sized pieces and put them into a jar of pickle prepared as for onions. Time to parboil, four or five minutes.

BOTTLED PICKLES.

Wash and wipe small cucumbers; put into a stone jar and cover with salt—allowing a pint of salt to a half bushel of cucumbers—and pour over them boiling water enough to cover. Place a gallon at a time on the stove, cover with vinegar, and add a lump of alum about the size of a hickory nut. Put on the stove in another kettle a gallon of the very best cider vinegar, to which add half a pint of brown sugar; have bottles cleansed and placed to heat on stove in a vessel of cold water; also have a cup of heated sealing-wax. Have spices prepared in separate dishes as follows: Green and red peppers sliced in rings; horse-radish roots washed, scraped and cut in small pieces; black and yellow mustard seed if liked, each prepared by sprinkling with salt and pouring on some boiling water, which let stand for fifteen minutes and then draw off; stick of cinnamon broken into pieces and a few cloves. When pickles come to boiling point, take out and pack in bottles, mixing with them the spices. Put in a layer of pickles, then a layer of spices, shaking the bottles occasionally so as to pack tightly. When full, cover with the boiling hot vinegar from the other kettle (using a bright funnel and tin cup), going over them a second time and filling up, in order to supply shrinkage, for the pickles must be entirely covered with vinegar. Put in the corks, which should fit very snugly; lift each bottle and dip the corked end in the hot sealing-wax; proceed in this manner with each bottle, dipping each a second time into the wax so that they may be perfectly secure. Glass cans, the covers of which have become defective, can be used by supplying corks. Pickles prepared in this way are superior to imported pickles.

MARY'S PICKLED BLACKBERRIES.

Three quarts blackberries, one quart vinegar, one quart sugar. No spice is required; put all together at the same time into your kettle and boil ten or fifteen minutes. After standing a few weeks they are very nice.

To PUT UP CUCUMBERS IN BRINE.

Leave at least an inch of stem to the cucumbers, and wash well in cold water. Make a brine of salt and water strong enough to bear an egg; put your cucumbers in this as you gather them each day from the vines. Cut a board so as to fit inside of your barrel; bore holes here and there through it, and put this board on the cucumbers with a weight sufficient to keep it down. Each day take off the scum that rises. When wanted for use, take out what is necessary and soak them two or three days, or until the salt is out

13

of them, and then pour boiling spiced vinegar over them. A red
pepper or two is an improvement if one likes hot pickles.

PICKLED CABBAGE.

Select solid heads, slice very fine, put in a jar, then cover with
boiling water; when cold, drain off the water, and season with
grated horse radish, salt, equal parts of black and red pepper, cinnamon and whole cloves.

PICKLED CAULIFLOWER.

Choose such as are firm, yet of their full size; cut away all the
leaves and pare the stalks; pull away the flowers in bunches, steep
in brine two days, then drain them, wipe them dry, and put them
in hot pickle, or merely infuse for three days three ounces of curry
powder in every quart of vinegar. ·

PICKLED CAULIFLOWER, No. 2.

These should be sliced and salted for two or three days, then
drained, and spread upon a dry cloth before the fire for twenty-
four hours; after which they are put into a jar, and covered with
piced vinegar.

PICKED CABBAGE, No. 2.

Slice red cabbage very thin; put on it a little coarse salt, and let
it rest twenty-four hours to drain; add sliced onions, if you like
them.   Boil four spoonfuls pepper, and four of allspice in a quart
of vinegar, and pour it over.

PICKLED CUCUMBERS.

Wash with care your cucumbers, and place in jars.   Make a
weak brine (a handful of salt to a gallon and a half of water).
When scalding hot, turn over the cucumbers and cover; repeat this
process three mornings in succession, taking care to skim thoroughly.   On the fourth day have ready a porcelain kettle of
vinegar, to which has been added a piece of alum the size of a
valnut.   When scalding hot, put in as many cucumbers as may be
overed with the vinegar; do not let them boil, but skim out as

soon as scalded through, and replace with others, adding each time a small piece of alum. When this process is through, throw out the vinegar, and replace with good cider or white wine vinegar; add spices, mustard seed and red pepper. Sort the pickles and place them in stone or glass jars, turn over the hot spiced vinegar; seal and put away the jars not wanted for immediate use. Pickles thus prepared are fine and crisp at the expiration of a year. Those that are kept in open mouth jars may be covered with a cloth, which will need to be taken off and rinsed occasionally.

Chow-Chow.

Two quarts of tomatoes, two white onions, half-dozen green peppers, one dozen cucumbers, two heads of cabbage, all chopped fine; let this stand over night; sprinkle a cup of salt in it. In the morning drain off the brine, and season with one tablespoonful of celery seed, one ounce of turmeric, half teaspoonful of cayenne pepper, one cup of brown sugar, one ounce of cinnamon, one ounce of allspice, one ounce of black pepper, one-quarter ounce cloves, vinegar enough to cover, and boil two hours.

Chow-Chow, No. 2.

Two heads of cabbage, two heads of cauliflower, one dozen cucumbers, six roots of celery, six peppers, one quart of small white onions, two quarts of green tomatoes; cut into small pieces and boil each vegetable separately until tender, then strain them. Two gallons of vinegar, one-fourth pound of mustard, one-fourth pound of mustard seed, one pot of French mustard, one ounce of cloves, two ounces of turmeric; put the vinegar and spices into a kettle and let them come to a boil; mix the vegetables and pour over the dressing.

Pickled Cherries.

Take the largest and ripest red cherries, remove the stems, have ready a large glass jar, fill it two-thirds full with cherries, and fill up to the top with best vinegar; keep it well covered and no boiling or spice is necessary, as the cherry flavor will be retained, and the cherries will not shrivel.

FRENCH PICKLES.

One peck of green tomatoes, sliced, six large onions, sliced; sprinkle over them one cup of salt; let them stand over night; in the morning drain and boil for fifteen minutes in two parts water and one part vinegar; drain again; take two quarts vinegar, one pound sugar, one tablespoonful each of cloves, cinnamon and allspice; boil together for fifteen minutes and pour over the pickles.

PICKLED GRAPES.

Fill a jar with alternate layers of sugar and bunches of nice grapes, not too ripe; fill one-third full of good, cold vinegar and cover tightly.

PICKLED GRAPES, No. 2.

When grapes are not quite ripe, but dark colored, pick from the stem and wash; put in bottles; in a dish put sugar and vinegar, and boil a few minutes; add spices to taste; boil a few minutes, pour over the grapes and seal up the bottles.

TO HARDEN PICKLES.

After they are taken out of the brine take a lump of alum and a horse-radish cut in strips; put this in the vinegar, and it will make them hard and crisp. When you wish to make a few cucumber pickles quick, take good cider vinegar; heat it boiling hot and pour it over them. When cool, they are ready for use.

LEMON PICKLES.

Wipe six lemons, cut each into eight pieces; put on them a pound of salt, six large cloves of garlic, two ounces of horse-radish, sliced thin, likewise of cloves, mace, nutmeg, and Cayenne, a quarter of an ounce each, and two ounces of flour of mustard; to these put two quarts of vinegar. Boil a quarter of an hour in a well-tinned saucepan; or, which is better, do it in a strong jar, in a kettle of boiling water; or set the jar on the hot hearth till done. Set the jar by, and stir it daily for six weeks; keep the jar close covered. Put it into small bottles.

MANGOES OF MELONS.

Take green melons and make a brine strong enough to bear up an egg; then pour it boiling hot on the melons, keeping them under the brine; let them stand five or six days, slit them down on one side, take out all the seeds, scrape them well in the inside, and wash them clean; then take cloves, garlic, ginger, nutmeg and pepper; put all these proportionately into the melons, filling them up with mustard seed; then lay them into an earthern pot, and take one part of mustard seed and two parts of vinegar, enough to cover them, pouring it on scalding hot. Keep them closely covered.

IMITATION PICKLED MANGOES.

Large cucumbers, or small melons, are split so that a marrow-spoon may be introduced, and the seeds scooped out; they are then parboiled in brine strong enough to float an egg, dried on a cloth before the fire, filled with mustard seed and a clove of garlic, and then covered with spiced vinegar. Real mangoes are pickled in the same way.

PICKLED NASTURTIUMS.

Soak for three days in strong salt and water; then strain and pour boiling vinegar over them, omitting the spice. Vinegar for any pickle should never be allowed to boil over one minute.

PICKLED ONIONS.

Small silver-skinned onions; remove outer skin so that each one is white and clean; put them into brine that will float an egg for three days; bring vinegar to a boiling point, add a little mace and whole red peppers and pour hot over the onions, well drained from the brine.

PICKLED ONIONS, No. 2.

Peel the onions and let them lie in strong salt and water nine days, changing the water each day; then put them into jars and pour fresh salt and water on them, this time boiling hot; when it is cold, take them out and put them on a hair sieve to drain, after which put them in wide-mouthed bottles and pour over them vinegar prepared in the following manner: Take white wine vinegar and boil it with a blade of mace, some salt and ginger in it; when cool, pour over the onions.

PICKLES.

An excellent way to make pickles that will keep a year or more is to drop them into boiling hot water, but not boil them; let them stay ten minutes, wipe them dry, and drop them into cold, spiced vinegar, and they will not need to be put in salt and water.

STUFFED PEPPERS.

Chop a large cabbage finely, add one large spoonful grated horse-radish root and one ounce of white mustard seed; mix all this well; cut pieces out of the stem ends of large green peppers, large as a silver dollar; fill with the filling and sew the piece in again with cotton thread; then take vinegar enough to cover; spice with cloves, mace and allspice, whole; boil, and when nearly cold, pour over the peppers; no salt is to be used. Mangoes are pickled and stuffed in the same manner.

MIXED PICKLES.

One quart raw cabbage chopped fine; one quart boiled beets chopped fine; two cups of sugar, tablespoonful of salt, one teaspoonful red pepper, one cup of grated horse-radish; cover with cold vinegar and keep from the air.

MIXED PICKLES, No. 2.

Three hundred small cucumbers, four green peppers sliced fine, two large or three small heads cauliflower, three heads of white cabbage sliced fine, nine large onions sliced, one large horse-radish, one quart green beans cut one inch long, one quart green tomatoes sliced; put this mixture in a pretty strong brine twenty-four hours; drain three hours; then sprinkle in one-fourth pound black and one-fourth pound of white mustard seed; also one tablespoonful black ground pepper; let it come to a good boil in just vinegar enough to cover it, adding a little alum; drain again and when cold put in one-half pint ground mustard; cover the whole with good cider vinegar; add turmeric enough to color if you like.

INDIA PICKLES.

Take three quarts of vinegar, quarter pound mustard, half ounce of black pepper, one ounce cloves, one ounce allspice, one ounce turmeric, one ounce ginger, one ounce Cayenne pepper, handful of salt and the same of sugar; boil for twenty minutes. When cold put in the vegetables, cucumbers, onions, cauliflower cut up small, and cover closely. If the liquid should seem thin, boil again and add more mustard in three weeks after making.

PYPER PICKLES.

Salt pickles down dry for ten days, soak in fresh water one day; pour off water, place in porcelain kettle, cover with water and vinegar and add one teaspoonful pulverized alum; set over night on a stove which had fire in it during the day; wash and put in a jar with cloves, allspice, pepper, horse-radish, onions or garlic; boil fresh vinegar and pour over all. Ready for use in two weeks.

RAGAN PICKLES.

Two gallons of cabbage, sliced fine, one gallon of chopped green tomatoes, twelve onions, also chopped, one gallon best vinegar, one pound of brown sugar, one tablespoonful of black pepper, half an ounce of turmeric powder, one ounce celery seed, one tablespoonful of ground allspice, one tablespoonful of ground cloves, one-quarter pound white mustard, and one gill of salt. Boil all together, stirring well, for two hours; take from the fire and add the spices, then put in air-tight jars; set in a cool, dry place, and this delicious pickle will keep all winter.

SWEET PICKLES.

To every seven pounds of fruit allow three and one-half pounds of sugar and one pint of cider vinegar, two ounces whole cloves, two of stick cinnamon. This is for peaches, pears, apples or musk melons. Peaches, pears, and apples should be pared only, not divided. Then in each stick two whole cloves. The cinnamon should be boiled in the vinegar. Put the prepared fruit into a jar and pour the vinegar, scalding hot, over it. Repeat this for three mornings. These sweet pickles will be found delicious, and will keep any length of time. The melons should be cut in strips as if to serve fresh on the table, and should not be too ripe. Simmer them thirty minutes slowly in the prepared vinegar, and they will need no further attention except to keep them closely covered, and they will keep good a year.

Sweet Apple Pickle.

Pickled sweet apples can be made by taking three pounds of sugar, two quarts of vinegar, one-half ounce of cinnamon, one-half ounce of cloves; pare the apples, leaving them whole; boil them in part of the vinegar and sugar until you can put a fork through them; take them out; heat the remainder of the vinegar and sugar and pour over them. Be careful not to boil them too long or they will break.

Sweet Tomato Pickle.

Seven pounds of ripe tomatoes, peeled and sliced, three and a half pounds of sugar, one pound of mace and cinnamon mixed, one ounce of cloves, one quart of vinegar. Mix all together and stew an hour.

Green Tomato Pickles.

Slice one peck of tomatoes into a jar and sprinkle a little salt over each layer; let them stand twenty-four hours, drain off the liquor; put the tomatoes into a kettle with a teaspoonful of each of the following spices: Ground ginger, allspice, cloves, mace, cinnamon, a teaspoonful of scraped horse-radish, twelve small or three large red peppers, three onions, a cup of brown sugar; cover all with vinegar; boil slowly for three hours.

PICALILLI.

One peck green tomatoes, one large cabbage, one dozen onions; add half pint salt; after the above have been chopped fine let it stand over night; in the morning drain off the brine and scald in weak vinegar; drain this off and stir in ground spices to suit the taste; add six red peppers and a little horse-radish root; pack in a crock and cover with strong vinegar; a few small cucumbers put in whole are quite an addition.

PICKLETTE.

Four large crisp cabbages chopped fine, one quart of onions chopped fine, two quarts of vinegar, or enough to cover the cabbage, two tablespoonfuls each of ground mustard, black pepper, cinnamon, turmeric, celery seed, and one of allspice, pulverized alum and mace. Pack the onions and cabbage in alternate layers with a little salt between them. Let them stand until next day. Then scald the vinegar, sugar and spices together and pour over the cabbage and onions. Do this three mornings in succession. On the fourth put all together over the fire and heat to a boil; let them boil five minutes. When cold pack in small jars. It is fit for use as soon as cold and will keep well.

SPICED VINEGAR FOR PICKLES GENERALLY.

Bruise in a mortar two ounces black pepper, one ounce ginger, one-half ounce allspice, and one ounce salt. If a hotter pickle is desired, add one-half drachm Cayenne, or a few capsicums. For walnuts add also one ounce shallots. Put these in a stone jar, with a quart of vinegar, and cover them with a bladder wetted with the pickle, and over this a piece of leather. Set the jar near the fire for three days, shaking it three time a day; then pour it on the walnuts or other vegetables. For walnuts it is used hot; for cabbage, etc., cold.

PICKLED PEACHES.

To fourteen pounds of peaches peeled, put three pounds of brown sugar, three tablespoonfuls of cinnamon, same of powdered cloves, to one quart of strong cider vinegar. Let the vinegar, sugar, and spices boil a very little while; then put in your peaches and let them scald enough to stick a straw through them with ease. Take them out and put them in an earthen jar, seeing that the vinegar covers them well, which must be poured over the packed peaches. Put a cover over them lightly the first day; the second pour off the vinegar, heat and pour it boiling hot over the fruit. Repeat till the fruit is ready for use. Four or five times heating will generally cure them. Watch closely and if any fermentation occurs pour off the vinegar and scald it, skimming off any scum that arises.

Pickled Peaches that will Keep.

Four pounds sugar, one pint vinegar, to twelve pounds of fruit; put sugar and vinegar together and boil; then add the fruit and let it come to a boil; the next day drain off the liquor and boil again; do this three times and your pickles are delicious; add cinnamon to the liquor and stick two or three cloves in each peach.

To Pickle Plums.

For eight pounds of fruit take four pounds of sugar, two quarts of vinegar, one ounce cinnamon, and one ounce cloves; boil the vinegar, sugar, and spices together; skim, and pour scalding hot over your fruit; let it set three days, pour off the syrup, scald and skim and pour over again, and continue this process every three days till you have scalded it three times, after which it will be fit for use. Plums prepared in this way we think superior to the old method of preserving with sugar alone.

Green Tomato Soy.

Two gallons of green tomatoes sliced without peeling; slice also twelve good sized onions; two quarts of vinegar, one quart of sugar, two tablespoonfuls each of salt, ground mustard, and ground black pepper, one tablespoonful of cloves and allspice. Mix all together and stew until tender, stirring often lest they should scorch. Put up in small glass jars. A good sauce for all kinds of meat or fish.

To Keep Tomatoes Whole.

Fill a large stone jar with ripe tomatoes, then add a few whole cloves and a little sugar; cover them well with one-half cold vinegar and half water; place a piece of flannel over the jar well down in the vinegar, then tie down with paper. In this way tomatoes can be kept a year. Should mildew collect on the flannel it will not hurt them in the least.

Pickled Tomatoes.

Let the tomatoes be thoroughly ripe and let them lie in strong salt and water for three or four days; then put them down in layers in jars, mixing with them small onions and pieces of horseradish; then pour on vinegar, cold, after having spiced it. Use plenty of spice, cover carefully, and let stand for a month before using.

CHAPTER XVII.

PRESERVES.

PRESERVED APPLES FOR TEA.

MAKE a nice syrup of sugar and water, and put in some small pieces of ginger root or the yellow of orange peel; have some good firm apples pared and halved—pippins are best—and when the syrup has boiled up three or four times and been skimmed, drop in the apples and cook until transparent, but they must not go to pieces. Let them be quite cold before eaten, and good cream greatly improves it.

APPLE PRESERVES.

Take three-fourths pound of sugar to each pound of apples; make a syrup of the sugar and water, and a little lemon juice or sliced lemon; skim off all scum and put a few apples at a time into the syrup and boil until they are transparent; skim out and put in a jar. When all are done, boil the syrup down thick; pour boiling hot over the apples and cover closely. Well-flavored fruit not easily broken should be selected.

APRICOT PRESERVES.

Proceed the same as for preserving peaches, save that apricots, having a smooth, thin skin, do not require paring.

CITRON PRESERVES.

Pare and take out the seeds and cut them in pieces one inch thick and two inches in length; weigh them and put into a preserving kettle and cook them until they are clear, or steam them, then make a syrup of their weight in sugar with water and add two sliced lemons for each pound of fruit; put the citron into the syrup, a part at a time, and boil about fifteen minutes; skim out and put into a jar. When all has been thus cooked, boil the syrup down thick, and pour over it. Cover closely with paper which the air cannot penetrate, or use air-tight jars.

Citron Preserves, No. 2.

First, peel and cut the citron in pieces an inch square; then boil in water until soft; drain off the water and add one pound of sugar to each pound of citron; to every five pounds of the preserve add one pound of raisins, one lemon sliced, half an ounce of white cloves, one ounce of stick cinnamon; dissolve the sugar, and when hot, add the fruit and simmer slowly for two hours.

Currant Preserves.

Take ten pounds of currants and seven pounds of sugar; pick the stems from seven pounds of the currants and press the juice from the other three pounds; when the juice and sugar are made into a hot syrup, put in the currants and boil until thick and rich.

Brandied Cherries or Berries.

Make a syrup of a pound of sugar and a half gill of water for every two pounds of fruit. Heat to boiling, stirring to prevent burning, and pour over the fruit while warm—not hot. Let them stand together an hour; put all into a preserving kettle, and heat slowly; boil five minutes, take out the fruit with a perforated skimmer, and boil the syrup twenty minutes. Add a pint of brandy for every five pounds of fruit; pour over the berries hot, and seal.

Lemon Preserves.

One pound of pounded loaf sugar, quarter pound of butter, six eggs and the whites of four, well beaten, the rind of two lemons, grated, and the juice of three. Mix together and let it simmer till of the consistency of honey. Be careful to stir all the time or it will burn.

Preserved Oranges.

Take any number of oranges, with rather more than their weight in white sugar. Slightly grate the oranges and score them round and round with a knife, but do not cut very deep. Put them in cold water for three days, changing the water two or three times a day. Tie them up in a cloth, boil them until they are soft enough for the head of a pin to penetrate the skin. While they are boiling place the sugar on the fire, with rather more than half a pint of water to each pound; let it boil for a minute or two, then strain it through muslin. Put the oranges into the syrup till it jellies and is a yellow color. Try the syrup by putting some to cool. It must not be too stiff. The syrup need not cover the oranges, but they must be turned, so that each part gets thoroughly done.

Preserved Pine-Apple.

Pare, cut into slices, take out the core of each one, and weigh, allowing pound for pound of sugar and fruit. Put in alternate layers in the kettle and pour in water, allowing a cup to each pound of sugar. Heat to a boil; take out the pine-apple and spread upon dishes in the sun. Boil and skim the syrup half an hour. Return the pine-apple to the kettle and boil fifteen minutes. Take it out, pack in wide-mouth jars, pour on the scalding syrup; cover to keep in the heat, and, when cold, tie up, first putting brandied tissue paper upon the top.

To Preserve Plums or Cherries.

Make a syrup of clean, brown sugar, and clarify it; when perfectly clear and boiling hot, pour it over the plums, having picked out all the unsound ones and stems. Let them remain in the syrup two days, then drain it off; make it boiling hot, skim it, and pour it over again; let them remain another day or two, then put them into a preserving kettle over the fire, and simmer gently until the syrup is reduced, and thick or rich. One pound of sugar to each pound of plums. Small damsons are very fine preserved, as are cherries, or any other ripe fruit. Clarify the syrup, and when boiling hot, put in the plums; let them boil very gently until they are cooked, and the syrup rich. Put them in pots or jars the next day; secure as directed.

Purple Plums Preserved.

Take an equal weight of fruit and nice sugar. Take a clean stone jar and fill it with the fruit and sugar in layers. Cover them and set the jar in a kettle of water over the fire. Let them stand in the boiling water all day, filling up the kettle as the water boils away. If at any time they seem likely to ferment, repeat this process. It is a simple and excellent way of preserving plums.

To Preserve Pears.

Pare them very thin, and simmer in a thin syrup; let them lie a day or two. Make the syrup richer and simmer again. Repeat this till they are clear; then drain and dry them in the sun or a cool oven a little time; or they may be kept in the syrup and dried as wanted, which makes them richer.

Brandy Peaches.

Drop the peaches in hot water, let them remain till the skin can be ripped off; make a thin syrup, and let it cover the fruit; boil the fruit till they can be pierced with a straw; take it out, make a very rich syrup, and add, after it is taken from the fire, and while it is still hot, an equal quantity of brandy. Pour this, while it is still warm, over the peaches in the jar. They must be covered with it.

Peach Preserves.

Take any nice peaches that will not cook to pieces, pare them and take out the pits; take their weight in sugar, or, if they are to be canned, three-fourths pound of sugar to each pound of fruit, and a coffee-cup of water to each pound of sugar. Boil part of the pits in the water until the flavor is extracted, then remove the pits; add about as much water as has evaporated, then add the sugar; skim thoroughly, then add a small quantity of fruit at a time, cook slowly for about ten minutes, skim out into a jar, then add more. When all are done, pour the boiling syrup over them. The next day drain off the syrup and boil again and pour back; do the same for two or three days, then make them air-tight with paper as directed for jellies; or, if to be sealed in cans, the first boiling is sufficient. Cling stone peaches are preserved the same way, whole, except that they must be cooked longer.

QUINCE PRESERVES.

Pare and core the quinces, and cut into halves or quarters, as suits the size of your jars; let them stand over night in enough cold water to cover them; in the morning put them in the kettle with the same water and let them cook gently until you can just stick a fork in them; take the fruit out with a skimmer, weigh it and to each pound of fruit allow a pound of sugar; put the fruit and sugar into the kettle, with enough of the water to make a good syrup, and let them boil gently until they are clear; take out carefully with the skimmer and put into the jars; fill the jars to the top with the syrup. If there is a large quantity of fruit, and the kettle is not large, it is best to put the fruit in the syrup a little at a time.

PRESERVING STRAWBERRIES.

Select the largest and finest strawberries. Hull them, weigh and allow to each pound one pound of the best double refined loaf sugar finely powdered. Divide the sugar into two equal portions. Put a layer of strawberries into the bottom of a preserving kettle and cover them with a layer of sugar, until half the sugar is in; next set the kettle over a moderate fire and let it boil till the sugar is melted; then put in, gradually, the remainder of the sugar, and, after it is all in, let it boil hard for five minutes, taking off the scum with a silver spoon; but there will be little or no scum if the sugar is of the very best quality. Afterwards remove the kettle from the fire and take out the strawberries very carefully in a spoon. Spread out the strawberries on large, flat dishes, so as not to touch each other, and set them immediately in a cold place or on ice. Hang the kettle again on the fire, and give the syrup one boil up, skimming it if necessary. Place a fine strainer over the top of a mug or pitcher, and pour the syrup through it. Then put the strawberries into glass jars or tumblers; pour into each an equal portion of the syrup. Lay at the top a round piece of white paper dipped in brandy. Seal the jars tightly.

Raspberries may be preserved as above; also large ripe gooseberries. To each pound of gooseberries allow one and a half pounds sugar. Bury them in a box of sand, or keep in a dark, cool place.

GREEN TOMATO PRESERVES.

Eight pounds small, green tomatoes; pierce each with a fork; seven pounds sugar, juice of four lemons, one ounce of ginger and mace mixed; heat all together slowly and boil until the fruit is clear; remove from kettle with skimmer and spread upon dishes to cool; boil the syrup thick; put the fruit in jars and cover with hot syrup.

RIPE TOMATO PRESERVES.

Seven pounds round yellow or egg tomatoes, peeled, seven pounds sugar, juice of three lemons; let them stand together over night, drain off the syrup and boil it, skimming well; put in the tomatoes, and boil gently twenty minutes; take out the fruit with a perforated skimmer and spread upon dishes; boil the syrup down until it thickens, adding, just before taking it up, the juice of three lemons; put the fruit into the jars and fill up with hot syrup. When cold, seal up.

SPICED CURRANTS.

Four quarts ripe currants, three pounds brown sugar, one pint cider vinegar, one tablespoonful each of allspice and cloves, and a little nutmeg and cinnamon. Boil one hour, stirring occasionally.

SPICED GOOSEBERRIES.

Six quarts of gooseberries, ripe or green, nine pounds of sugar, one pint of vinegar (not too strong), one tablespoonful each of

14

cinnamon, cloves and allspice. Put the berries in the kettle with half the sugar and a little water; boil an hour and a half. When nearly done, add the rest of the sugar; set it off the fire and add the spices and vinegar.

SPICED GRAPES.

Five pounds of grapes, three of sugar, two teaspoonfuls of cinnamon and allspice, half teaspoonful of cloves; pulp grapes; boil until tender; cook pulps and strain through a sieve; add to it the spices, put in sugar, spices and vinegar to taste; boil thoroughly and cool.

SPICED NUTMEG MELON.

Select melons not quite ripe; open, scrape out the pulp, peel and slice; put the fruit in a stone jar, and, for five pounds of fruit take a quart of vinegar and two and a half pounds of sugar; scald vinegar and sugar together, and pour over the fruit; scald the syrup and pour over the fruit for eight successive days. On the ninth, add one ounce of stick cinnamon, one of whole cloves, and one of allspice; scald fruit, vinegar and spices together, and seal up in jars. This pickle should stand two or three months before using. Blue plums are very nice prepared in this way.

SPICED PEACHES.

Five pounds peaches, two of brown sugar, one quart vinegar, one ounce each of cinnamon, cloves, and mace. Wipe the peaches and boil until done in the vinegar and sugar, then take out, put in spices, boil well and pour over.

SPICED PLUMS.

Spiced plums are delicious with cold meat. Cook the plums in a little water until they are soft; then, so far as possible, remove the stones, sweeten and spice to your taste, and boil until thick; put in large-mouthed bottles and seal, or can in the usual way.

Spiced Plums, No. 2.

Nine pounds blue plums, six pounds sugar, two quarts vinegar, one ounce cinnamon; boil vinegar, sugar and spice together, pour over plums, draw off next morning and boil; pour back on plums; repeat the boiling five mornings, the last time boiling the fruit about twenty minutes.

CHAPTER XVIII.

VEGETABLES.

THE following excellent remarks on the cooking of vegetables are from the pen of Miss Corson:

Spinach is an excellent dish when well cooked; take two quarts, wash, boil for two minutes in salted boiling water, drain, chop and heat in a frying-pan for two minutes with an ounce each of butter and flour; half a pint of meat broth is added, the compound is stirred and heated for five minutes, and served with small pieces of fried bread. Second only to spinach are beet sprouts; we all know them boiled, but after they are boiled they gain in flavor by being fried for two or three minutes in butter. New cabbage scalded for five minutes in fast boiling water, coarsely chopped, sprinkled with flour, salt and pepper, and gently stewed for five minutes with milk or cream enough to cover it, is good. So, too, is red cabbage sliced, thrown for fifteen minutes into scalding salted water and vinegar, then drained and fried five minutes with butter, and served with a little hot meat gravy. Lettuce, which seems devoted to "salad days," is excellent stuffed; it is well washed in salted cold water, the roots trimmed off, two tablespoonfuls of cooked force-meat of any kind, or chopped cold meat highly seasoned, inclosed within the leaves, which are bound together with tape or strips of cloth; several heads thus prepared are placed in a saucepan, covered with broth or cold gravy well seasoned, and set over the fire to simmer about five minutes; the tapes are then removed and the lettuce heads and sauce are served hot. A link between cabbage and lettuce are Brussels sprouts, those tender, baby cabbages, which, stewed in cream, or quickly fried in butter, almost incline one's thoughts to vegetarianism.

Beets are familiar enough boiled and sliced, either served hot with butter, pepper and salt, or pickled, but a novelty is a beet pudding, made by mixing a pint of cooked sugar beets, chopped, with four eggs, a quart of milk, a little salt and pepper, a table-spoonful of butter, and baking them about half an hour. Cold boiled beets sliced and fried with butter are palatable; to cook them so that none of their color shall be lost, carefully wash them without breaking the skin or cutting off the roots or stalks, and boil them until tender, about an hour, in boiling salted water.

Turnips, either white or yellow, stewed in gravy, are excellent. Choose a quart of small, even size; peel them; boil fifteen minutes in well salted boiling water; drain them; put them into a frying-pan with sufficient butter to prevent burning; brown them; stir in a tablespoonful of flour; cover them with hot water; add a palatable seasoning of salt and pepper, and stew them gently until tender. Or peel and cut them in small regular pieces; brown them over the fire with a little butter and a slight sprinkling of sugar; add salt and pepper and boiling water enough to cover them, and gently stew them until tender; serve them hot.

Parsnips are not sufficiently appreciated, perhaps because of their too sweet taste; but this can be overcome to a palatable extent by judicious cookery; they are excellent when sliced, after boiling, and warmed in a sauce made by mixing flour, butter and milk, over the fire, and seasoning it with salt and pepper; as soon as warm they are served with a little chopped parsley and a squeeze of lemon juice. For parsnips fried brown in an old-fashioned iron pot with slices of salt pork and a seasoning of salt and pepper, several good words might be said.

Carrots boiled and mashed and warmed with butter, pepper and salt deserve to be known; or sliced and quickly browned in butter; or tossed for five minutes over the fire with chopped onion, parsley, butter, seasonings and sufficient gravy to moisten them; or boiled, quartered, heated with cream, seasoned, and, at the moment of serving, thickened with the yolk of eggs.

Onions are capital when sliced and quickly fried in plenty of smoking hot fat, or roasted whole until tender, and served with butter, pepper and salt; or chosen while still small, carefully peeled without breaking, browned in butter, and then simmered tender with just boiling water enough to cover them; or boiled tender in broth and then heated five minutes in nicely seasoned cream.

Oyster plant, scraped under cold water, boiled tender in salted water containing a trace of vinegar, and then heated with a little highly seasoned melted butter, is excellent; the tender leaves which it often bears make a nice salad. Somewhat like oyster plant are Jerusalem artichokes, which are good and cheap in this market. Like oyster plant, they must be peeled under water, boiled tender, and then served with melted butter, or quickly browned in butter, either plain or with chopped herbs, or served with an acid sauce of any kind.

Celery we know best in its uncooked state, but it is very good stewed in any brown or white gravy or sauce, or rolled in fritter batter and fried brown.

Squash and pumpkin are very good either boiled, sliced, and broiled or fried, or made into fritters like oyster plant.

Potatoes, most important of all hardy vegetables. Lives there a cook with soul so dead as not to be willing to expend all the powers of fire, water and salt to produce mealy potatoes? If so, the writing of her epitaph would be a cheerful task. And if cold ones are left they can rehabilitate themselves in favor by appearing chopped, moistened with white sauce or cream, and either fried in butter or baked quickly, with a covering of bread crumbs. Steam-fried, that is sliced raw, put into a covered pan over the fire, with butter and seasoning, and kept covered until tender, with only enough stirring to prevent burning, they are capital. To fry them Lyonnaise style they are cooled in their jackets to keep them whole, sliced about a quarter of an inch thick, browned in butter with a little sliced onion, sprinkled with chopped parsley, pepper and salt, and served hot. Larded, they have bits of fat ham or bacon inserted in them, and are baked tender. Note well that the more expeditiously a baked potato is cooked and eaten the better it will be.

Boiling is the ordinary mode of cooking vegetables. The rule is to throw them (whether the roots, flowers, foliage, or unripe seeds) into cold water, after trimming or other preparation; to let them lie there, if shriveled or drooping, until they have recovered their natural crispness; then to throw them into soft water, or, if hard water, made soft by the addition of a small pinch of carbonate of soda; to keep them boiling without the lid (with roots this is immaterial, though it is one means of keeping greens a good color); to remove all scum as it rises; to cook them enough; and to take them up as soon as they are done through, instead of leaving them to seethe, and lose their natural juices in the water.

To this there are exceptions. Peas and beans may be thrown into cold water when they are dried, but when green are best not thrown into cold water; and the former should be boiled in the least quantity of water possible. Potatoes require different treatment, according to their kind and the soil in which they grew. Very mealy or large potatoes, if thrown into boiling water, will fall to pieces outside, while still raw in the center; while small, firm, or waxy varieties are best thrown into boiling salt water. If you buy of the grower, he will often tell you what treatment suits them. At any rate, an experiment both ways will soon settle the difficulty. But the qualities of potatoes vary, not only with soil and kind, but also with the period in the season. We have known potatoes, waxy and watery when first dug up, become light and floury in February and March, after the eyes have sprouted three or four inches. The reason is plain: Superabundant moisture had been drawn off, and the starch, which forms one of its component elements, had had time to mature itself.

How to Cook Potatoes.

It is well known that a good potato may be spoiled by bad cooking; and by good management a bad one may be rendered comparatively good. In fact, no vegetable depends more on the cooking than a potato. In the first place, if the skin is taken off them before boiling, it should not be peeled, but scraped, for the following reasons: If peeled, it is reduced in size considerably; besides, the outside removed is the very best part of the root. An iron saucepan is preferable to a tin one for cooking them, as it prevents their boiling so fast; but the best way is, first to wash them very clean, then to put them on the fire with just cold water enough to cover them; when it has begun to boil, throw in a handful of salt, and add a pint of cold water, which checks their boiling and gives them time to be done through, without allowing them to crack. As soon as done, rather under than over, which may be ascertained with a fork, pour the water off from them, and replace the pan on the fire for a short time, until the remaining moisture is evaporated. If not immediately wanted, do not place the lid upon them, or the steam will be confined, but cover them with a cloth. New potatoes require great caution not to over-boil them, or they will be tasteless and watery.

Artichokes (Jerusalem), Fried.

Pare and cut the artichokes into slices about an eighth of an inch in thickness, and fry them in sufficient boiling oil or lard for them to swim in until they are a rich brown. Strew a little salt over them, pile high on a dish, and send to the table hot.

They may also be peeled and cut pear-shaped and stewed in a little salt water, to which a little butter has been added, and used as a garnish for a dish of mashed potatoes.

Asparagus, Boiled.

Choose bunches of asparagus which have been cut fresh and the heads straight. If the cut end is brown and dry, and the heads bent on one side, the asparagus is stale. It may be kept a day or two with the stalks in cold water, but is much better fresh. Scrape off the white skin from the lower end, and cut the stalks of equal length; let them lie in cold water until it is time to cook them; put a handful of salt into a gallon of water, and let it boil; tie the asparagus into bundles and put them into it; toast a slice of bread brown on each side, dip it in the water, and lay it on a dish. When the asparagus is sufficiently cooked, dish it on the toast, leaving the white ends outward each way. Serve with melted butter.

ASPARAGUS, FRICASSEED.

Wash twenty-five heads of asparagus, cut off the tender portion and lay them into cold water until they are required. Drain them and chop them with a young head of lettuce, half a head of endive and a small onion. Put a piece of butter the size of an egg into a saucepan, melt it, then mix with it smoothly a dessert-spoonful of flour, and half a pint of stock. Add the chopped vegetables, with pepper and salt, and let all stew gently until the sauce is thick and good. Serve hot. Time to stew, half an hour.

EGG BROCCOLI.

Take half a dozen heads of broccoli, cut off the small shoots or blossoms and lay them aside for frying; trim the stalks short and pare off the rough rind up to the head; wash them well, and lay them in salt water for an hour; then put them into plenty of boiling water (salted) and let them boil fast till quite tender. Put two ounces of butter into a saucepan, and stir it over a slow fire till it is melted; then add gradually six or eight well-beaten eggs, and stir the mixture until it is thick and smooth. Lay the broccoli in the center of a large dish, pour the egg around it, and having fried the broccoli blossoms, arrange them in a circle near the edge of the dish.

BEETS AND POTATOES.

One of the most delicious ways to serve these early vegetables is this: Take new potatoes and young beets, boil until done in separate kettles, then slice into the dish in which they are to be put on the table; first put a layer of potatoes, sprinkled with pepper and salt and little lumps of butter, then a layer of beets, treated in the same way, and so on until the dish is full, then pour over all a very little sweet cream or milk.

Lima Beans.

Shell, wash, and put into boiling water with a little salt; when boiled tender, drain and season them, and either dress with cream or large lump of butter, and let simmer for a few moments.

String Beans.

Choose fine young beans, and be careful they are the right sort. The best kind is the case-knife, because they have no strings and need only to be broken in two and not cut. Should these not be obtainable take the youngest that can be procured; remove the thread or string that runs along the pod, then cut them in a slanting direction lengthwise in very thin slices, throw them into boiling water well salted, and to preserve their color boil without the lid of the saucepan. When tender, drain in a colander, put in a small piece of butter and a dash of pepper, and give the whole a shake. This dish may be varied in a great many ways and with great success. Cold beans, with oil and vinegar, make an excellent and refreshing salad. They may also, when cooked and drained, be mixed with some good brown gravy, and served alone as a course after the meat.

Brussels Sprouts.

Pick, trim, and wash a number of sprouts. Put them into plenty of fast boiling water; add a tablespoonful of salt, keep the saucepan uncovered and boil very fast for fifteen minutes. Drain as soon as done and serve with melted butter.

Stewed Carrots.

Scrape and boil whole forty-five minutes. Drain and cut into round slices a quarter of an inch thick. Put on a cup of weak broth—a little soup if you have it—and cook half an hour. Then add three or four tablespoonfuls of milk, a lump of butter rolled in flour, with seasoning to taste. Boil up and dish.

CELERY.

Wash, trim, and scrape the stalks, selecting those that are white and tender. Crisp by leaving in ice cold water until they are wanted for the table. Arrange neatly in a celery glass. Pass between the oysters and the meat.

FRIED CELERY.

Boil the celery entire until tender; drain it, divide into small pieces and fry in dripping until lightly browned.

STEWED CELERY.

Clean the heads thoroughly. Take off the coarse, green, outer leaves. Cut in small pieces, and stew in a little broth. When tender, add some rich cream, a little flour, and butter enough to thicken the cream. Season with pepper, salt, and a little nutmeg if that is agreeable.

CREAM CABBAGE.

Beat together the yolks of two eggs, one-half cup of sugar, one-half cup of vinegar, butter size of an egg, salt and a little Cayenne pepper. Put the mixture into a saucepan and stir until it boils; then stir in one cup of cream; let it boil, and pour over the cabbage while hot.

CABBAGE A LA CAULIFLOWER.

Cut the cabbage fine as for slaw; put it into a stewpan, cover with water and keep closely covered; when tender, drain off the water; put in a small piece of butter with a piece of salt, one-half a cup of cream, or one cup of milk. Leave on the stove a few minutes before serving.

BOILED CABBAGE.

Cut off the stalk, remove the faded and outer leaves, and halve, or, if large, quarter the cabbages; wash them thoroughly and lay them for a few minutes in water, to which a tablespoonful of vinegar has been added, to draw out any insects that may be lodging under the leaves. Drain them in a colander; have ready a large pan of boiling hot water, with a tablespoonful of salt and a small piece of soda in it, and let the cabbage boil quickly until tender, leaving the saucepan uncovered. Take them up as soon as they are done, drain them thoroughly and serve. Time to boil: young summer cabbages, from ten to fifteen minutes; large cabbages, half an hour or more.

Baked Cabbage.

Cook as for boiled cabbage, after which drain and set aside until cold. Chop fine, add two beaten eggs, a tablespoonful of butter, pepper, salt, three tablespoonfuls rich cream; stir well and bake in a buttered dish until brown. Eat hot.

Hot Slaw.

One small, firm head of cabbage, shred fine, one cup of vinegar, one tablespoonful of butter, one tablespoonful of sugar, two tablespoonfuls of sour cream, one-half teaspoonful of made mustard, one saltspoonful of pepper, and the same of salt. Put the vinegar and all the other ingredients for the dressing, except the cream, in a saucepan and heat to a boil; pour scalding hot over the cabbage; return to the saucepan, and stir and toss until all is smoking again; take from the fire, stir in the cream, turn into a covered dish and set in hot water ten minutes before you send to the table.

Cauliflower.

This favorite vegetable should be cut early, while the dew is still upon it; choose those that are close and white, and of medium size. Whiteness is a sign of quality and freshness. Great care should be taken that there are no caterpillars about the stalk, and to insure this, lay the vegetable with its head downward in cold salt and water for an hour before boiling it; or, better still, in cold vinegar and water. Trim away the outer leaves, and cut the stalks quite close. Cauliflowers are in season from the middle of June till the middle of November.

Cauliflower a la Francaise.

After preparing as above, cut the cauliflower into quarters and put into a stewpan and boil until tender; drain and arrange it neatly on a dish. Pour over it melted butter.

Cauliflower with Stuffing.

Take a saucepan the exact size of the dish intended to be used. Cleanse a large, firm, white cauliflower and cut it into sprigs; throw those into boiling salt water for two minutes; then take them out, drain, and pack them tightly with the heads downwards, in the saucepan, the bottom of which must have been previously covered with thin slices of bacon; fill up the vacant spaces with a stuffing made of three tablespoonfuls of finely minced veal, the same of beef suet, four tablespoonfuls of bread crumbs, a little pepper and salt, a teaspoonful of chopped parsley, a teaspoonful of minced chives, and a dozen small mushrooms, chopped fine. Strew these ingredients over the cauliflowers in alternate layers, and pour over them three well-beaten eggs. When these are well soaked, add sufficient nicely-flavored stock to cover the whole; simmer gently till the cauliflowers are tender, and the sauce very much reduced; then turn the contents of the saucepan upside down on a hot dish, and the cauliflowers will be found standing in a savory mixture.

Cauliflower with Sauce.

Boil a large cauliflower—tied in netting—in hot salted water, from twenty-five to thirty minutes; drain, serve in a deep dish with the flower upwards and pour over it a cup of drawn butter in which has been stirred the juice of a lemon and a half teaspoonful of French mustard, mixed up well with the sauce.

Corn, for Winter Use.

Cut the corn from the cob (raw) before it gets too hard; to each gallon of cut corn add two scant cups of salt, pack tightly in a jar (don't be afraid of getting the jar too large), cover with a white cloth, put a heavy weight to keep the corn under the brine which soon forms; now the most important part is to wash the cloth every morning for two weeks, or the corn will taste queerly. If the corn is too salty, freshen before cooking. This is as good as canned corn, and is much easier put up. Put tomatoes in jugs and seal with good corks and sealing wax; get a large funnel, and you can put up as fast and as much as you please.

Baked Corn.

Grate one dozen ears sweet corn; one cup milk, small piece butter; salt, and bake in pudding dish one hour.

Green Corn on the Cob.

Take off the outside leaves and the silk, letting the innermost leaves remain on until after the corn is boiled, which renders the corn much sweeter. Boil for half an hour in plenty of water, drain, and, after removing the leaves, serve.

Corn Oysters.

Eight ears of sweet corn, grated; two cups of milk, three eggs, salt and pepper; flour enough to make a batter. Put a tablespoonful of butter into a frying pan and drop the mixture into the hot butter—a spoonful in a place; brown on both sides. Serve hot for breakfast or as a side dish for dinner.

Stewed Corn.

Stew one quart of canned corn in its own liquor, setting the vessel containing it in an outer one of hot water; should the corn be dry, add a little cold water; when tender, pour in enough milk to cover the corn, bring to a boil, and put in a tablespoonful of butter rolled in flour, and salt to taste. Stew gently, stirring well, three or four minutes and turn into a deep dish. Keep the vessel containing the corn closely covered while it is cooking; the steam facilitates the process and preserves the color of the corn.

Stewed Cucumbers.

Cut the cucumbers fully half an inch thick right through; put

them in a saucepan, just covering them with hot water, and let them
boil slowly for a quarter of an hour, or until tender, but not so as
to break them; then drain them; you want now a pint of good cream,
and put your cream, with a teaspoonful of butter, in a saucepan,
and when it is warm put in the cucumbers; season with a little salt
and white pepper, cook five minutes, shaking the saucepan all the
time, and serve hot. It is just as delicate as asparagus, and a very
nice dish indeed.

CELERY.

This vegetable imparts an agreeable and peculiar flavor to soups,
sauces, etc. It is generally eaten raw, the brittle stalks with salt;
but there are many ways in which it may be nicely prepared, and
when cooked it is more digestible and equally palatable. When
the roots are not to be had, the pounded seed is an excellent substitute for flavoring. It is in season from October to February, and
is better when it has been touched by the frost.

FRIED CELERY.

Cold boiled celery will answer for this purpose. Split the heads
and dip them into clarified butter, or dip them into a batter, and
fry a light brown. Garnish the dish prettily with parsley.

CARROTS.

This vegetable should be served with boiled beef. When the
carrots are young they should be washed and rubbed, not scraped,
before cooking, then rubbed with a clean, coarse cloth after boiling.
Young carrots need to be cooked about half an hour, and full grown
ones from one hour and a half to two hours. They are excellent
for flavoring, and contain a great amount of nourishment.

CARROTS BOILED.

Wash and prepare the carrots. Throw them into plenty of
boiling water with salt. Keep them boiling till tender, and serve
with melted butter; or they may be boiled with beef and a few
placed round the dish to garnish, and the rest sent to table in a
tureen.

DANDELIONS.

Cut off the leaves, pick over carefully, wash thoroughly, put into boiling water and boil a half hour; drain well and put into salted boiling water and boil till tender. When done drain in a colander, season with butter, salt and pepper; or they may be boiled with salt pork or corned beef, omitting the butter. They are good from early spring until they blossom.

ENDIVE STEWED.

Strip off the outer green leaves from the heads of endive. Wash thoroughly, soak in salted water to dislodge the insects; then drain and boil for twenty-five minutes in water salted slightly. Have ready a stewpan with an ounce of butter, drain the endive and put it into the pan, and add a saltspoonful of salt, pepper, and a gill of cream. Serve hot.

EGG PLANT.

Pare and cut in slices half an inch thick; sprinkle with salt; cover and let stand for an hour. Rinse in clear cold water; wipe each slice dry; dip first in beaten egg, then in rolled cracker or bread crumbs. Season with pepper and salt, and fry brown in butter.

EGG PLANT, No. 2.

Boil until quite tender, then mash and add bread crumbs, pepper, salt, onions and butter or lard; put in a pan and bake until brown. You can put in all these things to your own taste, then you can boil and mash as before; season with salt and pepper, and add a little flour or meal as you like best. Make into little cakes and fry. These are nice. They should be picked when full grown, but before they are ripe.

FRICASSEED EGG PLANT.

Having peeled and sliced the egg plants, boil them in water with a saltspoonful of salt, until they are thoroughly cooked. Drain off the water, pour in sufficient milk to cover the slices, and add a few bits of butter rolled in flour; let it simmer gently, shaking the pan over the fire till the sauce is thick, and stir in the beaten yolks of two or three eggs just before it is served.

Stuffed Egg Plants.

Halve and parboil. When soft enough to stick with a fork remove from the water and let cool. Then cut out the inside, being careful not to break the skin. Next take bread that has been previously soaked in water. Squeeze as dry as possible and mix with the pulp of the vegetable. Add to that a good sized tomato, the juice of an onion, a little parsley and two or three eggs, season with pepper and salt, and the filling is ready for use. Before putting into the stove sprinkle with toasted bread crumbs. Another and quicker way to make the stuffing is to mix the pulp with the juice of an onion, a tomato and a couple of eggs. Thicken with boiled rice and season to taste.

Garlic.

Garlic requires to be used most judiciously, or it will spoil whatever is cooked with it. If used carefully, however, it will impart a most delicious flavor to salads and sauces; but it is so strong that, for many dishes, all that is necessary is to rub the dish which is to be sent to table sharply round with a slice of it; or, better still, to rub it on a crust of bread, and put the bread into the soup, etc., for a few minutes. A very general prejudice exists against garlic, probably on account of its being used in the same way as an onion. If it is desired to diminish the strength of the flavor, this may be done by boiling the garlic in two or three waters.

Greens, Stewed.

Take a bunch of fresh greens, wash in several waters; drain them well and throw them into plenty of fast boiling water, salted and skimmed, and boil them for ten minutes. Take them up, press the water from them, and throw them into cold water for half an hour: drain them, cover with stock, and add a bunch of herbs, an onion,

15

one clove, a slice of fat bacon, and a little pepper and salt. Stew very gently until tender. Serve with mutton, lamb, or veal.

Horse-radish as Garnish.

Wash and scrub the horse-radish thoroughly; let it lie for an hour in cold water; then scrape it very finely with a sharp knife; arrange it in little bunches around the dish, or, if there is gravy with the meat, put it in a small glass dish near the carver.

Lettuce.

There are two sorts of lettuces, the cabbage and the cos. They are chiefly used for salad, but may be also boiled or stewed, and served as a vegetable. They may be had all the year, but are in full season from April to September.

Lettuce, Stuffed.

Wash four or five large heads of lettuce; boil them in plenty of salt and water for fifteen minutes; throw them at once into cold water, and afterwards let them drain. Open them, fill them with good veal forcemeat, tie the ends securely, and put them into a stewpan with as much good gravy as will cover them, a teaspoonful of salt, half a teaspoonful of pepper, and a teaspoonful of vinegar. Simmer gently for another fifteen minutes, remove the strings, place them on a hot dish, and pour the gravy around them.

Macaroni.

Three long sticks of macaroni, broken in small pieces; soak in a pint of milk two hours; grate bread and dried cheese. Put a layer of macaroni in a pudding dish; add pepper, salt and butter; then sprinkle the bread and cheese crumbs over it, and so continue until the dish is filled. Bake until brown.

Macaroni as a Vegetable.

Simmer one-half pound of macaroni in plenty of water till tender, but not broken; strain off the water. Take the yolks of five and the whites of two eggs, one-half pint of cream, white meat and ham chopped very fine, three spoonfuls of grated cheese; season with salt and pepper; heat all together, stirring constantly. Mix with the macaroni; put into a buttered mold and steam one hour.

MACARONI WITH OYSTERS.

Boil macaroni in salt water, after which draw through a colander; take a deep earthen dish or tin; put in alternate layers of macaroni and oysters; sprinkle the layers of macaroni with grated cheese; bake until brown.

MACARONI WITH TOMATOES.

Boil one-half pound of macaroni till tender, pour off all the water, then add one-half cup sweet cream, one-third of a cup of butter, pepper and salt; let simmer for a short time, but be careful that it does not become much broken; turn into vegetable dish; have ready one pint stewed tomatoes, season with butter, salt and pepper, pour over the macaroni.

STEWED MACARONI.

Boil two ounces of macaroni in water, and drain well; put into a saucepan one ounce of butter, mix with one tablespoonful of flour, moisten with four tablespoonfuls of veal or beef stock, one gill of cream, salt and white pepper to taste; put in the macaroni, let it boil up, and serve while hot.

BOILED ONIONS.

Skin them thoroughly. Put them to boil; when they have boiled a few minutes, pour off the water and add clean cold water, and set them to boil again. Pour this away, and add more cold water, when they may boil till done. This will make them white and clear, and very mild in flavor. After they are done, pour off all the water, and dress with a little cream; salt and pepper to taste.

Boil in two waters, drain, and if they are large, cut into quarters and pour over them a cup of scalding milk in which a pinch of soda has been stirred; set over the fire, add a tablespoonful of butter, half teaspoonful corn starch wet with milk, a little minced parsley, with pepper and salt. Simmer and pour out.

BOILED OKRA.

Put the young and tender pods of long, white okra into salted boiling water in a porcelain or tin-lined saucepan (as iron discolors it), boil fifteen minutes, take off stems, and serve with butter, pepper, salt and vinegar if preferred; or, after boiling, slice in rings, season with butter, dip in batter and fry; season and serve; or stew an equal quantity of tomatoes and tender sliced okra, and one or two sliced green peppers; stew in porcelain kettle fifteen or twenty minutes, season with butter, pepper and salt and serve.

ONION ORMOLOO.

Peel ten or twelve large white onions, steep them an hour in cold water, then boil them soft. Mash them with an equal quantity of boiled white potatoes, adding half a pint of milk and two or three well-beaten eggs. Stir the mixture very hard, season it with nutmeg, pepper and salt, and bake it in a quick oven; when half done pour a little melted butter or gravy over the top.

SCALLOPED ONIONS.

Boil till tender six large onions; afterward separate them with a large spoon; then place a layer of onion and a layer of grated bread crumbs alternately in a pudding dish; season with pepper and salt to taste; moisten with milk; put into the oven to brown.

Wash but do not peel the onions; boil one hour in boiling water slightly salt, changing the water twice in the time; when tender, drain on a cloth, and roll each in buttered tissue paper, twisted at the top, and bake an hour in a slow oven. Peel and brown them; serve with melted butter.

VEGETABLE OYSTER.

One bunch of oysters; boil and mash. One pint sour milk, half a teaspoonful soda; flour to make a batter; add two eggs, beaten, and the oysters. Fry in hot lard—drop in spoonfuls.

Mock Stewed Oysters.

One bunch oyster plant, eight teaspoonfuls butter, a little flour or corn starch, vinegar and water for boiling, pepper and salt, one-half cup milk. Wash and scrape the oyster plant very carefully; drop into weak vinegar and water, bring quickly to a boil, and cook ten minutes; turn off the vinegar water; rinse the salsify in boiling water; throw this out and cover with more from the tea-kettle; stew gently ten minutes longer; add pepper and salt and two tablespoonfuls of butter; stew in this until tender. Meanwhile heat in a farina kettle the milk, thicken, add the remaining butter, and keep dry until the salsify is done, then transfer it to this sauce; pepper and salt; let all lie together in the inner kettle, the water in the outer at a slow boil, for five minutes; pour into a covered dish.

Parsley.

The foliage of parsley is of use in flavoring soups, etc.; it is nutritious and stimulating.

Crisp Parsley.

This is used for garnishing dishes. Pick and wash young parsley, shake it in a cloth to dry it thoroughly, and spread it on a sheet of clean paper and put in the oven. Turn the bunches frequently until they are quite crisp. Parsley is much more easily crisped than fried.

Parsley, Fried.

Wash and dry the parsley thoroughly; put it into hot fat and let it remain until it is crisp; take it out immediately and drain it in a colander. If the parsley is allowed to remain in the fat one moment after it is crisp it will be spoiled. Parsley is best fried in a frying basket.

Parsnips.

Parsnips may be dressed in the same way as carrots, which they very much resemble. When boiled, they are generally served with boiled meat, or boiled salt fish; when fried, with roast mutton. If

young, they require only to be washed and scraped before they are
boiled. If old and large, the skin must be pared off, and the roots
cut into quarters. Carrots and parsnips are often sent to the table
together It should be remembered that parsnips are more quickly
boiled than carrots.

FRIED PARSNIPS.

Boil until tender in hot water slightly salted; let them get almost
cold, scrape off the skin, and cut in thick, long slices; dredge with
flour and fry in hot dripping, turning as they brown; drain very dry
in a hot colander; pepper and salt to serve.

PARSNIP STEW.

Three slices of salt pork, boil one hour and a half; scrape five
large parsnips, cut in quarters lengthwise, add to the pork and let
boil one-half hour, then add a few potatoes, and let all boil together
until the potatoes are soft; the fluid in the kettle should be about
a cupful when ready to take off.

CANNED PEASE.

Open a can of pease an hour before cooking them, that there may
be no musty, airless taste about them, and turn into a bowl. When
ready for them, put on a farina-kettle—or one saucepan within
another—of hot water. If dry, add cold water to cover them, and
stew about twenty-five minutes; drain, stir in a generous lump of
butter; pepper and salt.

FRENCH WAY OF COOKING PEASE.

Put your pease in a nice dish, where they will not turn black in
cooking. Cut up fine one small head of lettuce; put in a few sprigs
of parsley, tied up; salt and pepper; enough of water to cover the
pease. Cook gently until tender, one and three-quarters of an hour,
then drain off most of the water; dissolve one full teaspoonful of
flour in water and stir in; add one-half tablespoonful of butter,
one-half cup of sweet milk and one lump of sugar; cook about ten
minutes; just before serving stir in one yolk of an egg, previously
beaten with a little water.

No. 2.—Put some thin slices of bacon in a skillet and brown a little on both sides; then put in your pease, with one large onion cut in four, one head of lettuce, and a few sprigs of parsley, tied up, water enough to cover them; salt and pepper (not much salt, as the bacon salts them); cook one hour. Ten minutes before serving sprinkle a little flour to thicken the gravy. Remove the bunch of lettuce and parsley.

GREEN PEASE.

Boil a quart of young, freshly-gathered pease in slightly salted water until they are tender; then drain them in a colander. Melt two ounces of fresh butter over the fire, mix smoothly with a dessert-spoonful of flour, and add very gradually a cup of thick cream, or, failing this, use new milk. When the sauce boils, put in the pease, stir them until they are quite hot, and serve immediately.

POTATO BALLS.

Bake the potatoes, mash them very nicely, make them into balls, rub them over with the yolk of an egg, and put them in the oven or before the fire to brown. These balls may be varied by the introduction of a third portion of grated ham or tongue.

BROWNED POTATOES.

While the meat is roasting, and an hour before it is served, boil the potatoes and take off their skins; flour them well, and put them under the meat, taking care to dry them from the drippings before they are sent to the table. Kidney potatoes are best dressed in this way. The flouring is very essential. They should always be boiled a little before being put into stews, as the first water in which they are cooked is thought to be of a poisonous quality. Potatoes when boiled, if old, should be peeled and put whole upon the gridiron until nicely browned.

ENGLISH POTATO BALLS.

Boil some potatoes very dry; mash them as smoothly as possible; season well with salt and pepper; warm them, with an ounce of butter to every pound of potatoes, and a few spoonfuls of good cream; let them cool a little, roll them into balls; sprinkle over them some crushed vermicelli or macaroni, and fry them a light brown.

Southern Baked Potatoes.

Parboil, or take the cold ones left over from dinner; place in a deep pie pan; between each layer sprinkle sugar; over the top drop small drops of butter and more sugar, about one small cup of sugar and one spoonful of butter to a plate of potatoes. Then pour over all one-half cup of butter and set in oven to bake. The common pumpkin is delicious prepared in the same way, using, instead of sugar, syrup or molasses. The pumpkin must be thoroughly steamed before baking, and requires two hours' baking. Some cooks add spice.

Cream Potatoes.

Pare and cut the potatoes into small squares or rounds, cook twenty minutes in boiling water and a little salt. Turn this off, add a cup of milk, and when this bubbles up a tablespoonful of butter, with a teaspoonful of water, wet up with cold milk; also a little chopped parsley; simmer five minutes and pour out.

Potato Croquettes.

Take six boiled potatoes, pass them through a sieve; add to them three tablespoonfuls of ham grated or minced finely, a little grated nutmeg, pepper and salt to taste, and some chopped parsley; work into this mixture the yolks of three or four eggs, then fashion it into the shape of balls, roll them in bread crumbs, and fry in hot lard, and serve with fried parsley.

Potato Cake.

Take potatoes, mashed ones are best, but boiled ones can be mashed, immediately after dinner, before getting too cold; add about an equal amount of flour and a small piece of butter or lard; rub thoroughly together, roll out and cut as for biscuit—not too thick—and bake in a rather quick oven. When done to a light brown, cut open, butter and eat warm.

FRIED POTATOES.

Take cold boiled potatoes, grate them, make them into flat cakes, and fry them in butter. You may vary these cakes by dipping them in the beaten yolk of an egg and rolling them in bread crumbs, frying them in boiling lard.

FRIED POTATOES, No. 2.

Raw potatoes, peel, cut in rings the thickness of a shilling, or cut in one continuous shaving; throw them into cold water until you have sufficient; drain on a cloth; fry quickly in plenty of hot fat, and with as little color as possible; dry them well from the grease, and sprinkle with salt. When nicely done, and piled up properly, they make a fine side dish, which is always eaten with great relish.

Or cut a potato lengthwise the size and shape of the divisions of an orange, trim them neatly and fry them; they are an excellent garnish for meat. Cold potatoes may be cut in slices somewhat less than an inch thick, and fried in like manner. They can also be fried with onions, as an accompaniment to pork chops, sliced cod, red herring, or with a rasher of bacon.

Another nice way is to boil them and let them become cold, then cut them into rather thin slices. Put a lump of fresh butter into a stewpan, add a little flour, about a teaspoonful for a moderate-sized dish; when the flour has boiled a short time in the butter add a cup of water and a little cream; boil all together; then put in the potatoes covered with chopped parsley, pepper and salt; stew them for a few minutes, and then take them from the fire and send to the table.

MASHED POTATOES.

Steam or boil potatoes until soft, in salted water; pour off the water and let them drain perfectly dry; sprinkle with salt and mash; have ready some hot milk or cream in which has been melted a piece of butter; pour this on to the potatoes, and stir until white and very light.

POTATO SURPRISE.

Scoop out the inside of a sound potato, leaving the skin attached at one side of the hole, as a lid. Mince finely the lean of a juicy mutton chop with a little salt and pepper; put it in the potato, fasten down the lid, and bake or roast. Before serving (in its skin) add a little hot gravy if the mince seems too dry.

POTATO PUFF.

Take two cups of cold mashed potato, and stir into it two table-spoonfuls of melted butter, beating to a white cream before adding anything else. Then put with this two eggs whipped very light and a cup of cream or milk, salting to taste. Beat all well, pour into a deep dish, and bake in a quick oven until it is nicely browned.

POTATO PIE.

Butter a shallow pie dish rather thickly. Line the edges with a good crust, and then fill the pie with mashed potatoes, seasoned with pepper, salt, and grated nut-meg. Lay over them some marrow, together with small lumps of but-ter, hard-boiled eggs, blanched almonds, sliced dates, sliced lemon and candied peel. Cover the dish with pastry, and bake the pie in a well-heated oven for half an hour or more, according to the size of the pie.

PURÉE OF POTATOES.

Mash them and mix while quite hot with some fine white gravy drawn from veal, together with butter and cream. The purée should be rather thin and seasoned with salt and pepper.

POTATO LOAVES.

These are very nice when eaten with roast beef, and are made of mashed potatoes prepared without milk, by mixing them with a quantity of very finely-minced raw onions, powdered with pepper and salt; then beating up the whole with a little butter to bind it, and dividing it into small loaves of a conical form, and placing them under the meat to brown; that is, when it is so nearly done as to impart some of the gravy along with the fat.

Saratoga Potatoes.

Pare and cut into very thin slices four large potatoes (new potatoes are best); let stand for a few minutes in cold salt water, then take a handful of the potatoes, squeeze the water from them, dry in a napkin, and separating the slices, drop into a skillet of boiling lard, taking care that they do not stick together; stir till they are of a light brown color, take out with a wire spoon, drain well and serve immediately.

Lyonnaise Potatoes.

Boil the potatoes with their jackets on and allow them to cool in order to have them solid. Peel and cut into slices about a quarter of an inch thick; slice an ordinary sized onion for half a dozen potatoes. As soon as a tablespoonful of butter has melted in the pan, and the onion begun to color, put in the slices of potatoes. Stir them a little; season with salt and pepper; fry the potatoes until they are a golden brown, and then chop up a tablespoonful of parsley and sprinkle it over them just before taking them out.

Old Potatoes.

These can be made to look like young ones in this way: Wash some large ones and cut them into as many small slices as will fill a dish; boil them in two or three waters about three minutes each time, the water being put to them cold; then let them steam until tender; pour a white sauce over them. Potatoes prepared in this way have been mistaken for young ones.

Tossed Potatoes.

Boil some potatoes in their skins; peel them and cut into small pieces; toss them over the fire in a mixture of cream, butter rolled in flour, pepper and salt, till they are hot and well covered with the sauce.

Sweet Potatoes.

Sweet potatoes require more time to cook than common potatoes.

To Boil.—Take large, fine potatoes, wash clean, boil with the skins on in plenty of water, but without salt. They will take at least one hour. Drain off the water and set them for a few minutes in a tin pan before the fire, or in the stove, that they may be well dried. Peel them before sending them to the table.

To Fry.—Choose large potatoes, half boil them, and then, having taken off the skins, cut the potatoes into slices and fry in butter, or in nice drippings.

To Bake.—Bake as the common potato, except give them a longer time.

Baked Sweet Potatoes.

Select those which are nearly of a size, not too large; steam them until nearly done, and then bake them until they are soft at the heart.

A Farmer's Dainty Dish.

Peel and slice thin potatoes and onions (five potatoes to one small onion); take half a pound of sweet salt pork (in thin slices) to a pound of beef, mutton or veal; cut the meat in small pieces; take some nice bread dough and shorten a little; line the bottom of the stewpan with slices of pork, then a layer of meat, potatoes and onions, dust over a little pepper and cover with a layer of crust; repeat this until the stewpot is full. The size of the pot will depend on the number in the family. Pour in sufficient water to cover, and finish with crust. Let it simmer until meat, vegetables, etc., are done, but do not let it boil hard. Serve hot. This we are assured by one who knows is a dish fit to set before a king.

Rice as a Vegetable.

It should first be picked over, washed, and dried. Then put in boiling water, and salt and boil twelve minutes. There should be plenty of water. At the end of ten or twelve minutes, pour off the water, cover up the rice, and set on the back of the stove on a brick; let it steam there for fifteen minutes; if it has been in a sufficiently hot place to steam it will now be done, and every grain will be distinct; pour off the water, and, for every cup of rice, add half a cup of milk and stir. The milk is better warmed before adding it to the rice.

SUCCOTASH.

Ten ears green corn, one pint Lima beans; cut the corn from the cob, and stew gently with the beans until tender. Use as little water as possible. Season with butter, salt and pepper—milk, if you choose.

SPINACH.

When cooking spinach, substitute a little piece of bacon for the salt pork usually cooked with it to season it. The nicest way to serve it is to put a bit of the bacon in each dish. Hard-boiled eggs, sliced when cold, are also liked with the greens.

CREAM OF SPINACH.

Take the leaves of spinach—no stalks—wash thoroughly; put them into enough salt boiling water to cover them. When boiled tender, take them out and put them into cold water to fix the fresh green color. Let them remain until cold and then rub them through a colander with a potato-masher. The spinach is then ready for table use.

WINTER SQUASH.

Pare, cut up and cook soft in boiling water and a little salt. Drain, mash smooth, pressing out all the water; work in butter, pepper and salt, and mound in a deep dish.

STUFFED SQUASH.

Pare a small squash and cut off a slice from the top; extract the seeds and lay one hour in salt water; then fill with a good stuffing of crumbs, chopped salt pork, parsley, etc., wet with gravy; put on the top slice; set the squash in a pudding dish; put a few spoonfuls of melted butter and twice as much hot water in the bottom; cover the dish very closely and set in the oven two hours or until tender; lay within a deep dish and pour the gravy over it.

TURNIPS.

Pare and cut into pieces; put them into boiling water well salted, and boil until tender; drain thoroughly, and then mash and add a piece of butter, pepper and salt to taste, and a small teaspoonful of sugar. Stir until they are thoroughly mixed, and serve hot.

MASHED TURNIPS.

Pare, quarter and cook tenderly in boiling water; a little salt. Mash and press in a heated colander; work in butter, pepper and salt; heap smoothly in a deep dish and put pepper on top.

TOMATOES A LA CREAM.

Pare and slice ripe tomatoes—one quart of fresh ones or a pound can; stew until perfectly smooth, season with salt and pepper, and add a piece of butter the size of an egg; just before taking from the fire, stir in one cup of cream, with a tablespoonful of flour stirred smooth in a part of it; do not let it boil after the flour is put in. Have ready in a dish pieces of toast; pour the tomatoes over this and serve.

BROWNED TOMATOES.

Take large round tomatoes and halve them, place them, the skin side down, in a frying-pan in which a very small quantity of butter and lard have been previously melted, sprinkle them with salt and pepper, and dredge well with flour. Place the pan on a hot part of the fire, and let them brown thoroughly; then stir, and let them brown again, and so on until they are quite done. They lose their acidity, and their flavor is superior to stewed tomatoes.

BAKED TOMATOES.

One can of tomatoes, stale bread crumbed fine, one tablespoonful of butter, pepper, salt, a little chopped parsley, and white sugar. Drain off two-thirds of the liquor from the tomatoes (the rest can be saved for to-morrow's soup). Cover the bottom of a bake-dish with crumbs; lay the tomatoes evenly upon this bed; season with pepper, salt, sugar, and parsley, with bits of butter here and there. Strew bread crumbs over all, a thicker layer than at the bottom; put tiny pieces of butter upon this and bake, covered, about thirty-five minutes. Take off the cover and brown upon the upper shelf of the oven. Do not let it stay there long enough to get dry.

BAKED TOMATOES, No. 2.

Cut in slices good fresh tomatoes (not too ripe); put a layer of them in a dish suitable for baking; then a layer of bread crumbs over them, salt, pepper, and plenty of butter, another layer of tomatoes, and so on until the dish is full. Bake one hour.

BROILED TOMATOES.

Cut large tomatoes in two, crosswise; put on gridiron, cut surface down; when well seared, turn, and put butter, salt and pepper on, and cook with skin-side down until done.

FRIED TOMATOES.

Cut the tomatoes in slices without skinning; pepper and sa't them; then sprinkle a little flour over them and fry in butter until brown. Put them on a hot platter and pour milk or cream into the butter and juice. When boiling hot, pour over the tomatoes

SCALLOPED TOMATOES.

Butter an earthen dish, then put in a layer of fresh tomatoes, sliced and peeled, and a few rinds of onion (one large onion for the whole dish), then cover with a layer of bread crumbs, with a little butter, salt and pepper. Repeat this process until the dish is full. Bake for an hour in a pretty hot oven.

STUFFED TOMATOES.

Choose a dozen large, round tomatoes; cut them off smooth at the stem end; take out the seeds and pulp; take a pound of lean steak and two slices of bacon; chop them fine, with the inside of the tomatoes; season with a finely-chopped onion, fried, a dessert-spoonful of salt, half a teaspoonful of white pepper, as much Cayenne pepper as you can take on the end of a knife and a table-spoonful of finely-chopped parsley; add four rolled crackers, and if too stiff, thin with stock, water or cold gravy; fill the tomatoes with this forcemeat, packing tight; sift cracker crumbs over the top, and bake for an hour in a moderate oven.

French Batter for Frying Vegetables.

Moisten a little flour with water, and add to it a small quantity of salt, a tablespoonful of olive oil, and a spoonful and a half of French brandy. Beat up the mixture thoroughly, and, when you are ready to use it, beat into it the white of an egg previously beaten to a strong froth. This batter may be used for frying sweet *entremets*, in which case sugar must be used instead of salt.

Rules for Cooking Them.

Green vegetables should be thoroughly washed in cold water and then dropped into water that has been salted and is beginning to boil. There should be a tablespoonful of salt to each two quarts of water. If the water boils long before the vegetables are put in, it has lost all its gases, and the mineral ingredients are deposited on the bottom and sides of the kettle, so that the water is flat and tasteless, then the vegetables will not look well or have a fine flavor. The time for boiling green vegetables depends much upon the age and time they have been gathered. The younger and more freshly gathered the more quickly they are cooked. Below is a very good time-table for cooking vegetables:

> Potatoes boiled, thirty minutes.
> Potatoes baked, forty-five minutes.
> Sweet potatoes boiled, fifty minutes.
> Sweet potatoes baked, sixty minutes.
> Squash boiled, twenty-five minutes.
> Green pease boiled, twenty to forty minutes.
> Shelled beans boiled, sixty minutes.

String beans boiled, one to two hours.

Green corn, thirty to sixty minutes.

Asparagus, fifteen to thirty minutes.

Spinach, one to two hours.

Tomatoes, fresh, one hour.

Tomatoes, canned, thirty minutes.

Cabbage, forty-five minutes to two hours.

Cauliflower, one or two hours.

Dandelions, two or three hours.

Beet greens, one hour.

Onions, one or two hours.

Beets, one to five hours.

Turnips, white, forty-five to sixty minutes.

Turnips, yellow, one and a half to two hours

Parsnips, one or two hours.

Carrots, one or two hours.

CHAPTER XIX.

FISH.

ISH, when considered with reference to the nourishment which they contain, appear to rank between animals and vegetables. When fish is consumed as the principal article of food, larger quantities are required than when meat is used, owing to the smaller amount of nourishment that it contains. From this cause, and, also, because fish is so much more easily digested than meat, food is required much sooner after a meal of fish than when animal food is taken. Owing to its greater digestibility than meat, fish is better adapted to invalids, more especially as it does not produce feverishness like meat diet.

The most digestible kinds of fish are those with white flesh, such as the cod, turbot, sole, whiting, haddock and flounder, the flesh of all these presenting a whitish appearance. Of the fish just mentioned, the whiting, haddock and flounder are easiest of digestion.

The flesh of fish when in good condition is always fleshy and opaque; when it is of a bluish color, or appears slightly transparent after being boiled, it proves either that the fish is out of season, or of inferior quality.

Sometimes fish have been found to exert a poisonous action on the system, producing headache, giddiness, and an eruption on the skin resembling that produced by being stung with nettles. In some cases, even death has been caused by this means. Although it may be true in some cases, that the ill effects produced by fish may be due to the bad condition of health in which the patient happens to be at the time, yet in most cases it can only be attributed to some poisonous principle developed in the fish. This may be due to their being eaten in a season when the fish is out of health, and, therefore, unfit for food, or it may be produced by the poisonous nature of the food on which the fishes lived.

Oysters, when fresh and in season, are very nutritious; when, however, they have a bluish appearance, they are liable to produce affections of the bowels. Salmon contains much nourishment, which is due to the oily matter which its flesh contains; and for this reason this fish is less suited for invalids than the white kind.

Most kinds of fish lose their flavor soon after being taken from the water. The cod and one or two others are exceptions to this general rule. Fish are fresh when the eyes are clear, the fins stiff, the gills red, and without bad odor. Fresh shad have gills of quite a crimson red, bright scales and a firm body; and shad are unfit to eat when the gills are a whitish blue and the eyes are sunken. In a good salmon, when cut, the flesh should appear quite red, solid and flaky. The Dutch and French bleed the cod, which accounts for the better quality and whiteness of their codfish. All large fish, in fact, should be bled as soon as caught.

Almost every kind of fish is either boiled, broiled or fried. Any small fish of the size of a smelt, or smaller, is better fried than prepared in any other way. Fish like salmon trout are best when baked and some fine sauce poured over them. A cup of diluted cream, in which is stirred two tablespoonfuls of melted butter and a little chopped parsley, makes an excellent sauce for salmon trout.

Bass weighing from one-half pound to a pound are best fried; those weighing from one to three pounds are best broiled, and larger sizes are best when boiled. Very large bass are dry eating. They should be thoroughly cleansed, washed, and sprinkled with salt.

Before broiling fish, rub the gridiron with a piece of fat, to prevent its sticking. Lay the skin side down first.

The earthy taste often found in fresh-water fish can be removed by soaking in salt and water.

Most kinds of salt fish should be soaked in cold water for twenty-four hours—the fleshy side turned down in the water.

BAKED FISH.

Stuff it with plain dressing; put in a pan with a little water; salt, pepper, and butter. Baste while baking. A fish weighing four pounds will cook in an hour. Garnish with hard-boiled eggs and parsley, and serve with drawn butter or egg sauce.

TO BOIL FISH.

Sew them in a cloth, and put in cold water, with plenty of salt. Most fish will boil in thirty minutes.

BOILED FISH.

For four or five pounds of fish, nearly cover with water, and add two heaping tablespoonfuls of salt. Boil thirty minutes and serve with drawn butter.

BAKED BLACK FISH.

Rub a handful of salt over the surface, to remove the slime peculiar to the fish. For the stuffing, two ounces of beef drippings, two tablespoonfuls of chopped parsley, and one ounce of salt pork; put in a saucepan and fry brown; then add a teaspoonful of chopped capers, half a saltspoonful of white pepper, one-half teaspoonful of salt, five ounces of bread, and one gill of broth; then stir until scalding hot; place inside the fish; cut a quarter of a pound of pork in thin slices and lay on either side of the fish, holding in place by twine around it—a generous sprinkle of salt and pepper completing it for the baking pan. Bake in a hot oven one-half hour, and serve on slices of fried bread with a sauce made of stock seasoned with one tablespoonful each of walnut and Worcestershire sauce, one tablespoonful of chopped capers, and one tablespoonful of parsley.

BROOK TROUT.

If small, fry them with salt pork; if large, boil, and serve with drawn butter.

FLOUNDERS.

These may be boiled or stewed; but we hold that they never do themselves so much credit as when making their appearance really well fried.

HALIBUT.

Of all flat fish, a halibut is the largest, measuring sometimes about seven feet in length, and weighing from three hundred to four hundred pounds. In its proportions, the halibut is rather longer than other flat fish. The flesh has not much flavor, but is light and wholesome. To boil halibut plain, after scaling the skin on both sides, salt it for six hours, and (unless the piece is very large) plunge it in boiling water. The time of boiling, of course, will depend on the size. Serve, accompanied by white sauce made with milk instead of water, liberally dosed with butter and slightly seasoned with salt and a small pinch of scraped horse-radish. Shrimp or anchovy sauce goes well with it. Where there are the means and skill of frying well, halibut, cut into steaks of the proper thickness, and so prepared, is both sightly and palatable garnished with fried parsley. Some well-buttered sauce is desirable, to obviate its natural dryness. Slices from the middle of a halibut may be divided and trussed into convenient sized cutlets, by cutting them into equal halves directly through the vertebra. The same plan may be adopted with slices from the thick part of other large fish (cod, over-sized pike, and salmon), which it is customary to dress as steaks. We have never heard or read of halibut being in any way served whole.

PERCH, EELS AND SMALL PIKE

Are excellent fried.

POTTED EELS.

After cleaning your eels and cutting off their heads, cut them into pieces about two inches long. Put them into a brown earthen pot, to which, if there is not an earthen cover, have a tin one. Season them with salt, pepper, allspice, and a few sprigs of parsley

and thyme. Pour over the eels a little more vinegar and water
than will cover them; put on the lid and set the pot into a slow
oven. They should not be too much done. As soon as the flesh
will come away from the bones they are done enough. Herrings
may be potted in the same way.

COLLARED EELS.

These, though a little more trouble than potted eels, make a very
good and handsome dish. For this, the larger the eels the better;
quite small eels can hardly be collared. Clean the eel, cut off the
head, open it on the under side the whole of its length, wash it,
take out the backbone, tearing the flesh as little as possible. Dry
it by pressing it with a coarse cloth. You will then have a flat
strip of eel flesh, broad at one end and narrow at the other. Season
the inner surface of eel by dusting it with salt, pepper, and allspice.
Then roll it tightly upon itself, as you would a ribbon, beginning
at the broad end, until you have rolled it into a lump something
like a short, thick sausage, blunt at both ends; tie it with broad
tape (not with string, which would cut into the flesh when cooked)
to keep it from unrolling, and then cook in an earthen pot with a
lid exactly as you do potted eels.

STURGEON.

There are few people so poor that they will consent to eat stur-
geon, yet this fish, if properly cooked, affords, it is said, a luxurious
meal. Get a few slices, moderately thick, put them in a pot or pan
of water, and parboil them to get rid of the oil; then roll in crumbs
of cracker and egg, just as you would a veal cutlet, and fry. This
makes a veal cutlet that beats the original by far, and you are sure
that it is "full six weeks old," as the butcher always certifies in
regard to the veal.

CODS' HEAD.

In some places, fishmongers take the heads off their codfish before
they cut up the rest of the fish to retail it by the pound. In that
case the heads are sold cheap; and when they can be thus had they

are well worth the buying. We have enjoyed many a cheap fish treat with a dish of cods' heads, which contain several of the tit-bits prized by epicures, namely, the tongue, the cheek-pieces, and the nape of the neck. After taking out the eyes, wash the heads, drain them, and, if you can let them lie all night with a little salt sprinkled over them, they will be none the worse for it. Put them into a kettle of boiling water and boil from fifteen to twenty minutes, according to size. Dish them on a strainer, if you can, and help with a spoon.

For sauce, drawn butter is good.

For sharp sauce, take a few tablespoonfuls of the cods' heads boilings; put them in a saucepan with a lump of butter or dripping and a tablespoonful of vinegar; thicken with a little flour and keep stirring in one direction till they are all raised smooth and come to a boil. Both these sauces go well with any boiled fish. To these we will add a third which will be found equally simple and good.

For brown sauce, put a good lump of butter or dripping into a saucepan. Set it on a brisk fire, shake it around now and then, and keep it there until it is browned, not burnt. Take it off the fire and stir into it a good tablespoonful of vinegar. When they are well mixed, pour into your sauce-boat and serve. The mixing of the vinegar with the hot fat had better be done out of doors, on account of the quantity of vapor that arises when they are put together.

Any meat remaining on the cods' heads after a meal should be separated from the skin and bone before it gets cold. This rule applies to all other fish. Arrange it neatly on a plate and dust a little pepper and drop a little vinegar over it. It will furnish a nice little delicacy when cold, or you may warm it up with mashed potatoes, adding any sauce that may be left; or, after putting on it the cold sauce left, or a little butter, you may cover with mashed potatoes and sprinkle over it bread crumbs; pour over it beaten egg and brown in the oven.

Fresh Codfish.

Cut it in slices and fry or broil; if fried, roll it first in flour.

Salt Codfish.

Pick the fish up fine and let it soak for two hours, then rinse, and if fresh enough, cook in a little milk thickened with flour; add two tablespoonfuls of butter, and eggs to taste. The eggs may be beaten and stirred in, or dropped into boiling water, and then put into the codfish gravy whole, or laid on a platter and have the fish poured over them. It may also be boiled and served with a gravy made of melted butter and flour.

Scalloped Codfish.

One quart of pickled codfish, one pint of bread crumbs, or rolled crackers, one-half pint of cream, four ounces of butter, one teaspoonful of pepper; wash and freshen the fish. When ready, put it into a baking dish with the crumbs in alternate layers, with a little butter and pepper; have the top layer of crumbs and cover with beaten egg, then pour the cream over all and bake half an hour.

Codfish Balls.

Pick the fish fine, and freshen. Boil potatoes and mash them; mix fish and potatoes together while potatoes are hot, taking two-thirds potatoes and one-third fish. Put in plenty of butter; make into balls, and fry in hot lard.

Salt Mackerel.

Soak for a day or two, after taking out of the brine, in cold water, or buttermilk; lay in a pan with the flesh side down, and change the water occasionally. Just before cooking, lay it into a shallow dish and cover with hot milk, which removes the strong taste. Take it out of the milk and wipe dry with a napkin. Then lay on a gridiron and broil the same as fresh fish and serve with sauce with lemon juice.

BAKED COD.

When purchasing a four-pound cod ask your fishdealer to send you three or four codfish heads. Rub a little salt on the fish, chop the heads into six pieces each, and sprinkle a little salt over them. Place them in the center of the baking-pan (to be used as supports for the fish), with two ounces of butter, one carrot, a turnip, a potato, and one onion cut into slices, two blades of mace, a teaspoonful of white pepper, one tablespoonful of celery seed, six cloves, and a cup of red wine. Set the pan in the oven while you prepare the cod. Soak in cold water until soft a sufficiency of bread to fill the fish; drain off the water and pound the bread to a paste; mix with it two tablespoonfuls of melted butter, two raw eggs, a tablespoonful of Worcestershire sauce, with salt and pepper to taste. Put this stuffing inside the fish and sew it up; place the cod in the pan with two or three pieces of butter on the top, and baste it frequently; when it is cooked lay the fish on a hot platter, and garnish with fried oysters if convenient. Add two tablespoonfuls of prepared flour to the pan, a wineglass of sherry; mix and strain the gravy into a sauce-boat.

BOILED PIKE.

If the fish is sent home split through the underside sew it up. Then run a thread through the fish so as to draw it into the shape of a letter S. Tie it fast, and then tie it up in a cloth. Not having any fish kettle, lower it into the pot of boiling water if it is small or a small piece, if a large fish put it into cold water. If a large fish is put into hot water the outside cooks first, but in cold water it cooks evenly through. While boiling add a tablespoonful of salt, a slice of lemon or a half cup of vinegar and a few cloves. When done lift the fish from the pot upon a platter, untie the cloth, and by gently scraping the skin down the sides, from the top of the back, you can take the whole fish from the shell and place upon a dish for the table.

Turbot.

Take a fine large whitefish, steam until tender; take out the bones and sprinkle with pepper and salt. For the dressing heat one quart of milk and thicken with a half or two-thirds of a cup of flour. When cool add two eggs and a quarter of a pound of butter; put in the baking-dish a layer of fish, then a layer of sauce, until full. Season with garlic, parsley and thyme. Cover the top with bread crumbs and bake three-fourths of an hour.

To Fry White Fish.

One of the best ways to fry white fish, or any other fish, is to first fry some slices of salt pork, then roll the pieces of fish in fine Indian meal, and fry in the pork gravy. About three slices of pork for a medium-sized fish. White fish needs less fat than almost any other. Fish needs to be cooked a long time and very slowly to make it flaky and white.

Salmon.

A delicious way to cook salmon is to boil it and serve with a gravy made of butter, flour, pepper, salt, and plenty of oysters. Cook the oysters in a very little water, then stir into the sauce. You may prepare canned salmon in this way.

CHAPTER XX.

SHELL FISH.

CLAMS.

TO judge whether clams and oysters are fresh insert a knife, and if the shell instantly closes firmly on the knife the oysters are fresh. If it shuts slowly and faintly or not at all they are dying or dead. When the shells of raw oysters are found gaping open they are not good.

CLAM BAKE.

Lay the clams on a rock, edge downward, forming a circle; cover them with fine brush, cover the brush with dry sage, cover the sage with larger brush; set the whole on fire, and when the brush and sage are a little more than half burnt look at the clams by pulling some out, and if done enough brush the fire, cinders, etc., off; mix some tomato or cauliflower sauce or catsup with the clams after being taken out of their shells; add butter and spices to taste and serve.

CLAM CHOWDER.

Put in a pot some small slices of fat salt pork, enough to line the bottom of it; on that a layer of potatoes cut in small pieces; on the potatoes a layer of chopped onions; on the onions a layer of tomatoes in slices, or canned tomatoes; on these a layer of clams, whole or chopped (they are generally chopped), then a layer of crackers. Season with salt and pepper, and other spices if desired. Then repeat this process, layer after layer, in above order, seasoning each, until the pot is full. When the whole is in, cover with water set on a slow fire, and when nearly done stir gently, finish cooking and serve.

When done, if found too thin, boil a little longer; if found too thick, add a little water, give one boil and serve. *Fish Chowder* is made exactly like clam chowder, except that fish are used instead of clams.

CLAM FRITTERS.

Twelve clams, minced fine, one pint of milk, three eggs; add the liquor from the clams to the milk; beat up the eggs and add to this, with salt and pepper and flour enough for a thin batter; lastly add the chopped clams. Fry in hot lard, trying a little first to see if fat and batter are right. A tablespoonful makes a fritter of moderate size. Fry quickly and serve hot.

FRIED CLAMS.

Take large soft-shell clams, dry them in a napkin, and dip them first in beaten egg and then powdered cracker or bread crumbs, and fry in sweet lard or butter or both mixed.

CLAM PIE.

Take a quantity of clams, if large chop them, put in a saucepan and cook in their own liquor, or, if necessary, add a little water; boil three or four medium-sized potatoes until done, then cut in slices; line a pudding-dish half way up its sides; turn a small teacup bottom up in the middle of the dish to keep up the top crust, put in first a layer of clams and then a few potatoes, season with bits of butter and a little salt and pepper and dredge with flour; add another layer of clams, and so on till the dish is filled; add the liquor in which the clams were cooked and a little water if necessary. There should be as much liquid as for chicken or other meat pie. Cover with top crust, cut places for steam to escape and bake three-fourths of an hour.

CLAM STEW.

Put the clams in a stewpan with about the same quantity of water as the juice of the clams. Boil twenty-five or thirty minutes;

remove all the scum that rises, and season with butter, salt and pepper.

CLAM SOUP.

Take the required number of clams, chop them fine, then cook in a little water with butter, pepper and salt; when almost done put in milk or cream, and in soup enough for four persons put one cup of rolled crackers. Serve hot.

CRABS.

To fit them for the table, living crabs require to be boiled in salt water; they are either placed in cold water which is then made hot or put at once into boiling water; crabs cooked by the latter method are found to have the finest flavor. The male crab is the most valuable for the table, and may be distinguished by possessing larger claws. In purchasing crabs in the living state preference should be given to those which have a rough shell and claws. When selecting a crab which has been cooked it should be held by its claws and well shaken from side to side. If it is found to rattle, or feels as if it contained water, it is a proof that the crab is of inferior quality. The crab may be kept alive, out of water, two or three days.

SOFT CRABS.

Many will not eat hard-shell crabs, considering them indigestible, and not sufficiently palatable to compensate for the risk they run in eating them. And it must be owned that they are, at their best, but an indifferent substitute for the more aristocratic lobster. But in the morning of life, for him so often renewed, his crabship is a different creature, and greatly affected by epicures.

Do not keep the crabs over night, as the shells harden in twenty-four hours. Pull off the spongy substance from the sides, and the sand-bags. These are the only portions uneatable. Wash well and wipe dry. Have ready a pan of seething hot lard or butter and fry them to a fine brown. Put a little salt into the lard; the butter will need none. Send up hot, garnished with parsley.

SCALLOPED CRAB.

Pick out all the meat of the crab and mix thoroughly; add to it one-third its quantity of bread crumbs, a good lump of butter, divided into little bits; season with salt and pepper, a dust of grated nutmeg and a dessertspoonful of vinegar or lemon juice sprinkled over the mass. Mix all equally together. Clean out the bottom shell of your crab, and fill it with the mixture; what is left you may put into scallop-shells or tins. Set them into a moderately hot oven. When hot through and slightly browned on the surface they are fit to serve on a dish covered with a napkin, the crab-shell in the middle and the scallop-shells around it, garnished with sprigs of parsley.

FROGS.

Scald the hind quarters in boiling water, rub them with lemon juice and boil for three minutes, wipe them, dip them first in cracker dust, then in a mixture of two beaten eggs in half a cup of milk seasoned with pepper and salt, then again in cracker crumbs. When they are well covered with crumbs fry in a mixture of hot lard and butter.

LOBSTER CROQUETTES.

Chop the lobster very fine; mix with pepper, salt, bread crumbs and a little parsley; moisten with cream and a small piece of butter; shape with your hands; dip in egg, roll in bread crumbs and fry.

LOBSTER CUTLETS.

Mince the flesh of lobsters fine; season with salt, pepper and spice; melt a piece of butter in a saucepan; mix with it one tablespoonful of flour; add lobster and finely-chopped parsley; mix with some good stock; remove from the fire, and stir into it the yolks of two eggs; spread out the mixture, and, when cold, cut into cutlets, dip carefully into beaten egg, then into fine baked bread crumbs; let them stand an hour, and repeat, and fry a rich brown. Serve with fried parsley.

Fried Lobster.

If, when making a salad, you have more lobster than you wish to use for that, keep it in a cool place and fry in butter and bread crumbs for breakfast.

Lobster Patties.

Make some puff-paste and spread it on very deep patty pans. Bake it empty. Having boiled well two or three fine lobsters, extract all the meat and mince it very small, mixing it with the coral smoothly mashed, and some yolk of hard-boiled egg, grated. Season it with a little salt, some Cayenne, and some powdered mace or nutmeg, adding a little yellow lemon rind, grated. Moisten the mixture well with cream, fresh butter, or salad oil. Put it into a stewpan, add a very little water, and let it steam till it just comes to a boil. Take it off the fire, and the patties being baked, remove them from the tin pans, place them on a large dish, and fill them up to the top with the mixture. Similar patties may be made of prawns or crabs.

Lobster Rissoles.

Extract the meat of a boiled lobster; mince it as fine as possible; mix it with the coral pounded smooth, and some yolks of hard-boiled eggs, pounded also. Season it with Cayenne pepper, powdered mace, and a very little salt. Make a batter of beaten egg, milk and flour. To each egg allow two large tablespoonfuls of milk, and a large teaspoonful of flour. Beat the batter well, and then mix the lobster with it gradually, till it is stiff enough to make into oval balls about the size of a large plum. Fry them in the best salad oil, and serve them up either warm or cold. Similar rissoles may be made of raw oysters minced fine, or of boiled clams. These should be fried in lard.

Lobster Salad.

Pick the meat from the shell, cut into nice square pieces, cut up some lettuce and mix. Make a dressing of four tablespoonfuls of oil, two of vinegar, one of mustard, the yolks of two eggs and pep-

per and salt to taste; rub smooth together, forming a creamy looking sauce, and cover the lobster with it. Garnish with sliced
cucumber pickles, egg-rings, parsley and cold beet cut in fancy
shapes.

BROILED LOBSTER.

Cut the tail part of a lobster in two, rub a little sweet oil over
the meat and broil. When done, brush a little butter over it with
the juice of half a lemon and a very little Cayenne. Place the meat
back into the shell and send to the table with a dish of broiled
tomatoes and a fresh baked potato.

LOBSTERS EN BROCHETTE.

Cut up the tail of a lobster in square pieces; take a few thin
slices of bacon and cut into lengths to match the lobster; place
them on a skewer alternately and broil; baste as in broiled lobster
and send to the table on a bed of water-cresses.

ROASTED LOBSTERS.

When lobsters are half cooked, remove from the water and rub
thoroughly with butter; lay before the fire; continue basting with
butter until it has a fine froth and the shell becomes a dark brown.
Place on a dish and serve with plain melted butter in a sauce-boat.

GRATIN OF LOBSTER.

Take out all the meat from a large lobster, then wash the body,
tail, and shells, if the lobster is first cut in halves down the back,
then dry and butter them and sprinkle with bread crumbs; chop
the meat fine, with a little parsley and shallot, a few drops of
essence of anchovies, a spoonful of vinegar, Cayenne pepper and salt,
a little bechamel sauce, and boil all well together, add a yolk of
egg, put it to cool, then fill your shells or paper cases, cover with
bread crumbs and some pieces of butter; brown them in the oven,
and dish on a napkin.

BROILED OYSTERS.

Drain select oysters in a colander; dip them one by one into melted butter, to prevent sticking to the gridiron, and place them on a wire gridiron. Broil over a clear fire. When nicely browned on both sides, season with salt, pepper, and plenty of butter, and lay them on hot buttered toast, moistened with a little hot water. Serve very hot, or they will not be nice. Oysters cooked in this way and served on broiled beefsteak are nice. .

OYSTER CHOWDER.

Fry out three rashers of pickled pork in the pot you make the chowder; add to it three potatoes and two onions, both sliced; boil until they are nearly cooked; soak two or three dozen crackers in cold water a few minutes, then put into the pot half a can of oysters, one quart of milk and the soaked crackers. Boil all together a few minutes; season with salt, pepper and butter. Fish chowder can be made the same way by using fresh fish instead of oysters.

OYSTER CROQUETTES.

Take the hard end of the oyster, leaving the other end in nice shape for a soup or stew; scald them, then chop fine and add an equal weight of potatoes rubbed through a colander; to one pound of this add two ounces of butter, one teaspoonful of salt, half a teaspoonful of pepper, half a teaspoonful of mace, and one-half gill of cream; make in small rolls, dip in egg and grated bread, fry in deep lard.

FRICASSEED OYSTERS.

Drain the liquor from a quart of oysters, strain half a pint and put in a porcelain kettle, and when it boils put in the oysters. Have a tablespoonful of flour rubbed well into two tablespoonfuls of butter. When the oysters begin to swell, stir in the butter and flour, cook until the oysters are white and plump; then add a gill of cream and pepper and salt.

FRIED OYSTERS.

Take large oysters, wash and drain. Dip them into flour; put in a hot frying pan with plenty of lard and butter; season with salt and pepper; fry brown on both sides. Fried in this way, they are similar to broiled oysters.

Fried Oysters, No. 2.

Drain, remove all bits of shell, and sprinkle with pepper and salt, and set in a cool place for ten minutes. Then, if the oysters are small, pour them into a pan of crackers, rolled fine; add liquor, mix well and let stand five minutes; add a little salt and pepper, mold into small cakes, with two or three oysters in each, roll in dry crackers and fry in lard and butter. Serve hot in a covered dish.

Chicken and Oyster Pie.

Parboil a chicken; cut up and place in a pie dish; cover with oysters and season to taste; add two hard-boiled eggs cut into slices, with a piece of butter, size of an egg, in the center; dust the whole with flour, and pour on one-half pint of milk; put on a puff-paste crust and bake about three-quarters of an hour in a moderate oven.

Scalloped Oysters.

Prepare stale bread-crumbs, season to taste with pepper and salt; butter a deep dish; cover the bottom with the crumbs; add a layer of large-sized oysters, with butter; fill the dish alternately with oysters, crumbs and butter. Bake in a hot oven until cooked entirely through; if they become too brown on the top, cover with paper. If preferred, scallop the oysters separately and serve in the shells, observing that the shells are well cleaned. Instead of crumbs use slices of well-buttered bread, if you like, or bake with a crust of puff-paste.

Park Row Oyster Stew.

Put the oysters into a stewpan with a little liquor to cover them; add a little butter, pepper and salt; stir every now and then while on the fire, and when poured into the dish, put in about a table-spoonful of milk to every ten oysters.

Oyster soup is made in the same way, except that more liquor is added, and a tablespoonful of pounded butter crackers; add plenty of milk the last thing when the oysters are cooked, and let it boil up once.

MARYLAND STEWED OYSTERS.

Put the juice into a saucepan and let it simmer, skimming it carefully; then rub the yolks of three hard-boiled eggs and one large spoonful of flour well together, and stir into the juice. Cut in small pieces a quarter of a pound of butter, half a teaspoonful of whole allspice, a little salt, a little Cayenne, and the juice of a fresh lemon; let all simmer ten minutes, and just before dishing, add the oysters. This is for two quarts of oysters.

PLAIN STEW.

One quart of oysters with liquor, pint and a half of milk, piece of butter size of egg, pepper and salt; boil all together until done.

OYSTER SAUCE.

Set the oysters in their liquor over the fire for a few minutes; then remove them from the liquor and stir into it some flour and butter well rubbed together, add salt and pepper, and when it has boiled well for five minutes put in the oysters and serve immediately.

OYSTER PIE.

Make a rich puff paste; roll out twice as thick as for a fruit pie, for the top crust—about the ordinary thickness for the lower. Line a pudding dish with the thinner, and fill with crusts of dry bread or light crackers. Some use a folded towel to fill the interior of the pie, but the above expedient is preferable. Butter the edges of the dish, that you may be able to lift the upper crust without breaking. Cover the mock pie with the thick crust, ornamented heavily at the edge, that it may lie the more quietly, and bake. Cook the oysters as for a stew, only beating into them at the last, two eggs, and thickening with a spoonful of fine cracker crumbs or rice flour. They should stew but five minutes, and time them so that the paste will be baked just in season to receive them. Lift the top crust, pour in the smoking hot oysters, and send up hot.

Many consider it unnecessary to prepare the oysters and crust separately; but experience and observation go to prove that if the precaution be omitted, the oysters are apt to be wofully overdone. The maker can try both methods and take her choice.

PICKLED OYSTERS.

One ounce each of allspice, mace, cinnamon and cloves, one quart vinegar; scald all together, then put in the oysters, waiting until it is cool; next day scald all together.

OYSTER PATTIES.

Line small patty-pans with puff paste; into each pan put six oysters, bits of butter, pepper and salt; sprinkle over a little flour and hard-boiled eggs, chopped (allowing about two eggs for six patties), cover with an upper crust, notch the edges and bake; serve either in the pans or remove them to a larger platter.

OYSTER POT–PIE.

Have ready nice light-raised biscuit dough, cut into small squares. Season the oysters well with butter, pepper and salt, and thicken them with a little flour; drop in the pieces of dough and boil till done. This may be baked in the oven in a pudding-dish, allowing the dough to brown on the top.

ROASTED OYSTERS.

Take oysters in the shell, wash the shells clean, and lay them on hot coals; when they are done they will begin to open. Remove the upper shell, and serve the oysters in the lower shell, with a little melted butter poured over each.

OYSTERS, FANCY ROAST.

Toast a few slices of bread, and butter them; lay them in a shallow dish; put on the liquor of the oysters to heat; add salt and pepper, and just before it boils add the oysters; let them boil up once, and pour over the bread.

Oyster a la Poulette.

Scald a dozen oysters in their own liquor; salt and remove the oysters; add a tablespoonful of butter, the juice of half a lemon, a gill of cream, and a teaspoonful of flour. Beat up the yolk of one egg while the sauce is simmering; add the egg and simmer the whole until it thickens. Place the oysters on a hot dish, pour the sauce over them, sprinkle a little chopped parsley on the top and serve.

Raw Oysters.

For a party, serve on a handsome block of ice in which a cavity has been made with a hot flat-iron. Set the ice on a platter and garnish the edges with slices of lemon. Have pepper, salt and vinegar on hand; also serve with lemon juice.

Oysters with Toast.

Broil or fry as many oysters as you wish, and lay them on buttered toast; salt and pepper; pour over them a cup of hot, rich cream; keep them perfectly hot until eaten.

Oyster Flavor.

A German cook has discovered a way to have oyster flavor all the year round. Take fresh, large, plump oysters, beard them and place them in a vessel over the fire for a few moments in order to extract the juice, then put them to cool, and chop them very fine with powdered biscuit, mace, and finely minced lemon peel; pound them until they become a paste; make them up into thin cakes, place them on a sheet of paper in a slow oven and let them bake until they become quite hard; pound them directly into powder, and place the powder in a dry tin box, well covered; keep in a dry place, and it will be very much appreciated when the true oyster flavor is imparted to fish, sauces and dishes. This makes a delicious sauce for fresh cod.

New Way of Preparing Oysters.

The ways of preparing oysters are not many. This method,

however, is not widely known: Take two dozen oysters and throw them in a large deep dish; then take a small bunch of parsley chopped fine, a little lemon rind grated, half a nutmeg grated, and the crumbs of a stale French roll, also grated; let the latter be well incorporated, adding some Cayenne. Have in readiness the yolks of three fresh eggs beaten up into a foam; dip each oyster separately into the eggs and roll them into the bread crumbs until they are all covered with a good coat. Put a quarter of a pound of butter in the oven till it is melted while arranging the oysters in the pan, then turn them continually until they assume a perfect brown and crusty appearance. When fully cooked serve them with some celery, salt and thin slices of Graham bread and butter.

SCALLOPS.

The heart is the only part used. If you buy them in the shell, boil and take out the hearts. Those sold in our markets are generally ready for frying or stewing. Dip them in beaten egg, then in cracker crumbs, and fry in hot lard. Or, you may stew them like oysters. The fried scallops are generally preferred.

TERRAPINS, OR WATER TURTLES.

Land terrapins, it is hardly necessary to say, are uneatable, but the large turtle that frequents our mill-ponds and rivers can be converted into a relishable article of food. Plunge the turtle into a pot of boiling water, and let him lie there five minutes. You can then skin the under part easily, and pull off the horny parts of the feet. Lay him for ten minutes in cold salt and water; then put into more hot water salted, but not too much. Boil until tender. The time will depend upon the size and age. Take him out, drain and wipe dry; loosen the shell carefully, not to break the flesh; cut open also with care, lest you touch the gall-bag with the knife. Remove this with the entrails and sand-bag. Cut up all the rest of the animal into small bits; season with pepper, salt, a chopped onion, sweet herbs, and a teaspoonful of some spiced sauce, or a tablespoonful of catsup—walnut or mushroom. Save the juice that runs from the meat, and put all together into a saucepan with a closely-fitting top. Stew gently fifteen minutes, stirring occasionally, and add a great spoonful of butter, or a teaspoonful browned flour wet in cold water, a glass of brown sherry, and lastly, the beaten yolk of an egg, mixed with a little of the hot liquor, that it may not curdle. Boil up once and turn into a covered dish. Send around green pickles and delicate slices of toast with it.

CHAPTER XXI.

GAME.

To Select Game.

PHEASANTS.—A young cock pheasant will have short and blunt spurs, while an old one will have them long and sharp. A hen pheasant may be known by its plumage, and its flavor is preferred by many, though not by all, except when almost ready to lay.

Grouse.—These are judged of the same as pheasants.

Woodcock.—When these are fat they will feel thick and firm, and a streak of fat will appear on the side of the breast. Fresh birds will have supple feet, and the head and throat clear; whereas, when stale, the feet are stiff, and the head and throat nasty.

Pigeons.—Tame pigeons, when fresh and in good order, are plump, and have their feet pliable and of a dusky white. Wild pigeons are not reckoned so good as tame, but they improve with keeping. They are not so fat but are to be chosen by the same rules as the others.

Hares.—An old hare does very well for soup, but for ordinary purposes it is by no means desirable. It will be distinguished by its dry, tough ears, its blunted claws and its widely-parted lips. A young hare has soft and tender ears, sharpish claws, and the parting of the lip close.

Rabbit.—An old rabbit will have long, rough claws, and fur often inclining to grey. When fresh, the body will be rather stiff and the flesh dry and pale; but if stale, it will be limper and the flesh dark colored.

Venison.—Choose the dark-colored meat, not the black, but the rich reddish-brown, with fine grain, and well coated with fat. Keep it hung up in a cool, dark cellar, covered with a cloth, and use as soon as you can conveniently.

To Pot Birds.

Prepare them as for roasting; fill each with a dressing made as follows: Allow for each bird the size of a pigeon one-half of a hard-boiled egg, chopped fine, a tablespoonful of bread crumbs, a teaspoonful of chopped pork; season the birds with pepper and salt; stuff them and lay them in a kettle that has a tight cover. Place over the birds a few slices of pork, add a pint of water, dredge over them a little flour, cover, and put them in a hot oven. Let them cook until tender, then add a little cream and butter. If the sauce is too thin, thicken with flour. One pint of water is sufficient for twelve birds.

Reed Birds.

"These delicious lumps of sweetness, as they are appropriately called, are always acceptable, but to thoroughly appreciate a reed bird dinner one must mingle with the gunners on the Delaware river as guest or member of one of the many clubs whose houses are situated within a few hundred yards of the hunting grounds. After the judge's decision as to who has *high boat*, the birds are plucked (and at some of the club houses drawn), arranged neatly in a dripping-pan with bits of fresh country butter between them. They are allowed to cook on one side a few minutes, and with a long-handled spoon are turned over to brown on the other side. A little salt is added and they are then placed on a hot platter *en pyramide* and the gravy poured over them; they are then sent to the table with fried chipped potatoes."

Reed Birds a la Lindenthorpe.

On "ladies' day" the members of this club are more particular than on "member's day." They prepare the birds by drawing the trail and removing the head; they then take large sweet or Irish potatoes, cut them in two, scoop out the insides, and put an oyster or small piece of bacon inside of each bird and put the birds inside the potatoes, tie them up with twine and bake until the potatoes are done. The common twine is then removed and the potatoes are tied with a narrow piece of white or colored tape in a neat bow-knot and sent to the table on a napkin.

Roast Prairie Chicken.

The bird being a little strong, and its flesh, when cooked, a little dry, it should be either larded or wide strips of bacon or pork placed over its breast. A mild-seasoned stuffing will improve the flavor of old birds. Dust a little flower over them, baste occasionally and serve.

Pheasants may be managed in the same way.

Prairie Chicken.

Clean nicely, using a little soda in the water in which they are washed; rinse them and drain, and fill with dressing, sewing them up nicely, and binding down the legs and wings with cord. Put them in a steamer and let them cook ten minutes; then put them in a pan with a little butter, set them in an oven and baste frequently until of a nice brown. They should brown in about thirty-five minutes. Serve them in a platter with sprigs of parsley alternated with currant jelly.

Partridges and quails may be cooked in the same manner.

To Roast Partridges, Pheasants or Quails.

Pluck, singe, draw and truss them, season with salt and pepper; roast for about half an hour in a brisk oven, basting often with butter. When done, place on a dish together with bread crumbs fried brown and arranged in small heaps. Gravy should be served in a tureen apart.

Quail on Toast.

Pick and clean, cut in the middle of back, fry in butter to a nice brown, salt and pepper; now put in an earthern or porcelain-lined dish, one tablespoonful of nice butter and the same of flour; stir on a slow fire until butter is dissolved; then pour in slowly two-thirds glass of water and the same quantity of wine; salt and pepper; put in your birds that are nicely fried, simmer slowly one-quarter of an hour; toast some thin slices of bread (one toast to each bird); put in the dish you wish to serve, laying the birds on top; pour the gravy over all; serve very hot.

To Broil Quail or Woodcock.

After dresssing, split down the back, sprinkle with salt and pepper, and lay them on a gridiron, the inside down. Broil slowly at first. Serve with cream gravy.

Pigeon Pie.

Dress and wash clean, split down the back, and then proceed as for chicken pie.

Roast Pigeons.

When cleaned and ready for roasting, fill the bird with a stuffing of bread crumbs, a spoonful of butter, a little salt and nutmeg, and three oysters to each bird (some prefer chopped apple). They must be well basted with melted butter, and require thirty minutes of careful cooking. They are best in the autumn, and should be full grown.

To Roast Pigeons.

They should be dressed while fresh. If young, they will be ready for roasting in twelve hours. Dress carefully, and after making clean, wipe dry and put into each bird a small piece of butter dipped in Cayenne. Truss the wings over the back and roast in a quick oven, keeping them constantly basted with butter. Serve with brown gravy. Dish them with young water-cresses.

Pigeon Compote.

Truss six pigeons as for boiling. Grate the crumbs of a small loaf of bread, scrape one pound of fat bacon, chop thyme, parsley, an onion and lemon—peel fine—and season with salt and pepper:

mix it up with two eggs; put this forcemeat into the craws of the pigeons, lard the breasts and fry brown; place them in a stewpan with some beef stock and stew them three-quarters of an hour, thicken with a piece of butter rolled in flour.   Serve with force-meat balls around the dish and strain the gravy on to the pigeon.

WILD DUCK OR MALLARD.

This is one of the best of wild fowl.   Truss it as you would a tame luck, but it is not usual to stuff it.   As soon as you have plucked and emptied it, boil down the giblets with a little bit of beef, to make savory brown gravy, flavored with lemon juice and wine. Wild duck is better served a little more under-done than tame duck.   Some carvers slice the breast, and dose it with Cayenne, lemon juice and its own roast gravy—a mode of dressing admissible only when everybody likes high seasoning.   The bones of the wild duck are smaller than those of the tame.   The teal, the jewel of water fowl, if fat, should be laid each on its slice of toast, roasted before the fire; turn it over now and then, and serve on the toast. The coot, on account of its black and very downy skin, is best flayed, cut into joints, and stewed with wine as a matelote.   It then becomes excellent eating.

WILD GOOSE,

When to be had, is a treat for lovers of wild fowl; and yet, strange to say, there is a prejudice against it, as fishy.   Some few species of geese may indeed graze on seaweed, and perhaps even swallow a few shell-fish when they happen to alight on the shore, hard pressed by hunger; but, as a rule, there is no cleaner feeding bird than the goose, feeding upon herbs or grain, but preferring the former as the staple of its diet.   We know of no wild goose which is not excellent to eat, when obtained at the proper age and in good condition.

Wild geese are roasted and served in the same way as wild ducks.

A satisfactory combination is made by taking a little bone, some cartilage or tendon for the sake of its gelatine, sufficient fat—to be supplied, if the meat has none, from white bacon or fresh pork—and plenty of the flesh of whatever constitutes the pate. Pack these closely together, filling the interstices with minced fresh pork or veal, season well, but not in excess; flavor with bay-leaf, chopped shallot or onion, and lemon peel; with bits of truffle (when possible), hard egg, and button mushrooms interspersed here and there through its substance, and half a tumbler of wine, with a little catsup poured in to prevent too much drying up. Bake this in a gentle oven, and let it stand at least twenty-four hours before cutting it up. It will keep some time, especially if untouched, and will be found improved and ripened at the end of three or four days.

Roast Hare.

Broil the hare slightly over the coals, to give firmness to the flesh, then cover it with slices of fat pork from the neck to the legs. Then roast it for an hour, and serve it with sauce *piquante* prepared with the crushed liver.

A Nice Way to Prepare Cold Hare.

Remove the flesh from the roast hare, and cut it in strips. Afterward break the bones and cook with them some butter and flour, onions, parsley, thyme, chives, salt, pepper, red wine, and stock broth; boil them down to one-fourth, and having strained the gravy, put the slices of hare into it and serve it up without again boiling it.

Roast Rabbit.

Rabbits are roasted in the same manner as directed for hare.

Rabbit with Herbs.

Cut a rabbit in pieces and place it in a stewpan with butter, parsley, chives, mushrooms, bay-leaves, and thyme, chopped fine. When done add a spoonful of flour to thicken it.

Venison Chops.

Broiled and served with currant jelly are not to be despised. Trim the ends as you would a French lamb chop.

Venison Epicurean.

Cut a steak from the leg or a chop from the loin of venison about an inch and a half thick.   Put a walnut of butter, salt, and pepper, into a chafing-dish; light the spirit-lamp under it, and when the butter melts put in the chop or steak; let it cook on one side a few minutes, then turn it over, and add a wineglassful of sherry or port and a tablespoonful of currant jelly.   Simmer gently about seven minutes if it is to be eaten rare, and allow twelve minutes' cooking if required well done.

Venison Patties.

Make a nicely-flavored mince of the remains of cold roast venison; moisten it with a little sherry or gravy, and warm it in a saucepan; fill the patty-shells with the meat and serve, as oyster patties.

CHAPTER XXII.

MARKETING.

BEFORE going to market it is a very good rule to determine what shall be purchased and in what quantity. This is especially needful when the butcher is to be visited. Another rule is to deal at shops where good articles only are sold, and, if possible, to take your money with you, because a ready-money customer will, as a rule, be the best served. It is not always safe to let the butcher, poulterer, fishmonger, or other provision dealer, choose for you, because he may be over anxious to sell what is not in the best condition, or what is from some other cause hardly saiable. Experienced persons will not fail to observe carefully the quality of what they buy, and they will reflect upon the quantity of bone, gristle or other waste in it. They will also consider the requirements of the family and the uses to which they can put what is not consumed as soon as cooked. At the butcher's see the meat cut and weighed and placed ready to be sent home; you will then know what you have bought. Always buy good meat rather than inferior, and if possible from the best parts of the animal. To aid the inexperienced we will now enter somewhat into detail.

Beef.—Young and well-fed ox beef is the best. It may be known by the lean being of a fine, smooth or open grain, and the fat of a yellowish white. When the fat is either a mottled yellow or white, the meat is doubtful. The suet, however, must be very white. Cow beef is inferior, its fat is whiter, the lean closer in the grain and not of so bright a red. Bull beef has white and shining fat, close-grained lean of a dark red, and a stronger smell than other beef.

The principal parts are as follows:

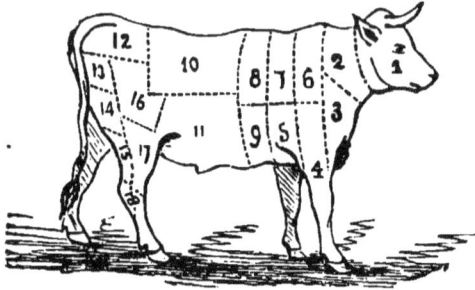

SECTION OF BULLOCK.

1. Cheek.	10. Surloin.
2. Neck or Sticking Piece.	11. Thin Flank.
3. Clod.	12. Rump.
4. Shin.	13. Aitch-bone.
5. Shoulder or Leg of Mutton Piece.	14. Round or Buttock.
6. Chuck Ribs.	15. Mouse Bullock.
7. Middle Ribs.	16. Veiny Piece.
8. Fore Ribs.	17. Thick Flank.
9. Brisket.	18. Leg.

Besides the above there are the kidneys, heart, tripe, sweet-breads, tongue, and palate.

Good beef is more elastic to the touch than that which is old or in bad condition, so that when pressed with the finger the impression will not be permanent. In poor meat, the lean is usually dark, the fat skinny, and the sinewy portions distinctly shown, especially a horny texture in the ribs. Beef should be perfectly sound, sweet and fresh, as taint rapidly spreads, and if frosted it will not cook properly. It is, perhaps, scarcely needful to say, that several of the joints which are enumerated above, are readily and commonly divided by the butcher and sold in portions for the convenience of small families and slender purses. If, at any time, more is bought than is wanted for present use, care should be taken to let it be from such parts as may be cut into two, the one for roasting and the other for salting and boiling; or let it be such as may be easily warmed a-fresh, or otherwise presented hot again at

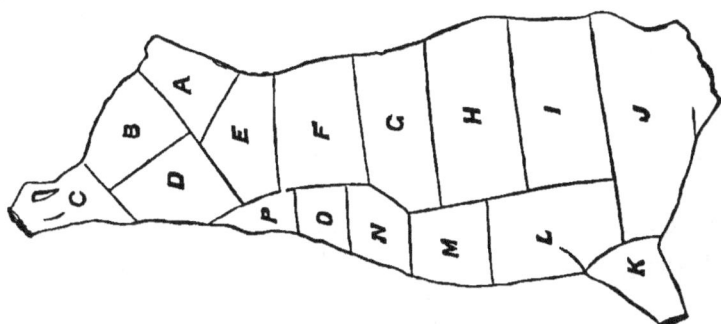

A. Rump.
B. Mouse Buttock.
C. Leg or Hock.
D. Buttock or Round.
E. Aitch-bone or Top.
F. Surloin.
G. Fore Ribs.
H. Middle Ribs.

I. Chuck Rib.
J. Neck, Clod, or Sticking Piece.
K. Shin.
L. Shoulder or Leg of Mutton Piece.
M. Brisket.
N. Thin Flank.
O. Thick Flank.
P. Veiny Piece.

table, which will be the case with such parts as are stewed, and such cheap portions as the heart, and cold roasted ox-heart cut into slices and warmed in gravy is as good as when first cooked.

SECTIONS OF SHEEP, OR LAMB.

1. Leg.
2. Shoulder.
3. Breast.
4. Scrag end of neck.

5. Best end of loin.
6. Best end of neck.
7. Chump end of loin.
8. Head.

18

Mutton.—Good mutton, of whatever breed, is known at a glance, the ham, dark, bright, crimson red; the fat, white and firm, and never too deficient in quantity according to the joint. Bad mutton is of an unsightly brownish color, and has a bad smell with a little fat, and that flabby and yellowish, often, but not always, the carcass looks as if the beast had been devoured by consumptive leanness. If you can get a sight of the liver, its state will sometimes tell you tales of the creature's healthfulness or the reverse.

Pork.—Pork, more than any other meat, requires to be chosen with the greatest care. The pig, from his gluttonous habits, is particularly liable to disease, and if it is killed and its flesh eaten when in an unhealthy condition, those who partake of it will probably have to pay dearly for their indulgence. It is generally understood that dairy-fed pork is the best. Where it is possible, therefore, it is always safest to obtain pork direct from some farm where it has been fed and killed. When this cannot be done, it should either be purchased from a thoroughly respectable and reliable person or dispensed with altogether. Pork is best in cold weather. It is in season from November to March. It should be avoided during the summer months. The fat should be white and firm, the lean finely grained, and the skin thin and cool. If any kernels are to be seen in the fat, the pig was diseased at the time it was killed. Pork should not be allowed to hang more than a day or two before it is cooked, as it will not keep unless it be salted. If cooked quite fresh, however, it will be hard. The head, heart, liver, etc., should be cooked as soon as possible. Care should be taken that the pork be thoroughly cooked.

Veal is best when the animal is from two to three months old. Veal, like all young meat, has a tendency to turn very quickly It is both unpalatable and most unwholesome when it is at all tainted, and it cannot be recovered, as brown meats sometimes can, by the use of charcoal. Therefore it ought not to be kept more than two days in summer and four in winter. If eaten quite fresh it is apt to be a little tough.

If there is any danger of the veal becoming tainted, wash it, and put it into boiling water for ten minutes. Plunge it into cold water till cool, wipe it dry, and put it into the coolest place that can be found. No meat is more generally useful for making soups and gravies than veal.

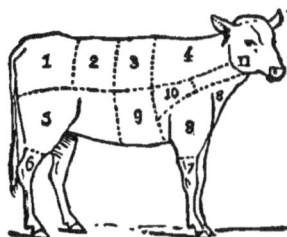

SECTIONS OF CALF.

1. Loin, chump end.	7. Fore knuckle.
2. Loin, best end.	8. Breast, brisket end.
3. Neck, best end.	9. Breast, best end.
4. Neck, scrag end.	10. Blade-bone.
5. Fillet.	11. Head.
6. Hind knuckle.	

Turkeys.—A young cock-turkey is the best, and may be known by its smooth, black legs and short spurs. The spurs must be closely looked into, because it is an old trick of the dealers to cut and scrape them in order to get rid of old birds as young ones. If in good condition the eyes will be bright and full and the feet soft and pliable; whereas where stale the eyes will be dim and sunken and the feet stiff and dry. The beak of a young turkey is somewhat soft, but hard and rigid in an old one. The legs of an old hen-turkey are red and rough. In other respects a hen-turkey may be judged of as a cock-turkey, spurs excepted.

Fowls.—A young cock will have short spurs, which will require the same inspection as turkeys. A fine bird will have a smooth comb, a full fat breast, and a large rump. The skin should be delicate and transparent. Pullets are best when about to lay, at which time they have partially formed eggs inside. Fowls with black legs are best roasted. Game birds should, also, be roasted.

Young Dorking, Spanish and Cochin should be provided for boiling. For broth, an old hen will do, if well cooked.

Geese.—A young goose will have its beak and feet yellow with a very few bristles about them; but an old bird will have the feet and bill red and bristly. When fresh, the feet are pliable, but stiff and dry when stale. The fat of a young bird is whiter and softer than that of an old bird, and the breast is plump, as is the case with all poultry in good condition; knowing which the dealers have a trick of breaking the breast bones to deceive their customers, and foist upon them old birds for young ones.

Ducks.—The feet and legs of a fresh killed duck are pliable and soft, but those of a stale one are stiff and dry. Freshness of the eye is an indication of a fresh bird. A wild duck has rather small, reddish feet, while those of a tame duck are a dusky yellow, and somewhat large. An old duck should be kept hanging a few days before it is cooked; it will generally be lean and thin as compared with a plump young bird.

CHAPTER XXIII.

MEATS.

BEEF, AITCHBONE OF, TO CARVE.

IN carving an aitchbone of beef it is necessary that it should be cut across the grain. In order to do this the knife should follow the line A to B in the illustration. The meat should be cut of a moderate thickness, and very evenly. Cut the lean and the fat in one slice, and if more fat is wanted it should be taken horizontally from the side. Before proceeding to serve, a slice of about a quarter of an inch in thickness should be cut from the top, so that the juicy part of the meat may be obtained at once.

BRISKET OF BEEF STEWED.

Take six pounds of beef, and, before dressing it, rub it over with vinegar and salt; place it in a stewpan with stock or water sufficient to cover it. Allow it to simmer for an hour, skimming it well all the time. Put in six each of carrots, turnips, and small onions; and allow all to simmer until the meat is quite tender, which will require about two hours more. As soon as it is ready the bones should be removed. Boil for a few minutes as much of the gravy as will be required with flour and a little butter, and season it with catsup, allspice and mace. Pour a little of it over the brisket, and send the remainder to the table in a separate dish.

MAKING TOUGH STEAK TENDER.

Take one teaspoonful of salad oil, two teaspoonfuls of vinegar and a very little Cayenne pepper. Lay the steak upon it and let it remain one hour; then turn it over and let it lie an hour. Then fry or broil as usual. The vinegar softens the fibre and the oil keeps it soft. Steak may stand over night this way if turned about ten o'clock. Pounding steak is a great mistake; it breaks up the fibre, but drives out the juice and destroys much of its nutriment.

BEEF, BRISKET OF, TO CARVE.

The accompanying engraving represents the appearance of a brisket of beef ready for the table. There is no difficulty in carving it. The only thing to observe is that it should be cut cleanly along the bones, in the direction indicated by the dotted line, with a firm hand, in moderately thick slices. Cut it close down to the bones, so that they may not have a rough and jagged appearance when removed.

BROILED STEAK.

Never put salt on a steak until after it is cooked. After trimming on each side equally, dress to taste with sweet fresh butter, pepper and salt, and add, if preferred, a teaspoonful of lemon-juice.

BROILED BEEFSTEAK.

To cook a good, juicy beefsteak, never pound it, but slash it several times across each way; have a nice bright fire and broil as quickly as possible, without burning; if the coals blaze from the drippings, sprinkle on a little salt, which will instantly extinguish the flames. Steak should be turned constantly while broiling, and to be rare should not cook over three minutes; butter and salt after taking up. This should be served very hot.

RUMP STEAK WITH OYSTER SAUCE.

Let your oysters give a turn or two with plenty of butter in a frying-pan, then add pepper and salt, a little flour, and the juice of half a lemon, with enough water to make up the quantity of sauce you want, stir till the oysters are done, and serve with the steak broiled in the usual way.

To Fry Steak, or Cook in Frying Pan.

If you have not a broiler, steak may be cooked nearly as well by heating the frying pan very hot and just greasing it with a little butter, or a little of the chopped suet, and lay in the steak and keep turning until sufficiently cooked; then transfer to a hot platter and season with salt and pepper, and cover with butter and serve.

German Way of Frying Beefsteak.

Pound the cut steak a little, salt it and fry quickly with hot lard on both sides; pour off the lard and place the steak on the dish; put into the pan some fresh butter and fry with it some finely cut onions and pour this over the steak.

Beefsteak Smothered with Onions.

Melt a lump of butter in a frying pan; cover the bottom of the pan with onions sliced very thin; then lay the steak over them. When the onions are fried until they are tender, put the beef on the bottom of the pan and cover it with the onions; add butter or lard as you need it. Liver cooked in this way is nice also. When it is done, lay it on a platter and heap the onions on the meat. A very little gravy made in the pan in which you have cooked the meat and onions is an addition, but make only a little and turn over the meat, seasoning it well with salt and pepper.

Beefsteak Pie.

Cut the steak into pieces an inch long, and stew with the bone (cracked) in just enough water to cover the meat until it is half done. Line a pudding dish with a good paste. Put in a layer of the beef, with salt and pepper, and a very little chopped onion; then one of sliced boiled potatoes, with a little butter scattered upon them, and so on until the dish is full. Pour over all the gravy in which the meat is stewed, having first thrown away the bone and thickened with flour. Cover with a crust thicker than the lower, leaving a slit in the middle.

Ribs of Beef, to Carve.

The rib should be cut in thin and even slices from the thick end towards the thin. This can be more readily and cleanly done, if the carving-knife is first run along between the meat and the end and rib bones.

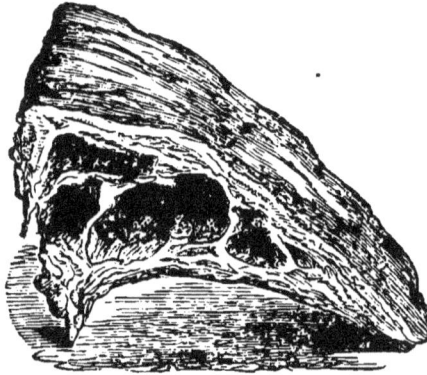

To Roast Ribs of Beef.

The best piece to roast is the fore-rib, and it should be hung for two or three days before it is cooked. The ends of the ribs should be sawn off, the outside fat fastened with skewers, and the strong sinew and chime bones removed. The joint should first be placed near the fire, and after a short time it should be drawn back and roasted steadily. Baste freely with clarified drippings at first, as there will not be sufficient gravy when first put down; keep basting at intervals of ten minutes until done. Care must be taken not to allow it to burn, as it is easily spoiled. Serve with horse-radish sauce.

To Roast Sirloin of Beef.

Take out the suet and lay it thickly over the fillet. Tie the flap under the fillet and make all firm before it is put into the oven. Should the oven be very hot place a paper over the meat while yet raw, in which case it will need very little basting; or turn the rib side up toward the fire for the first twenty minutes. The time it will take in cooking depends entirely upon the thickness of the joint and the length of time it has been killed. Skim the fat from the gravy and add a tablespoonful of prepared brown flour and a glass of sherry to the remainder.

SIRLOIN OF BEEF, TO CARVE.

A sirloin should be cut with one good, firm stroke from end to end of the joint, at the upper portion, making the cut very clean from A, B to C. Then disengage it from the bone by a horizontal cut exactly to the bone, B to D, using the tip of the knife. Bad carving bears the hand away to the rind of the beef, eventually, after many cuts, peeling it back to the other side, leaving a portion of the best of the meat adhering to the bone. Every slice should be clean and even, and the sirloin should cut fairly to the very end. Many persons cut the under side whilst hot, not reckoning it so good cold; but this is a matter of taste, and so is the mode of carving it. The best way is first of all to remove the fat, E, which chops up well to make puddings, if not eaten at table. Then the under part can be cut as already described, from end to end, F to G, or downwards as shown by the marks at H.

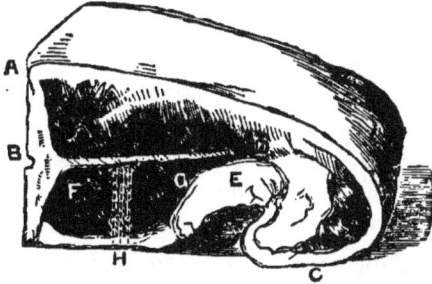

BEEF BALLS.

Mince very fine a piece of tender beef, fat and lean; mince an onion, with some boiled parsley; add grated bread crumbs, and season with pepper, salt, grated nutmeg and lemon peel; mix all together and moisten it with an egg beaten; roll it into balls, flour and fry them in boiling fresh dripping. Serve them with fried bread crumbs.

FILLET OF BEEF.

This is to be larded and dressed with a brown mushroom sauce. Trim the fat off a tenderloin of beef, and if you are going to dress it for dinner trim off the corners somewhat. It wants to be the shape of a fillet whole. A whole fillet is usually too large for a family dinner. Trim down the loin so it is smaller at each end.

Save the pieces of meat trimmed off, cut up in bits an inch square and make a stew with a few mushrooms or potatoes. Never by any means throw them away. After the fillet is trimmed lard it by inserting little strips of fat salt pork over the upper surface with a larding needle. After larding lay on a baking-pan with thin slices of salt pork under it, and put buttered paper over it to prevent burning the pork. Bake or roast it. It is usually served rare; then it should roast fifteen minutes to a pound. If it is to be well done it should roast twenty minutes for each pound. Season when brown, not before, with pepper and salt.

A Good and Cheap Way to Cook Beef.

A cheap dish can be made of a brisket or flank of beef. Cut a slice eight inches long and an inch thick, season highly, spread a stuffing of soaked bread highly seasoned over it, tie it up and lay in water enough to cover, and cook slowly a long time. This makes a very nice dish and should be served with red cabbage. Cut up the cabbage as for cold slaw. Put in a saucepan one table-spoonful of sugar, one of butter, half a cup of vinegar, half a dozen pepper corns, and half a dozen cloves; then put in the cabbage, cover tight and set on the back of the stove and let it steam an hour, when it will be tender. The beef may also be served with red beets, boiled till tender without breaking, peeled and laid around the dish of meat. A nice way to bake beef is to put in the pan under it a bed of vegetables and scraps of pork, a tablespoonful of carrot, turnip, sprigs of parsley, a half dozen cloves and a half dozen pepper corns; add a bay-leaf, if you wish, and a teaspoonful of onion. You will find that all these will give a nice flavor not only to the meat but also to the gravy made from the drippings.

Beef a la Mode.

Take a round of beef, remove the bone from the middle, also all the gristle and tough parts about the edges. Have ready half a pound of fat salt pork, cut into strips as thick and long as your finger. Prepare a nice dressing the same as for stuffing a turkey. With a thin sharp knife make perpendicular incisions in the meat about half an inch apart, thrust into them the pork, and work in with them some of the dressing. Proceed thus until the meat is thoroughly plugged. Put it into a baking pan with a little water at the bottom; cover tightly and bake slowly four hours; then uncover, and spread the rest of the dressing over the top, and bake until a nice brown. After taking up, thicken the gravy and pour over the beef. It should be sliced horizontally. Is good either hot or cold.

POUNDED BEEF.

Boil a shin of twelve pounds of meat until it falls readily from the bone; pick it to pieces; mash gristle and all very fine; pick out all the hard bits. Set the liquor away; when cool, take off all the fat; boil the liquor down to a pint and a half. Then return the meat to it while hot; add pepper and salt and any spice you choose. Let it boil a few times, stirring all the while. Put into a mold or deep dish to cool. Use cold and cut in thin slices for tea, or warm it for breakfast.

BEEF COQUETTES.

Use cold roast beef; chop it fine; season with pepper and salt; add one-third the quantity of bread crumbs, and moisten with a little milk. Have your hands floured; rub the meat into balls, dip it into beaten egg, then into fine pulverized cracker, and fry in butter; garnish with parsley.

DEVILED BEEF.

Take slices of cold roast beef, lay them on hot coals, and broil; season with pepper and salt, and serve while hot, with a small lump of butter on each piece.

BEEF SAUSAGES.

To three pounds of beef, very lean, put one and one-half pounds of suet, and chop very fine; season with sage in powder, allspice, pepper and salt; have skins thoroughly cleaned, and force the meat into them.

BEEF AU GRATIN.

Take cold beef, either boiled or roasted, and cut it in thin slices. Grease a tin pan with butter, dust with bread crumbs, put in a little chopped parsley, and lay on the slices of beef. Put salt, pepper, and parsley on top, dust with bread crumbs, drop on lemon-juice, and a little broth, just to cover the bottom of the pan, and place it in the oven.

BEEF HEART.

Wash it carefully and stuff it nicely with dressing as for turkey; roast it about one and a half hours, and serve with the gravy, which should be thickened with some of the stuffing. It is very nice hashed.

DRIED BEEF IN CREAM.

Shave your beef very fine; pour over it boiling water; let it stand for a few minutes; pour this off and pour on good rich cream; let it come to a boil. If you have not cream, use milk and butter, and thicken with a very little flour; season with pepper, and serve on toast or not, as you like.

BEEF OMELETTE.

Three pounds of beefsteak, three-fourths of a pound of suet, chopped fine, salt, pepper, and a little sage, three eggs, six Boston crackers, rolled; make into roll and bake.

BROILED BEEF TONGUE.

Put a fresh tongue on the fire with just cold water enough to cover it, and with it a carrot, an onion, a bay-leaf, a couple of slices of lemon, some black pepper, salt and a little garlic. Let it simmer gently for about two hours till quite tender. Skin and trim it. Either serve it whole or cut it in slices, and arrange in a ring with the following thick sauce in the center: Strain the liquor in which the tongue was cooked (this should be reduced by simmering to a mere gravy); brown a large tablespoonful of flour in a good sized piece of butter; braize two or three cloves of garlic, and let them steam a little while in the browning; then add the strained gravy by degrees, stirring it quite smooth. Add a little lemon-juice or vinegar; and whether it be served whole or sliced, dish the sauce with the tongue. If garlic is objected to, make a sauce of grated horse-radish, a carrot bruised fine, capers and a little wine. Garnish with lemon slices and parsley.

To Boil Beef.

Put fresh beef into boiling water (unless you wish to make soup, then it should be put into cold water) and bring quickly to a boil, then set on back part of the stove and simmer gently till done. Corned beef, if very salt, should be soaked over night, then put into lukewarm, not boiling, water. Simmer from the time of boiling till it is served up. Skim the pot thoroughly and turn the meat twice during the simmering. The meat will be much better if allowed to cool in the liquor in which it is cooked.

Tongue Roasted.

Parboil a tongue that has been salted about ten days; roast, baste with red wine, and cover it at last with butter. Serve with a rich gravy and sweet sauce.

Tripe.

This may be served in a tureen, stewed tender with milk and onions, or fried in bits dipped in butter. In both the above ways serve melted butter for sauce. Or cut the thin parts in oblong bits and stew in gravy; thicken with butter rolled in a very little flour, and add a spoonful of mushroom catsup. Or boil it tender in milk, and serve in milk-white sauce.

Tripe a la Lyonnaise with Tomatoes.

This economical dish, which is in reach of every family, is also very fine. Take two pounds of dressed and boiled tripe, cut into small strips two inches long and put into a saucepan. Parboil and drain off the first water; chop a small onion fine, and let all stew twenty minutes; add half a cup of thickening and then stir in half a can of tomatoes; season with salt and pepper. This dish has become very popular in all the hotels throughout the country.

BULLOCK'S HEART, ROASTED.

Wash the heart in several waters, clean the blood carefully from the pipes, and put it to soak in vinegar and water for two hours or more. Drain it and fill it either with ham forcemeat or sage and onion stuffing. Fasten it securely, tie it in a cloth, put into a pan of boiling water, and let it simmer gently for two hours. Take off the cloth and roast the heart while hot, basting it plentifully with good dripping for two hours longer. Serve with good brown gravy and currant jelly. The stewing may be omitted and the heart simply roasted for three or four hours, but the flesh will not then be so tender.

CALF'S HEART, ROASTED.

Wash the heart very clean, soak it in vinegar and water, fill it with a forcemeat made of four ounces of bread crumbs, two ounces of butter, two tablespoonfuls of chopped parsley, half a teaspoonful of finely-minced lemon rind, and a little salt and Cayenne. Fasten the heart securely and bake for two hours. Serve it with good melted butter, mixed with a tablespoonful of lemon-juice or vinegar. A calf's heart is improved by partially boiling before it is roasted.

CALF'S HEART, FRIED.

Wash and soak the heart, cut it into slices about a quarter of an inch thick and fry these in a little hot dripping or butter. About five minutes before they are done, put a slice of bacon into the pan for each slice of heart and when they are sufficiently cooked, serve on a hot dish and cover each piece of heart with a slice of bacon. Boil two or three tablespoonfuls of thin flour and water in the pan in which the meat was fried. Season it with pepper and salt; add one tablespoonful of red currant jelly and serve as hot as possible. The slices of heart will fry in fifteen minutes.

Sheep's Heart, Baked.

Wash two or three sheeps' hearts in lukewarm water, fill them with veal forcemeat, and skewer them securely. Fasten a rasher of fat bacon around each, place them in a deep dish, and with them a little good stock, and an onion stuck with two cloves. Bake in a moderate oven for two hours; draw off the gravy; thicken with a little flour and butter, and season it with salt and pepper and a tablespoonful of mushroom or walnut catsup. Put the hearts on a hot dish, pour the gravy over them, and send red currant jelly with them to the table.

Sweetbreads.

Sweetbreads should be chosen as fresh as possible, as they very quickly spoil. There are two sorts—heart sweetbreads and throat sweetbreads. The heart sweetbreads are the best. In whatever way sweetbreads are dressed, they should first be soaked in luke-warm water for a couple of hours. They should then be put into boiling water and simmer gently for five or ten minutes, according to size, and then taken up and laid in cold water. Sweetbreads are quite as frequently employed as ingredients in sundry made dishes as served alone, and as they do not possess a very decided natural flavor, they need to be accompanied by a highly seasoned sauce, or they will taste rather insipid. They are in full season from May to August.

Sweetbreads Fried.

Prepare them as usual. Cut them in slices, egg and bread crumb them, dip them in clarified butter, bread them again, and fry in plenty of hot fat till they are brightly browned on both sides. Drain them, and then dish on toast. Serve with cucumber sauce.

Sweetbreads Baked.

After preparing the sweetbreads as above, brush them over in every part with beaten egg, roll them in bread crumbs, sprinkle clarified butter over them, and bread-crumb them again. Put them in a baking-tin with about two ounces of butter, and bake in a well-heated oven; baste them till they are done enough and brightly browned. Take as many slices of hot toast as there are sweetbreads, put them in a dish, lay the sweetbreads upon them, pour brown gravy round, but not over them, and serve immediately.

SWEETBREADS BROILED.

Take moderate-sized sweetbreads and prepare them in the usual way. Stew them in good stock till they are done enough. Then drain them and press them between two dishes till they are cold. Split them in halves and trim them neatly; brush them over with butter, and broil them over a clear but very gentle fire. Have a plate with clarified butter on it near the gridiron and keep dipping the sweetbreads in it, turning them frequently. When they are brightly browned all over they are done enough. Dish the slices in a circle, and send brown sauce, flavored with lemon-juice, to table in a tureen.

SWEETBREADS AND CAULIFLOWERS.

Take four large sweetbreads and two cauliflowers. Split open the sweetbreads and remove the gristle. Soak them awhile in luke-warm water; put them into a saucepan of boiling water, and set them to boil ten minutes. Afterwards lay them in a pan of cold water to make them firm. The parboiling is to whiten them. Wash, drain and quarter the cauliflowers. Put them in a broad stewpan with the sweetbreads on them; season with a little Cayenne and a little nutmeg and add water to cover them. Put on the lid of the pan and stew one hour. Take a quarter of a pound of fresh butter and roll it in two tablespoonfuls of flour; add this with a cup of milk to the stew, and give it one boil up and no more. Serve hot, in a deep dish. This stew will be found delicious.

TOMATO SWEETBREADS.

Cut up a quarter of a peck of fine ripe tomatoes; set them over the fire, and let them stew in nothing but their own juice till they go to pieces—then strain them through a sieve; have ready four or five sweetbreads that have been trimmed nicely and soaked in warm water. Put them into a stewpan with the tomato juice, and a little salt and Cayenne; add two or three tablespoonfuls of butter rolled in flour. Set the saucepan over the fire, and stew the sweetbreads till done. A few minutes before you take them up, stir in two beaten yolks of eggs. Serve the sweetbreads in a deep dish, with the tomato poured over them.

Kidneys, Broiled or Roasted.

Split the kidneys in two without separating the halves; peel off the thin outer skin. Season them with salt and pepper; broil them, laying the flat sides first on the gridiron, to keep the gravy in; or, fry them the same. Or place them with the flat side upwards in a baking dish and put them in the oven. When done, serve in the same dish in which they were baked. Immediately before serving, put on each half-kidney a piece of butter and a little finely-chopped parsley.

Stewed Kidneys.

Split the kidneys and peel off the outer skin as before; slice them thin on a plate; dust them with flour, pepper and salt; brown some flour in butter in a stewpan; dilute with a little water; mix smooth and in it cook the sliced kidneys. Let them simmer, but not boil. They will cook in a very short time. Butter some slices of toast and lay on a hot dish and pour over it the stewed kidneys, gravy and all.

Fried Liver.

Cut one pound of liver into slices one-fourth inch in thickness, and dredge some flour over them. Take an equal number of slices of bacon; fry the bacon first, and when it is done enough remove from the fat and place them on a hot dish. Fry the slices of liver in the same fat, and when lightly browned on both sides, dish bacon and liver in a circle, a slice of each alternately. Pour the fat from the pan and dredge a little flour into it; add a quarter of a pint of

19

broth, a little salt and pepper and a tablespoonful of mushroom catsup. Stir smoothly together until the sauce boils, and pour into the dish with the liver. Garnish with sliced lemon. If liked, a tablespoonful of finely-minced gherkins or pickled walnuts may be added to the sauce.

FRIED LIVER, No. 2.

Take one egg to one pound of liver; cut the liver thin, scald with hot water and wipe dry; beat up the egg, dip the slices of liver into the egg, then into powdered cracker, and fry brown.

ROAST QUARTER OF LAMB.

Trim the joint and skewer three or four slices of bacon securely to the outer side, brush three ounces of clarified butter over the inner part and strew upon it a thick covering of finely-grated bread crumbs seasoned with pepper, salt and a little finely-minced parsley. Put in the oven, and when nearly done remove the bacon and baste the meat with the beaten yolk of egg mixed with the gravy, throw some more bread crumbs over it and let it remain until nicely browned. If liked, squeeze the juice of a lemon over it and serve with mint sauce.

LAMB CHOPS, FRIED.

Cut a loin or neck of lamb into chops from half to three-quarters of an inch in thickness. Dip each one into beaten egg and afterwards into bread crumbs, flavored as follows: Mix three ounces of finely-grated bread crumbs with a saltspoonful of salt, half a saltspoonful of pepper, a tablespoonful of finely-chopped parsley and a quarter of a teaspoonful of finely-mixed lemon rind. Fry the chops in good drippings until lightly browned on both sides. Serve on a hot dish and garnish with slices of lemon or crisped parsley.

Lamb Chops, Broiled.

Cut the chops about half an inch thick, trim them neatly, removing the superfluous fat, place them on a hot gridiron over a clear fire and brown them nicely on both sides. Season them with salt and pepper, and serve as hot as possible. Garnish with parsley. Mashed potatoes, asparagus, green pease, or spinach, are usually served with lamb chops.

Stewed Lamb with Green Pease.

Take two pounds of lamb, put it into a stewpan and cover with cold water; after removing the scum add a little pepper and salt, then let the meat stew for an hour and a half or nearly two hours; now add some boiling water (to make gravy); add your green pease (half a peck before shelling); let these cook about twenty minutes; stir up a tablespoonful of flour into half a cup of milk and mix with the stew. Let this cook two minutes.

Lamb Cutlets.

Trim the slices free from fat, beat up the yolk of an egg with rasped bread or crackers, seasons with pepper and salt, dip in the cutlets and fry in butter gently, until thoroughly done.

Boiled Breast of Mutton.

Take out the bones, gristle, and some of the fat; flatten it on the kneading-board, and cover the surface thinly with a forcemeat made of bread crumbs, minced savory herbs, a little chopped parsley, pepper, salt and an egg. The forcemeat should not be spread too near the edge, and when rolled, the breast should be tied securely, to keep the forcemeat in its place. If gently boiled, and served hot, it will be generally liked. Serve with good caper sauce.

Haunch of Mutton a la Venison.

Mix two ounces of bay salt with half a pound of brown sugar; rub it well into the mutton, which should be placed in a deep dish for four days, and basted three or four times a day with the liquor that drains from it; then wipe it quite dry, and rub in a quarter of a pound more of sugar, mixed with a little common salt, and hang it up, haunch downwards; wipe it daily till it is used. In winter it should be kept two or three weeks and roasted in paste, like venison. Serve with currant jelly. The paste (made with flour and water) should be removed fifteen minutes before serving.

BREAST OF MUTTON WITH PEASE.

Cut about two pounds of the breast of mutton into small square pieces. Put them into a stewpan with about an ounce of butter, and brown them nicely, then cover with weak broth or water, and stew for an hour. Remove the meat from the stewpan, and clear the gravy from fat. Put the meat into a clean stewpan, add an onion or shallot sliced finely, a bunch of sweet herbs, some pepper and salt, and strain the gravy over all. Stew for another hour, then put in a quart of young pease, and serve in about twenty minutes. Macaroni may be used in the place of pease.

MUTTON CURRIED.

Put four ounces of butter into a stewpan, and chop fine, or pound in a mortar four onions; add the onions to the butter with an ounce of curry powder, a teaspoonful of salt, a dessertspoonful of flour, and half a pint of cream; stir until smooth. Fry two pounds of mutton—cut in neat pieces without bone—to a light brown color. Lay the meat into a clean stewpan, and pour the curry mixture over; simmer until the meat is done.

MUTTON CHOPS.

First select well-fed mutton, but not too fat, and get the chops evenly cut; if not, beat them into shape with the chopper. Not more than one-third of the chop should be fat. Put an ounce of butter or lard into the frying-pan; when it is entirely melted seize the chop at the bone end with a fork, and dip it for half a minute into the fat, then turn on one side, sprinkle with salt and pepper, and if liked, finely-chopped shallot or onion, and savory herbs. In three minutes turn, and serve the other side the same; equalize the cooking by frequent turning, but give the chop altogether not more than ten minutes. A piece of garlic, if the flavor be approved, may be rubbed across the dish when hot, or it may be rubbed lightly across the chop. Serve with plain or maitre d'hotel butter.

Mutton Cutlets a la Minute.

The mutton for these cutlets should be cut from the middle of the leg, and sliced thin; season slightly with salt and pepper. Fry the meat quickly over a brisk fire, to make it crisp, turning it often. Let the cutlets be kept warm in the oven while the gravy is preparing. Have ready some mushrooms, chopped with a shallot, a sprig or two of parsley and thyme, minced fine. Stew these in the butter for a few minutes, and season with salt and pepper; add flour and water, strain and serve round the cutlets.

Mutton Cutlets and Puree of Potatoes.

Boil or steam two pounds of mealy potatoes, mash them smooth, put them into a stewpan with two or three ounces of butter, two or three tablespoonfuls of cream or broth, pepper and salt; make them hot, and pile them in the center of a hot dish. The cutlets may be bread-crumbed and fried, or, if preferred, broiled and served round the puree.

Boiled Leg of Mutton.

Cut off the shank bone, put it into a large stewpan or kettle, with as much boiling water as will cover it. When restored to its boiling state, skim the surface clean, and set the stewpan back and allow the contents to simmer until done. Allow for a leg of mutton of nine or ten pounds, from two and a half to three hours from the time it boils. Boil very young turnips for a garnish, also boil larger turnips to mash. Place the young turnips, which should be of equal size, round the dish with the mutton and send the mashed ones to the table separately. Melted butter, with capers added, should accompany the dish. The liquor from the boiling may be converted into good soup at a trifling expense.

MUTTON KEBBOBED.

Take a loin of mutton; joint well; take the following dressing and put between each joint: Two tablespoonfuls chopped parsley, a little thyme, a nutmeg grated, a cup of bread crumbs; mix well with two eggs; roast one hour. If there is a large flap to the loin, some of the dressing may be put in and then skewered securely.

LEG OF MUTTON, TO CARVE.

The leg of mutton comes to the table as shown in Fig. 1. Take the carving fork, as usual, in your left hand, and plant it firmly in the joint, as shown by A, in Fig. 1, placing it rather over to the other side of the joint, and drawing the leg over toward you on the dish about one-third, which brings the position of the fork from A to B. Cut straight down across the joint at the line marked C, not quite to the bone. Make the second cut a little on the slant, as shown in D, and take the piece out; continue cutting from each side slantingly as the line marked D, either from the thick or the knuckle end, according to the taste of the person to be helped. A very small piece of the fat should be given with each slice of meat to those who like it. The knuckle, if any one asks for it, is first cut off in a lump, as shown by the circular line at F, and afterwards in slices. Mutton should be cut thick, but it should not be cut to the bone; the slice in the centre should not penetrate so far

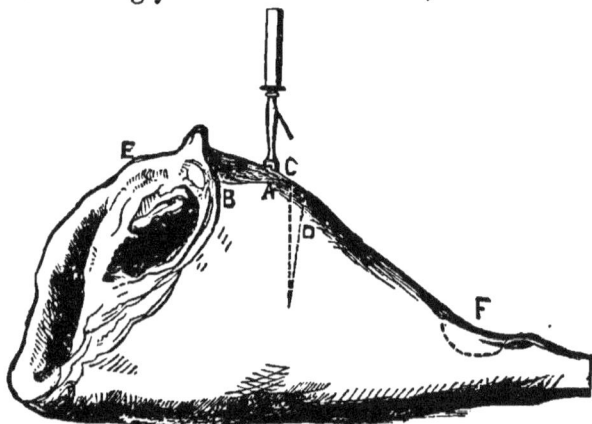

as the circular kernel of fat found there, and called the "pope's eye," which is generally considered best to leave for hashing.

The back of a leg of mutton is not generally cut until cold, when it is best sliced lengthwise, as shown in Fig. 2; the meat is still cut thick, but not quite so thick as in the cuts previously described. Cold mutton should be served with mashed potatoes and pickles, and the re-mains hashed, as there is much left on the bone that does not cut up well hot or cold. There is a part called the "crump bone" in a leg of mutton, which may be removed by a circular cut from H to J in Fig. 2; it is usually relished cold. Fig. 2 shows the joint when turned three parts over, held by the fork as previously described, and the dotted line at J indicates the direction of the first cut.

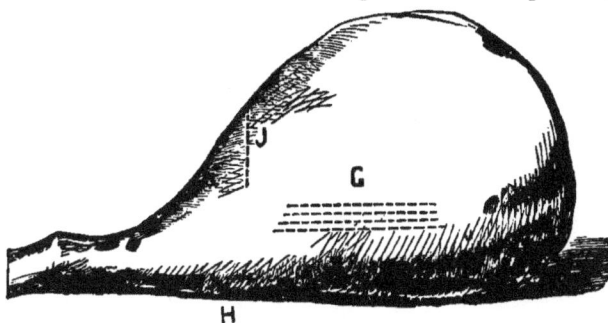

Roast Leg of Mutton.

Get a leg of about eight pounds, which has hung at least a week, weather allowing. During hot summer weather this joint gets quickly tainted. Rub it lightly with salt, and put it at once into a hot oven for the first few minutes, then allow the oven to cool, and roast more slowly until done. Baste continually with a little good dripping until that from the joint begins to flow. When within twenty minutes to being done, dredge it with flour, and baste with butter or dripping; and when the froth rises serve on a hot dish. Make a gravy and pour round the meat, not over it.

Mutton Cutlets with Provincale Sauce.

Use one-fourth of a medium-sized onion, tablespoonful of butter; put over the fire and gradually add a spoonful of flour, cup of water, one-half cup thyme, season with pepper and salt and stir constantly; add the yolks of two raw eggs and cook until about as thick as cream. This sauce can be used on cold meats, or in cooking raw meat. When used in cooking cutlets or other meats, the meats should be very slightly cooked on both sides in a hot skillet, then have a pot of fat large enough for the meat to swim in. Dip the cutlets in the sauce and put them in the boiling fat. Take them out and roll in cracker dust and bread crumbs; put them back, and do this occasionally until the meat floats on top of the fat. They are then done.

Pork—To Keep Fresh in Summer.

Take pork, when killed in the early part of the winter, and let it lie in pickle about a week or ten days, or until just sufficiently salted to be palatable; then slice it up and fry it about half or two-thirds as much as you would for present eating; now lay it away in its own grease, in jars properly covered, in a cool place, as you would lard. Re-fry when ready to use.

Pork, to Cook.

Large pork, such as portions of the shoulder, loin, or spare-rib, of large bacon hogs, may be cooked as follows: Rub the joint with pepper and salt, and put it into a large saucepan with a closely-fitting lid. When nearly done, add two or three onions and carrots, with half a dozen sticks of celery, four sage leaves, a bunch of parsley, a small sprig of marjoram and thyme, and as much stock or water as will cover the whole. Let the liquors boil up; skim carefully; then set back and simmer gently for three or four hours, according to size of joint. When the pork is done enough, lift it out, put the vegetables round it, strain and thicken a portion of the gravy, and pour it boiling hot over the pork. When the pork is removed from the table, trim it neatly and place on a clean dish to be eaten cold, or thicken the rest of the gravy and pour over the meat to be warmed over.

PORK, BELLY ROLLED AND BOILED.

Salt a belly of pork—young meat is the best—by mixing a salt-spoonful of powdered saltpetre with two tablespoonfuls of common salt, sprinkle the mixture over the pork, and let it lie for three days. When ready to dress the meat, wash it in cold water, and dry it with a cloth. Lay it, skin downwards, on the table, remove the bones, and cover the inside with pickled gherkins cut into thin slices. Sprinkle over these a little powdered mace and pepper. Roll the meat tightly and bind securely with tape. Put it into a saucepan with two onions stuck with six cloves, three bay-leaves, a bunch of parsley, and a sprig of thyme. Bring the liquid slowly to a boil, skim carefully, draw it to the back of stove, and simmer gently till the meat is done enough. Put it between two dishes, lay a weight upon it, and leave it until quite cold. The bandages should not be removed until the meat is ready to be served. Time to simmer, half an hour per pound.

PORK BRAWN.

Take a small pig's head with the tongue, and two pig's feet. Clean and wash them, sprinkle two tablespoonfuls of salt over them, and let them drain until the following day; dry them with a soft cloth and rub into them a powder made of six ounces of common salt, six ounces of moist sugar, three-quarters of an ounce of saltpetre, and three-quarters of an ounce of black pepper. Dry the powder well, and rub it into every part of the head, tongue, ears, and feet; turn them over and rub them again every day for ten days. Wash the pickle from them, cut off the ears, and boil the feet and ears an hour and a half; then put in the head and tongue, cover with cold water, and boil until the meat will leave the bones. Take them up, drain, cut the meat into small pieces; first remove all bones, and skin the tongue. Season the mince with a teaspoonful of white pepper, three saltspoonfuls of powdered mace, one saltspoonful each of powdered nutmeg and Cayenne. Stir all well together, press the meat while warm into a brawn tin, and lay a heavy weight on the lid. Put it in a cool place until the following day; dip the mold in boiling water, turn the brawn out, and serve with vinegar and mustard.

PORK CHOPS, BROILED.

Cut the chops rather less than half an inch thick. Have a clear fire; make the gridiron hot before putting the chops on it; pepper the chops, and when nearly done sprinkle salt, and a little powdered sage over them. Let them be done through, turn frequently, and serve hot. Tomato sauce eats well with pork chops.

PORK CHOPS, FRIED.

Cut pork chops a half an inch in thickness; trim them neatly; sprinkle them on both sides with a little salt and pepper. Melt a little butter in a frying-pan, put the chops in it and fry them until they are thoroughly done. If liked, a little powdered sage may be sprinkled over them before serving. Send apple sauce to table with them.

PORK CUTLETS, BROILED.

Pork cutlets are best taken from the neck or fore loin of small dairy-fed pork, not very fat. Neatly trim them. Score the skin at regular intervals and flatten the cutlets with a cutlet-bat. Brush them over with oil, season with salt and pepper, and place them on a hot gridiron over a clear fire. Turn them occasionally, that they may be equally browned on both sides, and let them be thoroughly cooked. Put them on a hot dish, and send tomato, piquant or any appropriate sauce to table with them.

LEG OF PORK, GOOD AS GOOSE.

Parboil a leg of pork and take off the skin. Make a stuffing as follows: Mince two ounces of onion very finely; mix with it half a chopped apple, four ounces of bread crumbs, half a dozen chopped sage leaves, an ounce of butter, and a little pepper and salt. Bind the mixture together with the yolk of an egg. Make a slit in the knuckle, put the stuffing into it, and fasten securely. Put the pork into the oven and baste liberally. Half an hour before it is taken up, sprinkle over it a savory powder made of two tablespoonfuls of bread crumbs mixed with one tablespoonful of powdered sage, and a little pepper and salt. Do not baste the meat after the powder is put upon it. Serve with good brown gravy and apple sauce.

PORK CUTLETS, FRIED.

Melt two ounces of butter in a saucepan, and stir into it a teaspoonful of chopped parsley, a teaspoonful each of chopped sage, and minced shallot. Move these ingredients about for a few minutes, then add a little salt and pepper, and two well-beaten eggs. Dip the cutlets first into this mixture, then into finely-grated bread crumbs, and let them stand ten minutes. Melt a little butter in a frying-pan, fry the cutlets in it, and when thoroughly done, serve with a good brown sauce.

BOILED LEG OF PORK WITH PEASE PUDDING.

Take a leg of pork and rub it over with salt; put it into a vessel and cover with salt and let it stand for ten days. At the end of that time boil it in soft water, and serve with cabbage all round it, and a pease pudding made as follows: Take a quart of dry pease, wash them, tie them in a clean bag, and boil with the pork. When the pease are done, strain them through a colander, put in a large lump of butter, some salt, and two yolks of eggs, and put back into the bag, and boil again for half an hour. The pease must be put into cold soft water for two hours before being boiled, otherwise they will never boil tender.

PORK PIES.

Make a crust as for chicken pies. Cut the meat into pieces the size of a small nut, and keep the lean and fat separate. Season the whole with pepper and salt and a teaspoonful of powdered sage. Pack the fat and lean closely into the pie in alternate layers until it is filled; put on the top crust and ornament according to taste; brush over with well-beaten egg, and bake in a slow oven as the meat is solid and requires to be cooked through, the outside pieces will be hard unless cut very small and pressed closely together. Take the bones and trimmings of the pork and stew them to make gravy; boil it until it will jelly when cold, strain, thicken and flavor, and when the pie is done raise the top crust and fill it with the gravy, and send the balance of the gravy to table in a tureen.

Roast Loin of Pork.

Score the skin of a fresh loin of pork at equal distances about a quarter of an inch apart. Brush it over with salad oil, season with salt and pepper, and place in a moderate oven. Baste liberally with butter or dripping at first, and when done serve on a hot dish, and serve with brown gravy and apple sauce. If liked, a little sage and onion stuffing may be served on a separate dish.

Pork Cake.

Cut the meat, fat and lean, from a cold joint of roast pork, and mince it very finely; mix with it a couple of large potatoes freshly boiled and mashed, a little salt and pepper, a chopped onion, and a little powdered sage. Add two or three eggs, a little milk, sufficient to make a very thick batter. Fry the cake like an omelet, or bake in a buttered dish. Serve with pickled onions or gherkins.

Pork Sausages.

Have two-thirds lean and one-third fat pork; cnop very fine. Season with one teaspoonful pepper, one of salt, three of powdered sage to every pound of meat. Warm the meat so that you can mix it well with your hands, do up a part in small patties, with a little flour mixed with them, and the rest pack in jars. When used, do it up in small cakes, flour the outside and fry in butter, or alone. They should not be covered, or they will fall to pieces. A little cinnamon to a part of them will be a pleasant addition. They should be kept where it is cool, but not damp. They are very nice for breakfast.

Pork and Beans.

Take two pounds side pork, not too fat nor too lean, and two quarts of marrowfat beans; put the beans to soak the night before you boil them in a gallon of milk-warm water. After breakfast, scald and scrape the rind of the pork, and put on to boil an hour before putting in the beans; as soon as the beans boil up, pour off the water and put on one gallon of fresh water; boil until quite tender, adding more water if necessary; great care must be taken that they do not scorch. When nearly as stiff as mashed potatoes, put into a baking-dish, score the pork and put in the center; brown in the oven one hour. If preferred use corned beef instead of pork.

Pressed Head.

Boil the several parts of the entire head and the feet, in the same way as for souse. All must be boiled so perfectly tender that the meat will separate easily from the bones. After neatly separated, chop the meat fine while warm, seasoning with salt, pepper, and other spices, to taste. Put it in a strong bag, place a weight on it and let it remain till cold. Or put it in any convenient dish, placing a plate with a weight on it to press the meat. Cut in slices, roll in flour, and fry in lard.

Boiled Pig's Feet.

Take the fore feet, cut off the hocks, clean and scrape them well; place two feet together and roll them up tightly in common muslin; tie or sew them so that they will keep in perfect shape, and boil them seven hours on a moderate fire—they will then be very soft; lift them out carefully and let them cool off; then remove the muslin and you will find them like jelly. Serve with vinegar, or split them and roll in bread crumbs or cracker dust, and fry or broil them. Serve with a little tart sauce.

Pig's Foot Cheese.

Boil the hocks and feet of equal quantity loose in a pot till the meat will fall freely from the bones; season well with pepper and salt; put into a pan while hot and press it. Cut in slices and serve with vinegar or Worcestershire sauce. Both of the above are great delicacies if properly cooked.

To Roast a Sucking Pig.

If you can get it when first killed this is of great advantage Let it be scalded, which the dealers usually do; then put some sage, a large piece of stalish bread, salt and pepper in the inside and sew it up. Observe to skewer the legs back, or the underpart will not crisp. Lay it to a brisk fire till thoroughly dry; then have ready some butter in a dry cloth and rub the pig with it in every part. Dredge as much flour over it as will possibly lie, and do not touch it again till ready to serve; then scrape off the flour very carefully with a blunt knife, rub the pig well with a buttered cloth, and take off the head while at the fire; take out the brains and mix them with the gravy that comes from the pig. Then take it up and cut it down the back and breast, lay it into the dish and chop the sage and bread quickly as fine as you can, and mix them with a large quantity of melted butter, that has a very little flour. Put the sauce into the dish after the pig has been split down the back and garnished with the ears and the two jaws; take off the upper part of the head down to the snout. In Devonshire it is served whole, if very small, the head only being cut off to garnish with as above. It will require from an hour to an hour and a half to roast, according to size.

To Cure Hams.

Take coarse salt, with a sprinkle of saltpetre, pepper and sugar; powder and mix; rub this in well a few times; smoke and wrap closely in paper of four folds or more; pack in dry ashes four inches thick around each ham. They will keep through the hottest of weather and be as good as new.

Ham Pie.

Make a crust the same as for soda biscuit, line your dish, put in a layer of potatoes, sliced thin, pepper, salt, and a little butter, then a layer of lean ham; add considerable water, and you will have an excellent pie.

Boned Ham; Fine Substitute for Turkey.

Take a good salted but unsmoked ham, remove the bone so as to leave the meat as solid as possible. In place of the bone put dressing made same as for turkey, and bake. It is good hot or cold.

Baked Ham.

Make a thick paste of flour (not boiled) and cover the ham with it, bone and all; put in a pan on a spider or two muffin rings, or anything that will keep it an inch from the bottom, and bake in a hot oven. If a small ham, fifteen minutes for each pound; if large, twenty minutes. The oven should be hot when put in. The paste forms a hard crust around the ham and the skin comes off with it. Try this and you will never cook a ham any other way.

Smoked Meat on Toast.

Take a cold smoked tongue or ham that has been well boiled, and grate it with a coarse grater or mince it fine, mix it with cream and beaten yolk of egg, and let it simmer over the fire. Prepare some nice slices of toast, butter them rather slightly, lay them in a flat dish that has been heated over the fire, and cover each slice with the meat mixture, which should be spread on hot. Place on the table in a covered dish, for either breakfast or supper.

Ham and Eggs.

Cut the ham into thin slices and broil, and spread over it a little butter. Poach the eggs in salted water and lay neatly upon the ham.

Boiled Ham.

Soak twenty-four hours; put into a pot with cold water and boil gently for five or six hours; take it off the fire and let it remain in the water until cold. Peel off the skin and sprinkle with bread or cracker crumbs, and brown in the oven. Slice very thin for the table.

Ham Balls.

Take one-half cup of bread crumbs and mix with two eggs well beaten; chop fine some bits of cold boiled ham and mix with them. Make into balls and fry.

Ham Garnishing and Ornamenting.

The usual way of finishing a ham, when it is not glazed, is to draw off the skin carefully, dredge bread raspings all over the fat, and put the ham in the oven to become brown and crisp. Fasten a frill of white paper round the bone, and garnish with parsley or cut vegetables.

To Glaze Hams.

Remove the rind by taking hold of the thick end first. Trim it neatly, put it in the oven for a few minutes; and press a cloth over it to dry it; brush it over with a paste brush dipped in glaze (a strong clear gravy boiled down as thick as syrup). To melt the glaze, put the jar which contains it into a saucepan of boiling water, and stir until dissolved. Brush the ham with two or three coats.

Collared Breast of Veal.

Bone a breast of veal; lay it on the table and spread on it a thick layer of oyster forcemeat (*See oyster forcemeat*); roll the veal as tightly as possible, and bind it with a tape. Put it into boiling water; let it boil up once; skim the liquor carefully; set the saucepan back and simmer the contents gently until done; put the bones into a separate saucepan with a moderate-sized onion, a bunch of sweet herbs, and a little pepper and salt; let them simmer till the liquor is strong and pleasantly flavored; strain it, thicken with a little flour and butter, and stir into it two or three tablespoonfuls of thick cream, or, if milk has to be used, beat into it the yolk of an egg. Serve the meat on a hot dish with the sauce poured over. This dish may be garnished with forcemeat balls, and with the sweetbreads cut into slices, egged, and bread-crumbed and fried; or a little parsley and sliced lemon may be used instead. The meat may be baked instead of boiled, and then a little weak stock should be put into the pan with it, and it should be basted frequently.

BOILED BREAST OF VEAL.

If the sweetbread is to be boiled with the veal, let it soak in water for a couple of hours; then skewer it to the veal. Put this into a saucepan, with boiling water to cover it; let it boil up, and carefully remove the scum as it rises; add a handful of chopped parsley, a teaspoonful of pepper-corns, a blade of mace, and a little salt. Draw it back, and then simmer gently until done enough. Serve on a hot dish, and pour a little good onion sauce or parsley sauce over it. Send boiled bacon to the table on a separate dish. The sweetbread may, of course, be dressed separately.

RAGOUT OF BREAST OF VEAL.

Take off the under bone, and put the veal into a stewpan with as much boiling stock as will cover it; let the liquor boil up, then add a large carrot, sliced, three onions, a blade of mace, a bunch of sweet herbs, the thin rind of a lemon, and pepper and salt; skim the gravy and simmer it gently until the veal is quite tender. Thicken the gravy till it is of the consistency of sauce, and stir into it the strained juice of a lemon and a glass of sherry or Madeira. Put the veal into a dish, pour the gravy over it, and garnish with savory forcemeat balls and slices of lemon.

ROASTED BREAST OF VEAL.

If the sweetbread is retained, skewer it to the back; season and cover with a buttered paper. Put it into a moderate oven and baste liberally till it is done. When it is roasted about an hour and a half, remove the paper, flour the joint and let it brown. Serve on a hot dish with melted butter poured over. Garnish with sliced

20

lemon. Forcemeat balls may be served with the veal and mushroom sauce sent to the table with it. Time, twenty minutes to the
pound.

BUBBLE AND SQUEAK OF VEAL.

Take the remains of cold veal; cut the meat into neat slices; fry
them in hot fat; put them where they will keep hot. Take some
boiled spinach, fry this, also, and when it is quite hot, pile it on a
dish and arrange the pieces of meat around it. Send tomato or any
kind of piquant sauce to table with it.

VEAL CAKE.

Butter a plain earthenware dish or mold; fill it with alternate layers
of hard-boiled yolks of eggs, chopped parsley, and veal and ham,
minced, seasoned highly, mixed thoroughly and beaten to a smooth
paste. Pour a spoonful or two of seasoned stock upon the meat,
cover the pan closely and bake in a gentle oven. When done
enough, press firmly into the mold, put a plate with a weight upon
it, and let it remain untouched until cold. Turn it out, garnish
with parsley, and serve for luncheon or supper. Time to bake,
about one hour.

VEAL SCALLOP.

Chop fine some cold veal, and put a layer in the bottom of a
pudding dish, and season with pepper and salt. Next put a layer
of finely powdered crackers, and strew some bits of butter over it
and wet with a little milk; then more veal, seasoned as before, and
another round of cracker crumbs with butter and milk. When the
dish is full, wet well with gravy or broth, and spread over all a thick
layer of cracker, seasoned with salt, wet into a paste with milk and
a beaten egg or two, and stick bits of butter thickly over it, and
cover and bake a half or three-quarters of a hour; then remove the
cover and brown nicely.

CALF'S HEAD, BOILED.

Take a calf's head, cut it in two, and take out the brains; wash
the head in several waters, and let it soak in warm water for a

quarter of an hour. Place it in a saucepan of cold water, and when the water comes to the boil, skim carefully; season when nearly done. Half a head, without the skin, will require from an hour and a half to two hours. It must stew gently till tender. If you wish it full-dressed, score it superficially, beat up the yolk of an egg, and rub it over the head with a feather. Powder it with a seasoning of finely-minced or dried and powdered winter savory, thyme, or sage, parsley, pepper and salt, and bread crumbs, and brown in the oven; when dry, pour melted butter over. You may garnish the dish with broiled rashers of bacon.

Calf's Brains a la Ravigote.

Wash the brains in several waters, and free them from skin and fibre; boil them for ten minutes in salt and water mixed with a tablespoonful of vinegar, and when they are firm, cut them in slices, dip them in a batter, and fry them to a light brown. Place them in a circle on a hot dish with a little fried parsley in the centre, and send ravigote sauce (*See Savory Sauces*) to table with them.

CHAPTER XXIV.

POULTRY.

CHICKEN SAUTE, A LA MARENGO.

CAREFULLY pick and singe the chicken. Clean it with a wet towel, as washing takes away much of the nutriment. Cut the bird in pieces beginning with the wing. Cut a small piece of the breast out with the wing. This distributes the white meat with the wing, otherwise the wing is a poor part. Next cut off the wing side bone and then the legs, cutting the upper joint in two near the middle, and the lower the same, dividing the second joint, which many think the best part of the chicken. This is better than giving all the best meat to one person. Next cut through the ribs, first one side then the other, taking the breast bone off and cutting it in three equal parts, trimming off the ends of the rib bones. It will then be easy to remove the entrails. Then break the neck and cut the backbone in two pieces. Save the heart, liver and gizzard; cut out the little sand-bag from the latter, and remove it all, instead of splitting it open and leaving the skin. In removing the gall take a part of the liver to make sure of no accident. Then place all these pieces in a saucepan, moistened with salad oil. As soon as the chicken begins to be browned put in a tablespoonful of flour; stir together and let the whole become brown by cooking. Then cover the whole with hot water, and season well with salt and pepper. If too much salt should be added it may be counteracted by a little vinegar and sugar. If it is desired, olives or button onions may be added. If so, put them in when the hot water is put in and cook slowly. After the flour and water are added, stirring is necessary, and it should be done with a flat wooden stick, which will not scratch the pan like metal. White pepper is better than black, as it is more digestible and has not the hard pieces of shell. An apple corer can be used to take the stones out of the olives, but a more economical instrument is a small sharp knife with which the olive can be peeled off the stone. The onions should be used whole, carefully relieved of the dry shell. When the chicken is sufficiently cooked, add a glass of sherry or Madeira wine, but the wine should not be added until ready to serve. If the wine and olives are not used, you have a nice brown fricassee. Those chickens are the best which have small bones, short legs, and clean, white-looking flesh. Chickens with white legs should be boiled, those with black legs roasted. The flesh of chickens is generally considered more digestible than any other animal food.

CAPON RANAQUE.

Use a capon or nice chicken. Have it carefully picked, singed and wiped with a wet towel; cut off the legs just below the joint; split down the back, and take out the crop; then bone the capon, which is done in this way: Cut down the middle of the back all the way; take out the crop, without breaking the skin of the neck; turn back the skin and cut the joint of the wing; then cut along close to the bone, until you have reached the leg joint, which twist out of joint where it joins the body; cut down the side until you have reached the edge of the breast bone, taking care not to cut the entrails; then go up the other side of the chicken in the same manner that you came down. Leave the leg and wing bones in; replace the bones taken out by stuffing, and sew up the carcass. For boned chicken, remove all bones from the inside. To stuff a capon you can use enough fresh pork and veal, in equal quantity, chopped fine, to fill up the place in the carcass. For every pound of forcemeat use one glass of wine and one whole egg; one teaspoonful of salt, one teaspoonful of mixed ground spice, one-half saltspoonful of pepper. In the place of the spices you can use sweet herbs. You can use in the place of this forcemeat a nice stuffing of bread. When finished bake slowly about two hours. To make the stuffing use fresh pork and veal in equal quantities, chopped fine. If you have a five-pound chicken three pounds of forcemeat will be enough. Make two-thirds the weight of the chicken. Lean veal and lean pork, both raw. For one pound of forcemeat use one glass of wine—sherry or Madeira, one egg, one teaspoonful of salt, one teaspoonful of mixed ground spice, and one-half saltspoonful of pepper. The spice may be cloves, allspice, and nutmeg, and any sweet herb you wish—thyme, summer savory, or sweet marjoram. A regular boned chicken should be boiled, stuffed and sewed up. For the Ranaque, stuff, then sew up. Leave long ends in sewing so they will be easy to remove when it is done. Push the legs up to the breast as far as possible. Run a trussing needle through with a cord attached, which tie around the chicken. Then run a cord through the breast and wings, and pass it under the back and tie. A skewer may be used. Bake slowly two hours. It may be well to tie a slice of pork over the breast.

FRICASSEED CHICKEN.

Cut up chicken, and boil with a slice or two of bacon in sufficient water to cover till quite tender. Fry some pork, and, when cooked a little, drain the chicken and fry with the pork till brown. Then take out and pour the broth into the frying pan with the pork fat, and make a gravy thickened with browned flour, season well with butter, and put the chicken into the gravy. Be sure and have the fat quite hot when the chicken is put in, so it will brown readily.

CHICKEN PIE.

Take two full-grown chickens, or more, if they are small, disjoint them and cut the backbone, etc., as small as convenient; boil them with a few slices of salt pork in water enough to cover them; let them boil quite tender, then take out the breast bone. After they boil and the scum is taken off, put in a little onion, cut very fine, not enough to taste distinctly, but just enough to flavor a little; rub some parsley very fine, when dry, or cut fine when green—this gives a pleasant flavor. Season well with pepper and salt, and a few ounces of good fresh butter. When all is cooked well, have liquid enough to cover the chicken; then beat two eggs and stir in some sweet cream. Line a five-quart pan with a crust made like soda biscuit, only more shortening, put in the chicken and liquid, then cover with a crust the same as the lining. Bake till the crust is done, and you will have a good chicken pie.

FRYING CHICKENS.

Many people prefer chickens fried to any other way. Dissect, salt, and pepper; roll the pieces in flour and fry in lard. When done, pour off the lard and put in a quarter of a pound of butter, a cup of cream, a little flour, and some parsley, scalded and chopped fine for the sauce.

CHICKEN SALAD.

Cut the meat from two chickens, or one, if you want a small dish. Add an equal quantity of shred lettuce, after you have cut the chickens into narrow shreds two inches long; stir in a bowl. Prepare a dressing thus: Beat the yolks of two eggs, salt lightly, and beat in, a few drops at a time, four tablespoonfuls of oil; then, as gradually, three teaspoonfuls of hot vinegar, and half a teaspoonful of best celery essence. The mixture should be thick as cream; pour over the chicken, mix well and lightly; put into a salad dish and lay sections of two hard-boiled eggs on top, with a chain of sliced whites around the edge.

CHICKEN CROQUETTES.

One cold, boiled chicken, chopped fine; then take a pint of sweet milk, and when the milk is boiled, stir into it two large tablespoonfuls of flour, made thin in a little cold milk; after the flour is well cooked with the milk, put in a piece of butter the size of an egg, add salt and Cayenne pepper; stir all well into the chicken; roll up with your hand, and dip first into an egg beaten up, then into crackers rolled fine, and fry in hot lard, or lard and butter.

Baked Chicken.

Split open in the back, season with salt and pepper, and plenty of butter; pour a little water into the pan, and, while baking, baste often, turning the chicken so as to nicely brown all over. When done, take up the chicken; thicken the gravy with a little flour and serve in a gravy boat. Chickens are nice stuffed and baked in the same manner as turkey.

A Nice Way to Cook Chicken.

Cut the chicken up, put into a pan, and cover with water; let it stew as usual. When done, make a thickening of cream and flour. Add butter, pepper and salt. Have ready a nice shortcake, baked and cut in squares, rolled thin as for crust. Lay the cakes on the dish, and pour the chicken and gravy over them while hot.

Chicken Pudding.

Cut up the chickens and stew until tender. Then take them from the gravy, and spread on a flat dish to cool, having first well-seasoned them with butter, pepper and salt. Make a batter of one quart of milk, three cups of flour, three tablespoonfuls of melted butter, one-half teaspoonful of soda, one teaspoonful of cream of tartar, and a little salt. Butter a pudding dish and put a layer of the chicken at the bottom, and then a cup of the batter over it. Proceed till the dish is full. The batter must form the crust. Bake an hour, and serve the thickened gravy in a gravy boat.

Jellied Chicken or Veal.

Boil a chicken in as little water as possible, until the meat falls from the bones; chop rather fine, and season with pepper and salt; put in a mold a layer of the chopped meat and then a layer of hard-boiled eggs, cut in slices; then layers of meat and egg alternately until the mold is nearly full; boil down the liquor left in the pot one-half; while warm, add one-quarter of an ounce of gelatine, and when dissolved, pour into the mold over the meat. Set in a cool place over night, to jelly.

SCALLOPED CHICKEN.

Mince cold chicken and a little lean ham quite fine; season with pepper and a little salt; stir all together, add some sweet cream, enough to make it quite moist, cover with crumbs, put it into scallop shells or a flat dish, put a little butter on top, and brown before the fire or front of a range.

CHICKEN POT-PIE.

Cut and joint a large chicken; cover with water, and let it boil gently until tender; season with salt and pepper, and thicken the gravy with two tablespoonfuls of flour mixed smooth in a piece of butter the size of an egg. Have ready a nice, light, bread dough; cut with a biscuit-cutter about an inch thick; drop this into the boiling gravy, having previously removed the chicken to a hot platter; cover, and let it boil from one-half to three-quarters of an hour. To ascertain whether they are done or not, stick into one of them a fork, and if it comes out clean, they are done. Lay on the platter with the chicken, pour over the gravy, and serve.

BROILED CHICKEN.

Only young, tender chickens are nice broiled. After cleaning and washing them, split down the back, wipe dry, season with salt and pepper, and lay them inside down on a hot gridiron over a bed of bright coals. Broil until nicely browned and well cooked through, watching and turning to prevent burning. Broil with them a little salt pork, cut in thin slices. After taking them from the gridiron, work into them plenty of butter, and serve, garnished with the pork, slices of lemon and parsley.

DUCKS A LA FRANCAISE.

Lard the breast of a duck with bacon and put it in the oven for an hour, and then put it into a stewpan of gravy previously prepared in the following manner: To one pint of beef gravy add two dozen chestnuts, roasted and peeled; two onions, sliced and fried in butter; two sage leaves, and a sprig of thyme; pepper and salt.

When the duck has stewed till tender put it on a dish, add a quarter of a pint of port wine to the gravy, a little butter, and flour to thicken; pour it over the duck and serve.

PRESSED CHICKEN.

Boil two chickens until dropping to pieces; pick meat off bones, taking out all skin; season with salt and pepper; put in deep tin mold; take one-fourth box of gelatine, dissolved in a little warm water, add to liquid left in kettle, and boil until it begins to thicken; then pour over the chicken and set away to cool; cut in slices for table.

DUCK A LA MODE.

Take a couple of ducks, divide them into quarters and lay them in a stewpan with a sprinkling of flour, pepper and salt. Put a large lump of butter divided into pieces at the bottom of the stew-pan and fry the ducks until they are a nice light-brown color. Remove the frying-pan and put in half a pint of gravy and a glass of port; sprinkle more flour and add a bunch of sweet herbs, two or three shallots minced fine, an anchovy, and a little Cayenne when the ducks have stewed in the gravy till tender, put them on a dish, take out the herbs, clear off any fat, and serve with the sauce thrown over them.

BAKED DUCK.

To cook a duck satisfactorily boil it first, until tender; this can be determined by trying the wing, as that is always a tough part of a fowl. When tender take it out, rinse it in clean water, stuff and put it in the oven for about three-quarters of an hour, basting it often.

BRAISED DUCKS.

Prepare the ducks exactly like chickens for the dressing, which should be seasoned with butter, sage and onions, as well as salt and pepper. Put them in a pot with some chopped onions, a little butter and water enough to steam. Let them stew gently with the lid on, and then let the water evaporate and then brown them. Serve with green pease and jelly.

BRAISE OF DUCK WITH TURNIP.

Prepare a domestic duck as for roasting. Line a small pan, just large enough for the duck, with slices of bacon; strew over the bottom a little parsley, powdered herbs, and lemon peel; lay in the duck, and add a carrot cut into strips, an onion stuck with a few cloves and a dozen whole peppers; cover with stock and add a tablespoonful of strong vinegar; baste frequently and simmer until done. Fry some slices of turnip in butter to a light-brown, drain and add them to the stewpan after removing the duck, which should be kept hot. When the turnips are tender remove them, strain the gravy, thickening if necessary with a little flour or arrow-root; put the duck on a dish, turn the hot gravy over it, and garnish with the turnips.

FRICASSEED DUCK.

Most people think a duck must be roasted, but try this once instead: Cut a mallard or red duck into four quarters; chop an onion fine, and put all into a pot; cover with water, and add more as it boils away. Stir a little celery seed, or celery chopped up fine, three or four strips of salt pork, and when nearly done add a tablespoonful of Worcestershire sauce. Build a mound of mashed potatoes around your dish and carefully lay the contents of the fricassee in the center. Season with salt and pepper. This makes a juicy and delicious dish.

MOCK DUCK.

Take a round of beefsteak; salt and pepper; prepare a dressing as for turkey and lay it in the steak; sew up; lay two or three slices of fat pork upon it and roast; baste often and you cannot tell it from duck.

MINCED FOWLS.

Remove from the bones all the flesh of either cold, roast or boiled fowls. Clean it from the skin, and keep covered from the air until ready for use. Boil the bones and skin with three-fourths of a pint of water until reduced quite half. Strain the gravy and let cool.

Next, having first skimmed off the fat, put it into a clean saucepan with a half cup of cream, three ounces of butter, well mixed with one tablespoonful of flour. Keep these stirred until they boil. Then put in the fowl, finely minced with three hard-boiled eggs, chopped, and sufficient salt and pepper to season. Shake the mince over the fire until just ready to boil. Dish it on hot toast, and serve.

To Carve Roast Fowl.

Insert the knife between the leg and the body, and cut to the bone; then turn the leg back with the fork, and, if the bird is not old, the joint will give way. The wing is next to be broken off,

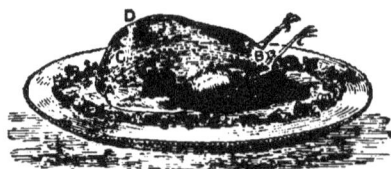

and this is done in the direction of A to B, only dividing the joint with a knife. The four quarters having been removed in this way, take off the merry-thought and the neck bones; these last are to be removed by putting the knife in at C and pressing it, when they will break off from the part that sticks to the breast. Next separate the breast from the body of the fowl by cutting through the tender ribs close to the breast, quite down to the tail. Turn the fowl now back upwards; put the knife into the bone midway between the neck and the rump, and on raising the lower end it will separate readily. Turn the rump from you and take off very neatly the two sidesmen, which completes the operation. The breast and wings are considered the best parts of a roast fowl, but in young fowls the legs are most juicy. In the case of a capon or large fowl, slices may be cut off the breast.

Croquettes.

Chop fine any cold pieces of cooked meat or chicken, or whatever you may wish to use, first removing all fat, bone, etc.; add half the quantity of fine bread crumbs, one egg, pepper and salt; make into balls and cook in a buttered spider; serve hot.

To Carve Roast Goose.

Begin by turning the neck end of a goose toward you, and cutting the whole breast in long slices, from one wing to another. (*See the lines A B.*) To take off the leg, insert the fork in the small end of the bone, pressing it to the body; put the knife in at A, turn the leg back, and if the bird be young it will easily come away; if old, we will not answer for it. To take off the wing, insert the fork in the small end of the pinion, and press it close to the body; put the knife in at B and divide the joint. When the leg and wing are off one side, attack those on the other; but, except when the company is very large, it is seldom necessary to cut up the whole goose. The back and lower side-bones, as well as the two side-bones of the wings, may be cut off; but the best pieces of a goose are the breast and thighs, after being separated from the drumstick. Serve a little of the seasoning from the inside, by making a circular slice in the apron at C. Should there be no stuffing, a glass of wine, a little orange gravy or vinegar, may be poured into the body of the goose at the opening made at the apron by the carver.

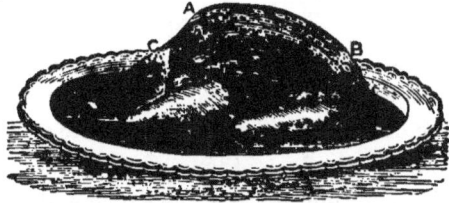

To Boil Goose.

Pick and singe a goose carefully. Let it soak in lukewarm milk and water for eight or ten hours. Stuff and truss it securely; put it into a saucepan with as much cold water as will cover it; bring to a boil, and let it simmer gently till done enough. Send good onion sauce to the table with it. Time, from an hour to an hour and a half after it has boiled.

Roast Goose.

Pluck the goose, carefully remove the quill-sockets and singe off the hairs; cut off the neck close to the back, leaving the skin long enough to turn over. After drawing, wash and wipe the bird both inside and out, and cut off the feet and pinions at the first joint; pull out the throat and tie the end securely; beat the breast-bone flat with a rolling-pin; draw the legs up closely, and put a skewer through them and through the body; cut off the end of the vent and make a hole in the skin large enough for the rump to go through. This will prevent the seasoning from escaping. Make a stuffing of bread crumbs, onions and potatoes cut fine; season with pepper, salt, sage, and butter the size of an egg; fill the goose and tie down the wings; roast two hours and a half. Boil the liver and heart and add to the gravy, which must be thickened with flour. Send to table with apple sauce and mashed potatoes.

STUFFING WITH SAGE AND ONION.

Boil four large onions until tender; drain them from the water, and mince them finely with four fresh sage leaves, or six dry ones, four tablespoonfuls of bread crumbs, a teaspoonful of salt, a teaspoonful of made mustard, and a teaspoonful of moist sugar, one-half teaspoonful of pepper, a large apple, pared and cored, and a quarter of a nutmeg, grated, may be added, if approved.

TURKEY.

The turkey is highly esteemed and usually commands a high price, especially at Christmas, when most extravagant prices are often demanded and obtained for large and well-fed birds. Turkeys are in season from September to March, and are at their best in December and January. If the weather is suitable they should be hung fully a week before being dressed. In very cold weather care must be taken that they are not frozen in hanging, and if this is the case, they should be brought into a warm place for some hours before being cooked, or they will be spoilt. The hen bird is considered the best.

"The turkey is the largest and, if not the most delicate, at least the most savory, of domestic poultry. It enjoys the singular advantage of assembling around it every class of society. When our farmers regale themselves on a winter's evening, what do we see roasting before the kitchen fire, close to which the white-clothed table is set? A turkey. When the useful tradesman or the hard-worked artist invites a few friends to an occasional treat, what dish is he expected to set before them? A nice roast turkey, stuffed with sausage meat and Lyons chestnuts. And in our highest gastronomical society, when politics are obliged to give way to dissertations on matters of taste, what is desired, what is awaited, what is looked out for at the second course? A truffled turkey. In my 'Secret Memoirs' I find sundry notes recording that on many occasions its restorative juice has illuminated diplomatic faces of the highest eminence."

Carving of Turkey.

The breast of a turkey is so large that slices taken neatly from it and from the wings generally suffice for all the company. They should be taken from each side alternately, beginning close to the wings, and a little forcemeat and a small portion of liver should be served to each guest. When it is necessary that the legs should be used, they should be separated from the body with a sharp knife and cut in slices, but it should be remembered that they, with the gizzard, will make an excellent devil.

Boiled Turkey or Capon.

When the poultry is plucked quite clean and singed, see that it is neatly trussed, and, before finally closing the vent, stuff the bird inside with as many raw oysters of the best quality as can be procured, adding to the same a lump of fresh butter, and a portion of bread crumbs from a stale loaf. Remove the turkey or capons into a clean cloth, fold them up carefully, place them into a saucepan of cold water, and let them boil over a moderately-heated fire until they are thoroughly done. Have a stick of white blanched celery at hand and chop it up very small; place it in a quart of new milk in a saucepan, and let it boil gently with a few black pepper corns, till the quantity is reduced to one pint; keep stirring the esculent up with the milk until it assumes the character of a consistent pulp. Thicken the whole with the yolk of a fresh egg, well beaten up, with half a cup of fresh cream. Have upon the table a sauce-boat of strong veal gravy.

Roast Turkey.

A young turkey, weighing not more than eight or nine pounds, is the best. Wash and clean thoroughly, wiping dry, as moisture will spoil the stuffing. Take one small loaf of bread grated fine, rub into it a piece of butter the size of an egg, one small teaspoonful of pepper and one of salt; sage, if liked. Rub all together, and fill only the breast of the turkey, sewing up so that the stuffing cannot cook out. Always put the giblets under the side of the fowl, so they will not dry up. Rub salt and pepper on the outside; put into dripping-pan with one cup of water, basting often, and turning it till brown all over. Bake about three hours. Have left in the chopping-bowl a little stuffing; take out the giblets and chop fine. After taking out the turkey, put in a large tablespoonful of flour; stir until brown. Put the giblets into a gravy-boat, and pour over them the gravy.

Roast Turkey, No. 2.

Rinse out the turkey well with soda and water, then with salt, lastly with clear water. Stuff with a dressing made of bread crumbs, wet up with butter and water and season to your taste. Stuff the craw and tie up the neck. Fill the body and sew up the vent. We need hardly say that the strings are to be clipped and removed after the fowl has been roasted. Tie the legs to the lower part of the body that they may not "sprawl" as the sinews shrink. Put into the dripping-pan, pour a cup of boiling water over it, and roast, basting often, allowing about ten minutes' time for every pound. Be careful not to have your oven too hot—especially for the first hour or so. The turkey would, otherwise, be dry and blackened on the outside and raw within. Much of the perfection of roasting poultry depends upon basting faithfully. Boil the giblets tender in a little water. When the turkey is done, set it where it will keep warm; skim the gravy left in the pan; add a little boiling water; thicken slightly with browned flour; boil up once and add the giblets minced fine. Season to taste; give another boil, and send to table in a gravy-boat.

Boiled Turkey.

Stuff the turkey as for roasting. A very nice dressing is made by chopping half a pint of oysters and mixing them with bread crumbs, butter, pepper, salt, thyme, and wet with milk or water. Baste about the turkey a thin cloth, the inside of which has been dredged with flour, and put it to boil in cold water with a tea-spoonful of salt in it. Let a large turkey simmer for three hours. Skim while boiling. Serve with oyster sauce, made by adding to a cup of the liquor in which the turkey was boiled the same quantity of milk and eight oysters chopped fine; season with minced parsley; stir in a spoonful of rice or wheat flour wet with cold milk; a table-spoonful of butter. Boil up once and pour into a tureen.

Turkey Dressed with Oysters.

For a ten-pound turkey take two pints of bread crumbs, half a cup of butter cut in bits (not melted), one teaspoonful of powdered thyme or summer savory, pepper, salt, and mix thoroughly. Rub the turkey well inside and out with salt and pepper, then fill with first a spoonful of crumbs, then a few well-drained oysters, using half a can for a turkey. Strain the oyster liquor and use to baste the turkey. Cook the giblets in the pan, and chop fine for the gravy. A fowl of this size will require three hours in a moderate oven.

Deviled Turkey.

The legs, back, gizzard and rump of cold dressed turkey may be used for this dish. Score the meat along in a cross at regular dis-tances, three-quarters of an inch apart, and three-quarters of an inch deep. Rub into the gashes a well-mixed seasoning made of a saltspoonful of white pepper, a saltspoonful of salt, a quarter of a

21

saltspoonful of Cayenne, and the strained juice of a lemon, and cover with freshly-made mustard. Brush the pieces of meat over with butter or oil and broil over a clear fire till they are brown and crisp without being at all burnt, and turn them over that they may be equally done on both sides. Send to table on hot dish with little pieces of butter on them. Dry toast may be served as an accompaniment. The devil will be all the more savory if it is prepared some hours before it is broiled. If liked, half a clove of garlic may be minced and mixed with the seasoning.

TURKEY SCALLOP.

Pick the meat from the bones of cold turkey, and chop it fine. Put a layer of bread crumbs on the bottom of a buttered dish, moisten them with a little milk, then put in a layer of turkey with some of the filling, and cut small pieces of butter over the top; sprinkle with pepper and salt; then another layer of bread crumbs, and so on until the dish is nearly full; add a little hot water to the gravy left from the turkey, and pour over it. Then take two eggs, two tablespoonfuls of milk, one of melted butter, a little salt, and cracker crumbs as much as will make it thick enough to spread on with a knife, put bits of butter over it, and cover with a plate. Bake three-quarters of an hour. About ten minutes before serving, remove the plate and let it brown.

PLAIN STUFFING.

Take stale bread, cut off all the crust, rub very fine and pour over it as much melted butter as will make it crumble in your hands; salt and pepper to taste.

APPLE STUFFING.

Take half a pound of the pulp of tart apples which have been baked or scalded; add two ounces of bread crumbs, some powdered sage, a finely-shred onion; season well with Cayenne pepper. For roast goose, duck, etc.

Potato Stuffing.

Take two-thirds bread and one-third boiled potatoes, grated, butter size of an egg, pepper, salt, one egg and a little ground sage; mix thoroughly.

Chestnut Stuffing.

Boil the chestnuts and shell them; then blanch them and boil until soft; mash them fine and mix with a little sweet cream, some bread crumbs, pepper and salt. For turkey.

For other stuffings, see "*Forcemeats.*"

CHAPTER XXV.

SALADS.

ANCHOVY SALAD.

WASH six anchovies in water, remove the bones and the insides, and also the heads, fins, and tails. Put them on a dish with two large heads of lettuce, cut small, half a dozen young onions, a saltspoonful of chopped parsley, and a sliced lemon. Pour over them the juice of a lemon mixed with salad oil, and send to table.

ARTICHOKE SALAD.

Wash thoroughly and quarter some very young artichokes, and serve them with salt, pepper, vinegar, and oil. They make a nice relish.

BEETROOT SALAD.

To some nicely-boiled and well-sliced beetroot, lay alternate rows of onions, also sliced, and pour over them any salad sauce, or simply oil and vinegar. Garnish with curled parsley.

CELERY SALAD.

Cut nice blanched salad very small. Wash clean and dry it; pour over it a Mayonnaise sauce (*See Savory Sauces*), or any salad dressing, and garnish with green celery leaves.

CHICKEN SALAD.

Use the white meat of two good-sized chickens, and celery enough to make the proportion one-third chicken and two-thirds celery; boil ten eggs hard, rub the yolks perfectly smooth with a silver spoon, adding gradually four tablespoonfuls of olive oil, one tablespoonful of made mustard, two teaspoonfuls of salt, one tea-spoonful of black pepper, half a teaspoonful of Cayenne pepper, and one tablespoonful of sugar; add sweet cream by degrees until about the consistency of batter. Just before sending to the table, mix the dressing with the chicken and celery, and moisten with sharp vinegar. The juice of two lemons is an improvement.

CHICKEN SALAD, No. 2.

Boil the white meat of two large chickens; cut it coarse, and add the white part of celery, cut coarse; a little more chicken than celery.

Dressing.—Three yolks of eggs, well beaten; one pint of oil added drop by drop, and beaten; the juice of two lemons, one tea-spoonful of dry mustard, a little Cayenne pepper, a little salt. If not moist enough, beat the whites of two eggs and add to it.

CABBAGE SALAD.

To a dish of chopped cabbage, four teaspoonfuls of celery seed, or one bunch of celery. Put in a bowl, yolks of two eggs, one tea-spoonful of sugar, one teaspoonful of butter, one teaspoonful of pepper, one teaspoonful of salt, one teaspoonful of made mustard, one-half cup of vinegar. Set the bowl into hot water, and stir care-fully until it begins to thicken. Let it get cold, and pour over the cabbage. If it does not moisten it enough, put in a little more vinegar.

FISH SALAD.

This consists of cold fish of any kind, mixed with well-dried salad, pickled gherkins, or any other green pickle. Oysters or shrimps may be added to the other fish, which should be separated neatly into flakes, and the whole moistened with a salad dressing. Garnish with some slices of lemon and parsley.

HOT EGG SALAD.

Put a tablespoonful of salad oil in a pan and let it get hot. Break in three eggs; stir a little with a fork, but not enough to mix the yolks and whites; these should be kept separate. Put the eggs out on a dish, and put over them a tablespoonful of chopped pickle and a tablespoonful of grated lemon rind. Make a salad dressing of one tablespoonful of lemon-juice, three of salad oil, a saltspoonful of salt, and one-quarter of a saltspoonful of pepper. Much of the niceness of this salad depends on its being served hot.

Endive with Winter Salad.

An ornamental and wholesome dish of salad may be made in winter principally by the aid of this plant. Only a little cress, celery, and beetroot will be necessary to form a striking contrast to the crisp, blanched leaves of the endive, which may be arranged (*en bouquet*) in the centre, or interspered with other materials, through the dish. Endive may be had good from November till March.

Lettuce Salad.

Wash and dry nice leaves of lettuce, and pour over a salad dressing, and garnish with slices of hard-boiled eggs.

Lettuce Salad, No. 2.

Wash, dry, and shred nice leaves of lettuce, and put them in a salad bowl. Cut four ounces of bacon into dice; fry these with a finely-minced onion, and do not allow them to burn, add a little salt, if needed, half a teaspoonful of pepper, a tablespoonful of vinegar; pour all over the lettuce and mix thoroughly. Serve immediately.

Lobster Salad.

Pick the meat from the body of a lobster, take out the tail part in one piece, and cut it, with the contents of the claws, into slices a quarter of an inch thick. Chop the whites of two hard-boiled eggs small; and rub the yolks smooth. Do the same with the spawn or coral of the lobster, but mix the soft part and any bits with the sauce. Pour the sauce into the bowl, put in a layer of shred lettuce and small salad, and place the slices of lobster, with hard-boiled eggs quartered and interspersed, with sliced beetroot, cucumber, etc., on the top. Repeat in the same manner till the bowl is full, sprinkling the egg and coral over and between the layers. To ornament, reserve some of the hard-boiled eggs, yolks and whites, arrange these with the coral, beetroot, and sliced lobster, so that the colors may contrast well. Before serving, pour some Mayonnaise sauce over the top.

GAME SALAD.

Take the remains of cold cooked game, pick up fine, and cover with a dressing made as follows: Take the yolk of a hard-boiled egg and mix it smoothly with a tablespoonful of salad oil; stir in a little salt and pepper, a little made mustard, a dessertspoonful of walnut catsup, and three dessertspoonfuls of vinegar.

ORANGE SALAD.

A very simple dish made of tart oranges. Some peeled and sliced and some sliced unpeeled, garnished with one tablespoonful of lemon-juice, three tablespoonfuls of salad oil and a little Cayenne pepper. This is a nice dish for breakfast, or with game or cold meats. The oil, lemon, juice and pepper should be mixed in a dish and poured over the oranges.

POTATO SALAD.

Take some cold boiled potatoes and slice very thin; add to them three hard-boiled eggs, also sliced thin; chop one small, fresh onion. In a glass bowl or salad dish put a layer of potatoes, then a layer of eggs, and sprinkle over them a little chopped onion, salt and pepper. For dressing, take the yolk of a raw egg and stir into it half a teaspoonful of made mustard. Beat into it, drop by drop, three tablespoonfuls of sweet cream; add one tablespoonful of strong vinegar and the white of the egg beaten to a stiff froth. If needed for supper make at noontime. Flakes of cold boiled salmon, cod, or halibut, substituted for the eggs, or added with them, will improve the salad.

SALMON SALAD.

One can of fresh salmon, four bunches of celery; chop as for chicken salad; mix with the salmon, and pour salad dressing over it.

SUMMER SALAD.

Cut up a pound of cold beef into thin slices, and half a pound of white, fresh lettuce; put in a salad bowl, season with a teaspoonful of salt, half that quantity of pepper, two tablespoonfuls of vinegar, and four of good salad oil. Stir all together lightly with a fork and spoon, and when well mixed it is ready to serve. Chaptal, a French chemist, says the dressing of a salad should be saturated with oil, and seasoned with pepper and salt, before the vinegar is added; it results from this process that there can never be too much vinegar, for, from the specific gravity of the vinegar compared with the oil, what is more than useful will fall to the bottom of the bowl, the salt should not be dissolved in the vinegar, but in the oil, by which means it is more equally distributed throughout the salad.

RUSSIAN SALAD.

Any three kinds of vegetables may be used—carrots, turnips and beets; string beans, carrots and turnips; or carrots, turnips and parsnips. The vegetables should be cut in slices about one and a half inches thick. These slices should be cut into cylinder-shaped pieces. This could be done with an apple-corer or with a knife. These pieces should be put in dishes, keeping each vegetable separate. As they are cut throw the pieces into cold water; take from the cold water and put into boiling water containing a spoonful of salt to a quart of water. Boil each vegetable by itself and boil until tender; drain off the juice and put the pieces into cold water until they are thoroughly cold. They are then ready to use for the salad. Beets must not be peeled or cut. When boiled tender the skins should be taken off by rubbing in a towel as soon as cool enough to handle, and then cut in pieces like the other vegetables. The pieces left after cutting out what is wanted can be saved by putting them in cold salt water. Pease, beans, spinach, and all vegetables, can be kept green by boiling and putting them in salt cold water until wanted to use. The dressing for the Russian salad is made plain, like that of orange salad, being a table-spoonful of lemon-juice or vinegar, three tablespoonfuls of salad oil, salt and Cayenne pepper. It is best not to put on the dressing until ready to serve.

SIDNEY SMITH'S RECEIPT FOR SALAD DRESSING.

Two boiled potatoes, strained through a kitchen sieve,
Softness and smoothness to the salad give;
Of mordant mustard take a single spoon—
Distrust the condiment that bites too soon;
Yet deem it not, though man of taste, a fault,
To add a double quantity of salt.
Four times the spoon, with oil of Lucca crown,
And twice with vinegar procured from town;
True taste requires it, and your poet begs
The pounded yellow of two well-boiled eggs.
Let onion atoms lurk within the bowl,
And, scarce suspected, animate the whole;
And lastly, in the flavored compound toss
A magic teaspoonful of anchovy sauce.
Oh, great and glorious! oh, herbaceous meat!
'Twould tempt the dying anchorite to eat;
Back to the world he'd turn his weary soul,
And plunge his fingers in the salad bowl.

VEGETABLES AND SALADS.

Upon the washing of green vegetables for salads much of their excellence depends; they should be shaken about without breaking in a large pan of cold water well salted, since the action of the salt will destroy all the minute inhabitants of their fresh green coverts, and, once dead, from sheer force of gravity they will fall to the bottom of the water. When the salad plants are free from sand

and insects they should be shaken without breaking their leaves, in a colander, a wire basket, or a dry napkin until no moisture adheres to them; then they may be used at once or kept until wanted in a very cold, dark place.

WATER-CRESS SALAD.

Gather the water-cress when young, cleanse it thoroughly in salt and water, and serve as fresh as possible. Place it in a bowl, either alone or mixed with other salad plants, and toss in lightly a simple salad sauce. When served at breakfast, water-cress is best sent to the table as it is, fresh and crisp.

SALAD DRESSING.

Take half a pint of vinegar and let it get hot; then beat up two eggs, half a tablespoonful of flour, half a tablespoonful of sugar, one teaspoonful of mustard, a little salt and pepper, and four tablespoonfuls of melted butter; stir this in the vinegar and let the whole boil up till it is like custard, then mix it with whatever you have for a salad. It is good for potatoes, meat or fish.

SALAD DRESSING, No. 2.

Yolks of two hard-boiled eggs, rubbed very fine and smooth, one teaspoonful English mustard, one of salt, the yolks of two raw eggs beaten into the other, dessertspoonful of fine sugar. Add very fresh sweet oil, poured in by very small quantities, and beaten as long as the mixture continues to thicken; then add vinegar till as thin as desired. If not hot enough with mustard, add a little Cayenne pepper.

CHAPTER XXVI.

SOUPS, SAUCES, AND FORCEMEATS.

Soups.

HERE is no part of cookery which is so imperfectly understood by ordinary cooks as the preparation of a soup. Amongst the wealthy it is considered a necessity, and, as a matter of course, forms part of the dinner. Amongst the middle classes it is more usually served than it used to be, and is, year by year, increasingly appreciated; but amongst the lower classes it is all but scorned; and mistresses of small households will testify that the maid-of-all-work, who, when at home is half starved instead of being properly fed, will consider herself most hardly used if part of the provision of the day's dinner consists of a portion of wholesome soup. This opinion is, of course, a sign of ignorance. Soup is both nourishing and wholesome, and it may also be prepared economically. With attention and a little trouble, it may be made from very inexpensive materials, and considering that when soup has been served, smaller inroads are made into the joint, the frugal housekeeper who has once calculated the difference in cost of a dinner consisting of an economically made soup, meat and vegetables, and one of meat and vegetables only, will never object to the introduction of soup at her table on account of the expense. Soup may be made of a large variety of different articles, including meat of all kinds, bones, game, and poultry; fish, shell-fish, all kinds of vegetables, herbs, and farinaceous articles, milk, eggs, etc. The basis of all soup is stock. Instructions in making this will be found in its proper place, and it will, therefore, not be considered here. Directions for making various soups will be found under their several headings; nevertheless, it may be found useful if a few rules of universal application are here given as an assistance in their manufacture.

There are three kinds of soups—celery soup, thick soup and purées. A purée is made by rubbing the ingredients of which it is composed through a sieve. A thick soup is stock thickened by the addition of various thickening ingredients. These soups are best suited to the winter season. Clear soup is thin and bright, and adapted for use in the summer months. In making soup it is most important that every culinary article used should be perfectly clean. The inside of the covers of saucepans, the rims and the handles particularly require attention. The lid of the saucepan should never be removed over a smoky fire. The meat used should be freshly killed, and should be as lean as it can be procured; it should never be washed. The bones should be broken up into small pieces. Cold water should be put upon fresh meat and bones; boiling water (a small quantity at a time) upon meat or vegetables that have been fried or browned. As it is very important that no fatty particles should be left to float on the surface of the soup, this should be made, if possible, the day before it is wanted, so that the fat may be removed after it has grown cold. Soup should be simmered very softly till it is done enough. A large fire and quick boiling are the great enemies of good soup. In flavoring soup, the cook should be careful to add the seasoning ingredients in moderation and gradually, especially such things as garlic, onions, shallots, spices, herbs, salt and Cayenne. An overdose of salt has spoilt' many a dish of soup, while a deficiency thereof has again and again nullified the effect of the most delicate combination of flavors. As a general rule, two ounces of salt will suffice for a gallon of soup stewed with large quantities of vegetables; an ounce and a half only will be needed if the vegetables are omitted, or if a small quantity only is used. It should be remembered that salt and all seasonings can be added when they cannot be taken out. For flavoring purposes, aromatic seasoning of herbs, and spices, and herb-powders for flavoring soups, will be found of great use. Whatever ingredients are added to soup, whether farinaceous articles, such as rice, vermicelli, macaroni, etc., or vegetables, all should be partially boiled in plain water before they are put into the liquor. This will insure their being perfectly clean and bright. The flavor of rich brown soups will be brought out better if a small piece of sugar be added to it. This must not be used for white soups. Cream or milk, when put with soups, should be boiled separately, strained, and added boiling. If, instead of cream, milk and the yolk of an egg are used, the egg must on no account be boiled in the liquor. Either it must be mixed thoroughly with a little of the soup which has cooled for a minute, then be stirred into the rest, or, better still, it must be put into the soup tureen, a spoonful of the soup mixed with the milk stirred into it, and the rest added gradually. If soups are to be kept for a few days they should be boiled up every day, according to the state of the weather, put into freshly-scalded dry earthenware crocks or pans and kept in a cool place; cover with a piece of gauze. Soup should never be kept in metal vessels.

STOCK.

Stock is the basis of all meat sauces, soups and purées. It is really the juice of meat extracted by long and gentle simmering, and in making it, it should be remembered that the object to be aimed at is to draw the goodness of the material out into the liquor. It may be prepared in various ways, richly and expensively, or economically. All general stock, or stock which is to be used for miscellaneous purposes, should be simply made, that is, all flavoring ingredients should be omitted entirely until its use is decided upon. The stock will then keep longer than it would do if vegetables, herbs, and spices were boiled in it, besides which the flavoring can be adapted to its special purpose. To ensure its keeping, stocks should be boiled and skimmed every day in summer, and every other day in winter. The pan and lid used in making it should be scrupulously clean. A tinned iron pan is the best for the purpose. Those who wish to practice economy should procure a digester, which is a kind of stock-pot made with the object of retaining the goodness of the materials, and preventing its escape by steam, when ready stock should be kept in an earthenware vessel, and never allowed to cool in a metal pan. Before being used, skim off all fat. Excellent stock is constantly made with the bones and trimmings of meat and poultry, with the addition or not of a little fresh meat, or a portion of extract of meat. In a house where meat is regularly used, a good cook will never be without a little stock. Broken remnants of all kinds will find their way to the stock-pot, and will not be thrown away until, by gentle stewing, they have been made to yield to the utmost whatever of flavor and goodness they possessed. When fresh meat is used it is better for being freshly killed. The liquor in which fresh meat has been boiled should always be used as stock.

BEAN SOUP.

Soak one and a half pints of beans in cold water over night. In the morning drain off the water, wash the beans in fresh water and put them into a soup kettle with four quarts of good beef stock, from which all the fat has been removed. Set it where it will boil slowly but steadily until dinner, or three hours at the least. Two hours before dinner slice in an onion and a carrot. Some think it improved by adding a little tomato. If the beans are not liked whole, strain through a colander and send to the table hot.

ASPARAGUS SOUP.

Select about two dozen of good asparagus stalks; boil these thoroughly in enough water to cover them; a quarter of an onion boiled with the asparagus is an improvement. When tender, take the asparagus out of the water, saving the water, and removing the onion; cut the asparagus into small pieces, of course only the tender part, and put them in a mortar, adding a little of the water; must be pounded until perfectly smooth; now take some sifted flour, a dessertspoonful, a bit of butter as big as an egg, and a very little pulverized sugar; mix well, and then put on the fire until it melts, stirring all the time; add this to the pounded asparagus and the rest of the water; when it has boiled a few minutes, mix the yolk of one egg with a tumblerful of cream, and add this; if properly made, it wants no straining; use salt and pepper to taste, and a very little nutmeg; one stalk of asparagus may be left, which may be cut in thin slices, and added last.

BEEF SOUP.

Boil a soup bone about four hours; then take out meat into a chopping-bowl; put the bones back into the kettle. Slice very thin one small onion, six potatoes, and three turnips into the soup; boil until all are tender. Have at least one gallon of soup when done. It is improved by adding crackers, rolled, or noodles, just before taking off. Take the meat that has been cut from the bones, chop fine while warm, season with salt and pepper, add one cup of soup, saved out before putting in the vegetables; pack in a dish, and slice down for tea or lunch when cold.

COMMON SOUP.

Take shank or neck of beef or meat of fowls; cut fine; crack the bones; put in a pot and stew slowly several hours, until all the meats are cooked to shreds. Pour on a little boiling water and keep boiling until nearly ready to serve; skim off all grease; add vegetables, potatoes, carrots, barley or rice as you may prefer—the vegetables having been previously cooked by themselves—and then add a little butter to give it richness.

CLAM SOUP.

Select five large, plump clams, and after chopping them finely; add the liquor to the meat. To every dozen allow a quart of cold water, and, putting meat, liquor and water into a clean vessel, allow them to simmer gently, but not boil, about one and one-half hours. Every particle of meat should be so well cooked that you seem to have only a thick broth.   Season to taste and pour into a tureen in which a few slices of well-browned toast have been placed.   If desired, to every two dozen of clams allow a cup of new milk and one egg.   Beat the latter very light, add slowly the milk, beat hard a minute or so, and when the soup is removed from the fire, stir the egg and milk into it.

CORN SOUP.

Twelve ears of corn scraped and the cobs boiled twenty minutes in one quart of water.   Remove the cobs and put in the corn and boil fifteen minutes, then add two quarts of rich milk.   Season with salt, pepper and butter, and thicken with two tablespoonfuls of flour.   Boil the whole ten minutes and turn into a tureen in which the yolks of three eggs have been well beaten.

FRENCH VEGETABLE SOUP.

To a leg of lamb of moderate size take four quarts of water.   Of carrots, potatoes, onions, tomatoes, cabbage and turnips, take a cup each, chopped fine; salt and pepper to taste.   Let the lamb be boiled in this water.   Let it cool; skim off all fat that rises to the top.   The next day boil again, adding the chopped vegetables. Let it boil three hours the second day.

EGG SOUP.

Boil a leg of lamb about two hours in water enough to cover it. After it has boiled about an hour and when carefully skimmed, add one-half cup of rice, and pepper and salt to taste.   Have ready in your tureen two eggs well beaten; add the boiling soup, a little at a time, stirring constantly.   Serve the lamb with drawn butter, garnished with parsley and hard-boiled eggs cut into slices.

CHICKEN SOUP.

Boil a pair of chickens with great care, skimming constantly and keeping them covered with water.   When tender, take out the chicken and remove the bone.   Put a large lump of butter into a spider, dredge the chicken meat well with flour, and lay in the hot pan; fry a nice brown, and keep hot and dry. Take a pint of the chicken water, and stir in two large spoonfuls of curry powder, two of butter and one of flour, one teaspoonful of salt and a little Cayenne; stir until smooth, then mix it with the broth in the pot. When well mixed, simmer five minutes, then add the browned chicken. Serve with rice.

Cabbage Soup.

Put into your soup kettle a couple of pounds of sweet bacon or pork that has not been too long in salt. Add, if you like, a bit of knuckle of veal, or mutton, or beef, or all three; skim well as they come to a boil. Shred into a pail of cold water the hearts of one or two cabbages, some carrots, turnips, celery and leeks. When the soup boils, throw all these in. When the vegetables are tender without falling to pieces, the soup is done. You may thicken with a few mashed, boiled potatoes. Simmer the meat two hours before adding the vegetables.

Green Pea Soup.

Boil a pint of green pease in water with salt, a head of lettuce, an onion, a carrot, a few leaves of mint, and a strip of parsley, some pepper and salt to taste, and a lump of sugar. When thoroughly done, strain off the liquor and pass the pease, etc., through a hair sieve; add as much of the liquor as will bring it to the right consistency; put the soup in a saucepan with a small pat of fresh butter; let it boil up, and serve with dice-shaped bread fried in butter.

Gumbo Soup.

Cut up a pair of good-sized chickens, as for a fricassee; flour them well, and put into a pan with a good-sized piece of butter, and fry a nice brown; then lay them in a soup-pot, pour on three quarts of hot water, and let them simmer slowly for two hours. Braid a little flour and butter together for a thickening, and stir in a little pepper and salt. Strain a quart or three pints of oysters,

22

and add the juice to the soup. Next add four or five slices of cold boiled ham, and let all boil slowly together for ten minutes. Just before you take up the soup, stir in two large spoonfuls of finely-powdered sassafras leaves, and let it simmer five minutes, then add your oysters. If you have no ham, it is very nice without it. Serve in a deep dish, and garnish the dish with rice.

PLAIN GUMBO SOUP.

Take a piece of ham half the size of your hand, and a knuckle of veal; put them in a pot with two quarts of cold water; simmer slowly two or three hours, then add two quarts of boiling water. Twenty minutes before serving, put in one small can of okra and as many oysters as you please. Season to taste.

LOBSTER SOUP.

One large lobster; pick all the meat from the shell and chop fine; take one quart of milk and one pint of water, and, when boiling, add the lobster, nearly a pound of butter, salt and pepper to taste, and a tablespoonful of flour. Boil ten minutes.

MACARONI SOUP.

Six pounds of beef put into four quarts of water, with one large onion, one carrot, one turnip, and a head of celery, and boiled three or four hours slowly. Next day take off the grease and pour into the soup-kettle, season to taste with salt, and add a pint of macaroni broken into small pieces, and two tablespoonfuls of tomato catsup. Half to three-quarters of an hour will be long enough to boil the second day.

MACARONI, OR VERMICELLI SOUP.

Two small carrots, four onions, two turnips, two cloves, one tablespoonful salt; pepper to taste. Herbs—marjoram, parsley and thyme; any cooked or uncooked meat. Put the soup bones in enough water to cover them; when they boil, skim them and add the vegetables. Simmer three or four hours, then strain through a colander and put back in the saucepan to re-heat. Boil one-half pound of macaroni until quite tender, and place in the soup tureen, and pour the soup over it—the last thing. Vermicelli will only need to be soaked a short time—not boiled.

MOCK TERRAPIN SOUP.

For the mock terrapin soup, take one and one-fourth pounds of calf's liver and put in salt boiling water for half an hour; add small herbs, one-half dozen grains of pepper, one teaspoonful of cloves, a few slices of onion, carrot, etc. When the vegetables are done, take them out and mash by putting them through a colander or sieve. Make a Spanish sauce of salt pork or bacon, fried enough to get the fat out of it; put into the fat a little slice of onion, a little celery, one-half dozen peppers, one-half cup of tomato, and cook brown. Take a teaspoonful of salad oil, a yolk of a hard-boiled egg, dust of Cayenne pepper, roll to paste, and make into small, round balls; put these into Spanish sauce, then put the sauce into the soup. When they come to the top, skim them out. Put in the tureen a glass of wine and slice of lemon, and pour in the soup; then cut the calf's liver into small bits and add it.

MOCK TURTLE SOUP.

Clean a calf's head well and let it stand in salt and water two or three hours; then soak it in fresh water. Put it to boil in cold water, and when sufficiently cooked, separate the meat from the bone. Strain the broth, cut the meat in small pieces, and add it to the broth; season with salt and Worcester sauce, both of which are particularly suited to this soup. Next take one pound of suet, and two pounds of veal, chopped fine, with sufficient bread crumbs. Seasoning as above, make some forcemeat balls and fry them in butter; chop three hard-boiled eggs fine, add these and a glass of wine.

MUTTON SOUP.

Boil a leg of mutton from two to three hours, and season with salt, pepper and about a tablespoonful of summer savory rubbed fine; add rice or noodles as desired.

Mushroom Soup.

Take a good quantity of mushrooms, cut off the earthy end, and pick and wash them. Stew them with some butter, pepper, and salt in a little good stock till tender; take them out, and chop them up quite small; prepare a good stock as for any other soup, and add it to the mushrooms and the liquor they have been stewed in. Boil all together and serve. If white soup be desired, use the white button mushrooms and a good veal stock, adding a spoonful of cream or a little milk, as the color may require.

Noodles for Soup.

Beat one egg light; add a pinch of salt, and flour enough to make a stiff dough; roll out in a very thin sheet, dredge with flour to keep from sticking, then roll up tightly. Begin at one end and shave down fine, like cabbage for slaw.

Okra Gumbo.

Cut one chicken; wash, dry and flour it thoroughly; salt and pepper; fry very brown in a skillet with a lump of lard large as an egg. Put it into your soup kettle with five quarts of water; add one onion cut up, and let it boil two hours; add two dozen okra pods, and let it boil another hour. Season to taste and serve with rice.

Ox-Tail Soup.

Take two tails, wash, and put into a kettle with about one gallon of cold water and a little salt; skim off the broth. When the meat is well cooked, take out the bones, and add a little onion, carrot and tomatoes. It is better made the day before using, so that the fat can be taken from the top. Add vegetables next day, and boil an hour and a half longer.

Oyster Soup.

Two quarts of oysters, three pints of new milk, three ounces of butter, one and one-half ounces of flour, salt and pepper to taste.

and mace, if liked. Put the milk over boiling water; drain the oysters and put the liquor in a saucepan on the stove; wash the oysters and remove every particle of shell that may adhere to them. When the milk is hot add the butter and flour, rubbed smoothly together and thinned with a little of the milk; let it cook, stirring slowly, until slightly thickened; the liquor, which must be well boiled, skimmed and hot, may then be added, and after that, the drained oysters. As soon as they are well puffed and the edges somewhat curled, serve the soup. Half a pint of rich cream is a great improvement and may be used instead of the butter. Serve with them a plate of small crackers, crisped in the oven.

Potato Soup.

Boil a half dozen potatoes, and mash thoroughly, mixing with it a quart of stock, seasoning with salt and pepper; boil it for five minutes, removing scum; add to this a tumblerful of milk last, and serve after the soup has come again to the boil; must be perfectly smooth.

Turkey Soup.

Take the turkey bones and boil three-quarters of an hour in water enough to cover them; add a little summer savory and celery chopped fine. Just before serving, thicken with a little flour (browned), and season with pepper, salt, and a small piece of butter.

Southern Gumbo Fela.

Take an onion and cut it up fine; have the lard quite hot, then drop the onion in and let it fry a light brown; dust in two table-spoonfuls of flour and stir all the time to keep from burning, and in a few minutes it will be brown; pour in boiling water as much as will serve the family, allowing for boiling down; have a nice fat chicken cut up, put it in the pot and let it boil until tender; take fifty oysters from th liquor and strain it to remove all pieces of shell; put the liquor in a stewpan, let it boil up once, then skim and put the liquor in the pot, season with salt, black and red pepper, also a small piece of garlic; after letting it boil some time, add the oysters; take two tablespoonfuls of fela and dust in, stirring all the time; as soon as it boils once it is ready to serve; always serve with boiled rice.

Fela is prepared by our Indians, and is simply the young leaves of the sassafras, dried in the shade, and pulverized with a few leaves of the sweet bay. In the summer, young okra pods are used in place of fela.

Tomato Soup.

Seven good-sized tomatoes to two quarts of milk; stew and season tomatoes highly with salt and pepper; have the milk hot; break into it a few crackers; stir in a large lump of butter; pour into a tureen, and just as you take to the table, add tomatoes, mixing them well together.

Tomato Soup, No. 2.

One quart of tomatoes, one onion, two ounces of flour, four ounces of butter, two tablespoonfuls of sugar, two of salt, one-third of a teaspoonful of Cayenne pepper, three pints or water, one-half pint of milk. Boil the tomatoes and onion in water for three-quarters of an hour. Add salt, pepper, sugar, butter, and flour; rub smoothly together like thin cream; boil ten minutes; boil milk separately. When both are boiling, pour the milk into the tomatoes, to prevent curdling. Serve with squares of toasted bread.

Green Turtle Soup.

A glass of Madeira, two onions, bunch of sweet herbs, juice of one lemon, five quarts of water. Chop up the coarser parts of the turtle meat with the entrails and bones. Add to them four quarts of water, and stew four hours with the herbs, onions, pepper and salt. Stew very slowly, but do not let it cease to boil during this time. At the end of four hours strain the soup, and add the finer parts of the turtle and the green fat, which has been simmered for one hour in two quarts of water. Thicken with browned flour; return to the soup-pot, and simmer gently an hour longer. If there are eggs in the turtle, boil them in a separate vessel for four hours, and throw into the soup before taking it up. If not, put in force-meat balls; then the juice of the lemon and wine; beat up once and pour out. Some cooks add the finer meat before straining, boiling all together for five hours; then strain, thicken, and put in the green fat, cut into lumps an inch long. This makes a handsomer soup than if the meat is left in. For the mock eggs, take the yolks of three hard-boiled eggs, and one raw egg well beaten. Rub the boiled eggs into a paste with a teaspoonful of butter, bind with a raw egg, roll into pellets the size and shape of turtle eggs, and lay in boiling water for two minutes before dropping into the soup.

Soyer's Cheap Soups.

Soyer, in his "Culinary Campaign," has given recipes for making palatable soups, which he says will not cost more than a cent a quart in London. Here is one of them: Take two ounces of dripping, quarter of a pound of solid meat, cut into pieces one inch square; quarter of a pound of onions, sliced thin; same of turnips (the peel will do) or a whole one cut into slices; two ounces of leeks (green tops will do) sliced thin; three ounces of celery; three-quarters of a pound of common flour; half a pound of pearl barley, or one pound of Scotch; three ounces of salt; quarter of an ounce of brown sugar; two gallons of water. First put two ounces of dripping into a saucepan capable of holding two gallons of water, with a quarter of a pound of leg-beef without bone, cut into square pieces of about an inch; and two middling-sized onions, peeled and sliced; then set the saucepan over the fire, and stir the contents around for a few minutes with a wooden or iron spoon until fried lightly brown. Have then ready washed the peelings of two turnips, fifteen green leaves or tops of celery, and the green part of two leeks (the whole of which, I must observe, are always thrown away). Having cut the above vegetable into small pieces, throw them into the saucepan with the other ingredients, stirring them occasionally over the fire for another ten minutes; then add one quart of cold water and three-quarters of a pound of com-non flour, and half a pound of pearl barley, mixing all well together; then add seven quarts of hot water, seasoned with three ounces of salt, and a quarter of an ounce of brown sugar, stirring occasion-ally until boiling, and allowing it to simmer gently for three hours; at the end of which time the barley will be perfectly tender. The above soup has been tasted by numerous noblemen, members of Parliament, and several ladies, who have lately visited my kitchen department, and who have considered it very good and nourishing. The soup will keep several days when made as above described; but I must observe, not to keep it in a deep pan, but within a flat vessel, when the air could act freely upon it. Stir it now and then until nearly cold, or otherwise the next day it will be in a state of fermentation. This does not denote the weakness of the soup, because the same evil exists in the strongest of stock, or sauce, if not stirred or confined in a warm place—a fact known to every first-rate cook. The expense may come to three farthings per quart in London; but as almost every thing can be had at less cost in the country, the price of the soup will be still more reduced. In that case, a little additional meat might be added. By giving with this a small portion of bread or biscuit, better support would be given to the poor at a trifling cost; and no one, it is to be hoped, here-after, would hear of the dreadful calamity of starvation.

Soup, No. 2.—Same Cost.

Quarter of a pound of beef cut into pieces one inch square; two ounces of dripping, or melted suet, quarter of a pound of turnips, or carrots, cut into fragments half an inch square, four drops essence of meat, one and a half pounds of maize flour, three ounces of salt, quarter ounce of brown sugar, one teaspoonful of black pepper, ground fine. Take two ounces of either drippings, Amer-ican lard, or suet, to which add the turnips and carrots; fry for ten minutes; add one quart of cold water, and the meal, well mixed, and moisten by degrees with seven quarts of hot water; boil five hours, and season with three ounces of salt, one-quarter ounce of brown sugar, one teaspoonful of black pepper, two drops of essence of garlic, one drop of essence of mint, a little celery; stir quickly, and serve directly.

By adding a pound of potatoes to this, a superior soup will be the result.

Aspic Jelly for Garnishing.

Take two pints of nicely-flavored stock, of a clear, firm jelly; put this into a saucepan with a blade of mace, a tablespoonful of vinegar and a glass of sherry. Let it boil; then stir into an ounce of the best gelatine, which has been soaked in a little cool water. When again cool, add the whisked whites of two eggs; let it boil; then set back to settle; strain through a jelly-bag until quite clear, and pour it on a dish which has been standing in cold water. Cut it into dice for garnishing.

Aspic Jelly, Stock.

Put a knuckle-bone of veal, a knuckle-bone of ham, a calf's foot, a large onion with four cloves stuck in, one large carrot, and a bunch of savory herbs, in two quarts of water, and boil gently till it is reduced rather more than half; strain, and put it aside to cool. Very carefully remove every particle of fat or sediment, and place the jelly in a saucepan with a glass of white wine, a tablespoonful of vinegar, salt and pepper to taste, and the whites of two eggs; keep stirring until it nearly boils, which may be known by its becoming white; then draw it back and let it simmer gently for fifteen or twenty minutes; put on the cover, let it stand to settle, and strain through a jelly-bag until it is quite clear. Put it into a mold.

Bechamel Sauce.

As white stock is the foundation of this sauce, it must be prepared first. Boil down an old fowl, two or three pounds of the knuckles of veal and three of very lean ham, with four carrots, two onions, one blade of mace, some white pepper-corns, two tablespoonfuls of salt and an ounce of butter, in four or five quarts of water. Cut up the fowl and veal, and put them with the ham to simmer in a small quantity of water till the juices are extracted; then put in the full quantity of water, about three and one-half quarts, to the other ingredients. Let the liquid simmer from four to five hours; skim and strain till clear, when it is ready for the bechamel. Mix a tablespoonful of arrowroot with a pint of cream, and when well blended, let it simmer in a carefully cleaned pan for four or five minutes. Make one pint of the stock hot and pour it to the cream; simmer slowly for ten minutes, or until it thickens. If too thick, add a little stock.

ANCHOVY SAUCE.

An easy way of making anchovy sauce is to stir two or three teaspoonfuls of prepared essence or paste of anchovy (which may be bought at your grocers) into a pint of melted butter; let the sauce boil a few minutes and flavor with lemon-juice.

BREAD SAUCE.

Take one pint of white stock; boil with an onion, a little mace, pepper-corns and salt; strain and pour it over six ounces of bread crumbs; boil for ten minutes and add three tablespoonfuls of cream.

BROWN SAUCE.

Melt two ounces of butter in a small saucepan and add one ounce of flour, stirring until it is of a brown color. Then add sufficient boiling stock to render it of a cream-like consistency, and season to taste with salt and pepper.

CUCUMBER SAUCE.

Take three young cucumbers, slice them rather thickly, and fry them in a little butter till they are lightly browned; dredge them with pepper, salt, and grated nutmeg, and simmer them till tender in as much good brown gravy as will cover them. White sauce or melted butter may be substituted for the gravy if these are more suitable to the dish with which the cucumber sauce is to be served. Time, about a quarter of an hour to simmer the cucumbers.

CHILI SAUCE.

Twelve ripe tomatoes, pared, two large peppers, chopped fine, one large onion, chopped fine, two cups of vinegar, one tablespoon. ful salt, one cup brown sugar, one teaspoonful each of allspice, nutmeg, cloves, and ginger. Boil all together.

CAPER SAUCE.

Two tablespoonfuls of butter, one tablespoonful of flour; mix well; pour on boiling water until it thickens; add one hard-boiled egg, chopped fine, and two tablespoonfuls of capers.

CELERY SAUCE.

Put two ounces of butter into a saucepan, melt it, and add two heads of celery cut up into inch pieces; stir the celery in the pan till it is quite tender; add salt and pepper, with a little mace. Mix a tablespoonful of flour in a cup of stock and simmer half an hour. A cup of cream may be used instead of stock.

EGG SAUCE.

Take yolks of two eggs, boiled hard; mash them with a table-spoonful of mustard, a little pepper and salt, three tablespoonfuls of vinegar, and three of salad oil. A tablespoonful of catsup improves this for some. This sauce is very nice for boiled fish.

FISH SAUCE.

One-quarter of a pound of fresh butter, one tablespoonful of finely-chopped parsley, a little salt and pepper, and the juice of two lemons. Cream the butter; mix all well together.

THE HOLLANDAISE SAUCE.

For one pint: one tablespoonful of salt, same of butter and flour; put them in a saucepan and put over the fire, and stir until the butter is melted. Add gradually one pint of hot water, about half a cup at a time, and stir each time for a minute while it is boiling; season with white pepper, nutmeg, and make sure it is cooked.

One great difficulty with sauces is they are raw. This makes the white sauce, which is the basis of many sauces. Add the yolks of two or three eggs, one tablespoonful of lemon-juice, or vinegar; three tablespoonfuls of salad oil. These may be added by putting them together in a separate dish and dipping a few spoonfuls of the white sauce upon them and stirring thoroughly, and then pouring back into the sauce. In this consistency the sauce makes a fine dressing for lobster or chicken salad. This sauce is suitable for any kind of boiled fish.

Hot Sauce for Meats.

Four onions, two cups of sugar, thirty-two tomatoes, one quart of vinegar, four peppers, two tablespoonfuls of salt, two tablespoonfuls of cinnamon, two tablespoonfuls of cloves, three tablespoonfuls of red pepper; cook, strain and bottle.

Horse-Radish Sauce.

Two teaspoonfuls of made mustard, two of white sugar, half a teaspoonful of salt and a gill of vinegar; mix and pour over grated horse-radish. Excellent with beef.

Mushroom Sauce.

To make a pint of mushroom sauce for the fillet of beef, use one tablespoonful of butter and one of flour; put over the fire and stir until brown. Then put in half a pint of water or chicken broth and half a pint of essence of mushroom or the liquor found in a can of mushrooms; stir till the sauce is perfectly smooth, season with a saltspoonful of salt and quarter of a saltspoonful of pepper. Put in the mushrooms and boil two minutes; take off, put in a glass of sherry or Madeira wine, and pour around the fillet of beef.

Mint Sauce.

Mix one tablespoonful of white sugar to half a cup of good vinegar; add the mint and let it infuse for half an hour before sending to the table. Serve with roast lamb or mutton.

Mustard Sauce.

One cup of sugar, one cup of vinegar, one tablespoonful of butter, four eggs and one tablespoonful of mustard; beat the eggs well; mix all together; turn into a new tin pail or basin and boil in water same as custard, only to a cream, not thick. Strain through a thin cloth and it is done.

Prepared Mustard.

Two tablespoonfuls of mustard, one of flour; mix thoroughly while dry. Have a cup two-thirds full of strong vinegar; fill with water, stir the flour and mustard into it and let it boil until as thick as custard; remove from the fire and add a tablespoonful of sugar.

Made Mustard.

Pour a very little boiling water over three tablespoonfuls of mustard; add one saltspoonful of salt, a tablespoonful of olive oil, stirred slowly in, and one tablespoonful of sugar; add the yolk of an egg; beat well together, and pour in vinegar to taste. It is best eaten next day.

Mayonnaise Sauce.

A mixture of egg yolks, oil, vinegar or lemon-juice. The principal point to be attended to in preparing this sauce is the mode of mixing, which demands time, patience and care. Break the yolk of a fresh egg into a bowl with a saltspoonful of pepper and salt mixed. Beat it till thick, then add from time to time during the mixing, two or three drops of the best olive oil until about four ounces have been used and the mixture is thick and yellow. When eight teaspoonfuls of oil have been used, stir in one teaspoonful of white wine vinegar, and continue adding oil and vinegar in these proportions until all the oil is used. The yolk of one egg would be sufficient for a pint of oil and vinegar in proportion. The addition of a few drops of lemon-juice makes mayonnaise look creamy. Mayonnaise will keep a long time if bottled closely and kept in a cool place.

MAITRE D'HOTEL BUTTER.

Knead together (on a plate with the point of a knife) equal quantities of chopped parsley and fresh butter. Add pepper, salt and a little lemon-juice. Keep in a cool place. When a dish is said to be a la Maitre d'Hotel it is generally served with this butter.

MAITRE D'HOTEL SAUCE.

Melt two ounces of fresh butter in a small enameled saucepan, and stir to it, by degrees, two tablespoonfuls of flour; continue stirring five or ten minutes, until the butter and flour are well blended, when add, also by degrees, a quarter of a pint of boiling cream and a quarter of a pint of good veal stock, also boiling; add a few spoonfuls of each at a time and stir well, allowing the sauce to simmer a minute or two between each addition. When perfectly smooth, put in the strained juice of a lemon, or, if preferred, a tablespoonful of Chili vinegar, a little pepper, a pinch of salt, and a tablespoonful of chopped parsley. The yolks of two eggs are a great improvement to this sauce, and are almost necessary when it is served with fish; but in that case only half the quantity of flour should be used, as the eggs help to thicken it.

OYSTER SAUCE.

Prepare some nice drawn butter; scald the oysters in a little water and mix them with the butter; mix well and let the sauce come nearly to a boil, after which serve with oyster crackers.

OLD CURRANT SAUCE FOR VENISON.

Boil an ounce of dried currants in half a pint of water, a few minutes; add a small cup of bread crumbs, six cloves, a glass of port wine and a bit of butter. Stir it till the whole is smooth.

PIQUANT SAUCE.

Dissolve an ounce and a half of butter in a small saucepan over a moderate fire. Throw in a tablespoonful of chopped onions, and stir them about for two minutes, sprinkle a teaspoonful of flour over them, and beat it with a wooden or iron spoon to prevent it from getting into lumps. Add half a pint of stock or broth, a small bunch of parsley, a sprig of thyme, a bay leaf, and a quarter of a teaspoonful of Cayenne. Simmer gently for twenty minutes, then lift out the herbs, pour in half a wineglassful of vinegar, and add a little pepper and salt if required; let all boil up together and serve.

TOMATO SAUCE.

Nine ripe tomatoes, peeled and cut small, red pepper chopped fine, one cup of vinegar, two tablespoonfuls brown sugar, one tablespoonful of salt, one teaspoonful ginger, one of cloves, one of allspice; put vinegar in last; stew one hour.

ALMOND FORCEMEAT.

Beat up the yolks of three eggs with a quarter of a pint of good cream, and flavor with a little nutmeg. Blanch and pound in a mortar three ounces of sweet almonds, using white of egg to moisten. Add these with three-quarters of a pound of light bread crumbs, and three ounces of butter broken into small bits, to the egg mixture. Stir in, lastly, the whites of the eggs whisked to a solid froth, and fill either capon or turkey.

FORCEMEAT BALLS.

Chop a quarter of a pound of beef suet, a little lemon peel, and parsley. Mix with a basin of bread crumbs, and flavor with pepper, salt, and nutmeg. Moisten with the yolks of two eggs, roll in flour, and make up into small balls. Bake in a hot oven, or fry till crisp. This recipe will do for fowls. The addition of a little ham, chopped or pounded, will be found a considerable improvement.

CHESTNUT FORCEMEAT.

Remove the outer skin from some chestnuts (they should be ripe and sound). Boil them for two or three minutes to get off the inner skin. Peel them, and to preserve their color throw them into cold water; drain and weigh them. Stew six ounces of them gently for about twenty minutes in veal gravy. Let them get cold, pound them till smooth with an equal quantity of butter, or half their weight in fat bacon, and add two ounces of bread crumbs, and a little salt, lemon rind, and nutmeg. Bind the mixture together with the unbeaten yolks of two eggs. If this forcemeat is formed into cakes, these should be dipped into flour before being fried.

FORCEMEAT FOR FISH, SOUPS AND STEWS.

Pound the flesh of a medium-sized lobster, half an anchovy, a piece of boiled celery, the yolk of a hard-boiled egg, salt, pepper, and Cayenne to taste. Mix these with a tablespoonful of bread crumbs, two ounces of butter, and two of raw eggs. Make into small balls, and fry a pale brown in butter. Two or three oysters may be added.

FORCEMEAT FOR GAME.

Take the livers of the game and pound them with half their weight of beef suet and good fat bacon, mixed together; season with salt, pepper, and ground cloves. Use a little of the meat of the game if enough of the livers cannot be obtained; moisten with cream, and bind with the yolks of two eggs. If the forcemeat be required stiff, stew over a gentle fire, keeping it constantly stirred until the proper consistency is gained.

FORCEMEAT FOR TURKEYS.

Take equal quantities of lean veal and pork, and mince them finely together; also cut into pieces a parboiled veal sweetbread, and mix with about three-quarters of a pound of each of the former meats. Add half a pound of bread, soaked, and the same amount of warm butter. Flavor with a little nutmeg, salt, pepper and half an ounce of grated lemon rind. Bind with three beaten eggs, and fill the turkey.

MUSHROOM FORCEMEAT.

Procure four ounces of young, fresh mushrooms. Peel them, cut off the stems. Dissolve two ounces of butter in a stewpan, and let them simmer very gently over a slow fire, with a slight flavoring of mace and Cayenne. Spread them over a dish placed in a slanting position to drain away the moisture. When cold mince them, and add four ounces of fine bread crumbs, a small seasoning of salt, Cayenne, mace, and nutmeg, a piece of butter, the yolks of two eggs. Put in as much of the mushroom gravy as will make the forcemeat of the proper consistency. Make into balls, poach and throw into soup; or fry, and serve round a dish of roast fowl or minced veal. It is also a good stuffing for boiled fowls.

OYSTER FORCEMEAT.

Get fresh oysters and cut them into quarters. Grate bread enough to fill half a pint, and one ounce and a half of finely shred suet or butter, which should be broken into bits. Mix all these ingredients together with a good flavoring of herbs, and a seasoning of salt, pepper, and grated nutmeg. Add two well-beaten eggs. This forcemeat is for boiled or roast turkey. It may be made into balls and used as a garnish. Twenty oysters are sufficient for one turkey.

WEIGHTS AND MEASURES.

Ten common-sized eggs weigh one pound.

Soft butter the size of an egg weighs one ounce.

One pint of coffee A sugar weighs twelve ounces.

One quart of sifted flour (well heaped) one pound.

One pint of best brown sugar weighs thirteen ounces.

Two tea cups (well heaped) of coffee A sugar weigh one pound.

Two teacups (level) of granulated sugar weigh one pound.

Two teacups of soft butter (well packed) weigh one pound.

One and one-third pints of powdered sugar weigh one pound.

Two tablespoons of powdered sugar or flour weigh one ounce.

One tablespoon (well rounded) of soft butter weighs one ounce

One pint (heaped) of granulated sugar weighs fourteen ounces.

Four teaspoons are equal to one tablespoon.

Two and one-half teacups (level) of the best brown sugar weigh one pound.

Two and three-fourths teacups (level) of powdered sugar weigh one pound.

One tablespoonful (well heaped) of granulated, coffee A, or best brown sugar, equals one ounce.

Miss Parloa says one generous pint of liquid, or one pint of finely-chopped meat packed solidly, weighs one pound, which it would be very convenient to remember.

Teaspoons vary in size, and the new ones hold about twice as much as an old-fashioned spoon of thirty years ago. A medium-sized teaspoon contains about a dram.

ALLOWANCE OF SUPPLIES FOR AN ENTERTAINMENT.

In inviting guests, it is safe to calculate that out of one hundred and fifty, but two-thirds of the number will be present. If five hundred are invited, not more than three hundred can be counted upon as accepting.

Allow one quart of oysters to every three persons present. Five chickens (or, what is better, a ten-pound turkey, boiled and minced), and fifteen heads of celery, are enough for chicken salad for fifty guests; one gallon of ice-cream to every twenty guests; one hundred and thirty sandwiches for one hundred guests; and six to ten quarts of wine jelly for each hundred. For a company of twenty, allow three chickens for salad; one hundred pickled oysters; two moulds of Charlotte Russe; one gallon of cream; and four dozen biscuits.

CONTENTS.

CONTENTS. 361